I0887222

Citizen of Empire

Citizen of Empire

Ethel Thomas Herold, an American in the Philippines

Theresa Kaminski

LEGACIES OF WAR
G. Kurt Piehler, Series Editor

The University of Tennessee Press · Knoxville

The Legacies of War series presents a variety of works—from scholarly monographs to memoirs—that examine the impact of war on society, both in the United States and globally. The wide scope of the series might include war's effects on civilian populations, its lingering consequences for veterans, and the role of individual nations and the international community in confronting genocide and other injustices born of war.

Copyright © 2011 by The University of Tennessee Press / Knoxville.
All Rights Reserved. Manufactured in the United States of America.
First Edition.

Unless otherwise credited, all photographs are courtesy of Betsy Herold Heimke.

The paper in this book meets the requirements of American National Standards Institute / National Information Standards Organization specification Z39.48-1992 (Permanence of Paper). It contains 30 percent post-consumer waste and is certified by the Forest Stewardship Council.

Library of Congress Cataloging-in-Publication Data

Kaminski, Theresa, 1958-
Citizen of empire: Ethel Thomas Herold, an American in the Philippines / Theresa Kaminski. — 1st ed.
p. cm. — (Legacies of war)
Includes bibliographical references and index.
ISBN-13: 978-1-57233-757-2 (hardcover)
ISBN-10: 1-57233-757-5 (hardcover)
1. Herold, Ethel Thomas, 1896-1988.
2. Americans—Philippines—Biography.
3. Women—Philippines—Biography.
4. Philippines—History—1898-1946.
5. Philippines—History—1946-1986.
I. Title.
DS685.8.H47K36 2011
959.9'03092—dc22
[B] 2011001956

In Loving Memory

Michael Carl Joseph Kaminski
1929–2009
Husband, Father, Citizen, Soldier

Contents

Illustrations

Foreword

THE UNITED STATES gained independence by fighting a war against an imperial power, Great Britain, and for over a century avoided formally taking on colonial possessions. True, the young country did resort to diplomacy and war to expand its boundaries, but even under Manifest Destiny the ideal remained that conquered territories should be incorporated into the republic. At the turn of the twentieth century, the United States followed the lead of many European powers, albeit on a smaller scale, and sought an empire. The Spanish-American War, which started as a conflict to liberate Cubans from Spanish domination, quickly led to war against the Filipino people to turn the Philippines into an American colony. Moreover, the U.S. Supreme Court in the insular cases declared that the new colonial peoples of the United States in Puerto Rico, Guam, and the Philippines were not entitled to the constitutional protections granted to residents of the continental United States. In short, the court held that the U.S. Constitution did not automatically follow the American flag.

Theresa Kaminski's *Citizen of Empire* tells the story of one woman, Ethel Thomas Herold, who believed in the American colonial enterprise in the Philippines. In 1901 she watched her brother leave home for the distant Philippines in response to the federal government's call for American teachers to travel to this newly acquired colony. After World War I, she and her husband Elmer followed in his footsteps. Although their careers as educators would be brief, Ethel and her husband remained in the Philippines until retirement with only an occasional trip back to the continental United States. When Elmer became a manager of a lumber company, Ethel not only assumed responsibility for raising her children and managing a household but also became active in civic affairs through women's clubs.

War remained a crucial legacy in the life of Ethel Thomas Herold. Growing up in a small town in Wisconsin, her earliest civic involvement began as a member of the Woman's Relief Corps. A suffragist during her college years, she married her college sweetheart and watched him go off to war in France in World War I. As a young schoolteacher she peppered her lessons with current events about the nature of the war against Germany and volunteered to teach neighbors about how to conserve food for the war effort. When the United States entered World War II in December 1941, Ethel and her family would, like other Americans living in the Philippines, be interned by the Japanese and suffer great hardship until the forces led by General Douglas MacArthur returned to liberate the islands. After World War II, Ethel became a Cold Warrior and, when she did permanently return to the United States, became active in Republican Party politics favoring Barry Goldwater in 1964.

Does living with people of another culture breed greater understanding and tolerance? Not only did Ethel spend most of her adult life in the Philippines, but she also took several world tours to Africa, Asia, and Europe. Although she remained in the Philippines after it gained full independence from the United States in 1946, she chafed at the loss of privileges once conferred on Americans by virtue of their citizenship. Despite her time abroad, Ethel clung to the notion of American exceptionalism and thought the Philippines had declined politically and economically after gaining independence from the United States. As a club woman, Ethel had spent hours raising funds for philanthropic projects but later in life embraced calls by Goldwater and others to cut spending on foreign aid.

This biography of Ethel Thomas Herold provides valuable insights into the first eight decades of the twentieth century. Whereas most governor generals and military officers only resided in the Philippines for a few years, as an ordinary civilian Ethel Herold spent decades there and witnessed the islands' transition from a colony into an independent nation. Her involvement in Republican Party politics sheds new light on the resurgence of modern conservatism in the 1960s. A keen observer if not often introspective, Ethel Thomas Herold led a remarkable life that is ably captured by Theresa Kaminski.

G. Kurt Piehler
The University of Tennessee

Acknowledgments

MANY FASCINATING WOMEN appeared in the pages of my first book, *Prisoners in Paradise: American Women in the Wartime South Pacific,* but it was Ethel Thomas Herold whom I could not get out of my head. I had a rather vague idea that an examination of her entire life, which spanned most of the twentieth century, would provide an interesting way of looking at key issues of American women's history. For help with sharpening that notion, I am deeply grateful for the cooperation and encouragement of Betsy Herold Heimke and the late Bill Herold, the children of Ethel and Elmer Herold, who provided me with the documents of their mother's life and shared their memories.

Financial support for research for this project came from the University Personnel Development Committee at the University of Wisconsin–Stevens Point and from a year-long sabbatical leave. The Bentley Historical Library at the University of Michigan in Ann Arbor awarded me a Bordin/Gillette Researcher Travel Fellowship in 2005–06. The extremely resourceful staff of the Interlibrary Loan Department at the University of Wisconsin–Stevens Point kept my research travel to a minimum.

Many scholars provided help and encouragement along the way, including Beth Bailey, Frances Cogan, Stacy Cordery, Simon Cordery, Kimberly Jensen, Barbara Steinson, Christopher Capozzola, Jessica Weiss, and Kurt Piehler. The late James J. Halsema, an amateur historian and a lifelong friend of the Herolds, graciously passed on his unrivaled knowledge of Baguio and of the Philippines and shared his own vast collection of documents. A seminar with Professor Fumiko Fujita's Project on Reconstructing U.S. History at the Institute for Research in Language and Culture at Tsuda College in Tokyo in 2003 helped me see that Ethel Thomas Herold's expatriate life was central to understanding her perceptions of nationalism and the place of the

United States in the world. When I despaired of finding a publisher, mystery novelist and dear friend Joanna Slan baited me with the always-inspiring Winston Churchillism, "We will never, ever, ever, ever give up." She was right, as usual, but it still took a long time and a bit of luck to place this manuscript. A fortuitous discussion with Janis Appier, then a member of the History Department at the University of Tennessee–Knoxville, led me to the University of Tennessee Press. It was a real-life publishing fairy tale, and I am very grateful that Janis and UT Press director Scot Danforth were just as intrigued with Ethel's story as I was.

Susan Brewer, Leslie Midkiff DeBauche, and Valentina Peguero have redefined Ladies Who Lunch. Through the years our regular meetings, as friends and as colleagues, offered stimulating conversation on topics as serious as current research projects and as frivolous as imaginary shopping excursions in Paris. These three women have enriched my life beyond measure. And Susan gets credit for coming up with the main title of the book.

Charles E. Clark, historian, administrator, and husband (only he knows the true order of those descriptors), read the manuscript and let me know when it was ready to go out. Our son, Sam Clark, took all of my book-related absences and distractions in stride and grew into a fine young man in the time it took Ethel's story to go to press. Nothing is possible without their love and support.

My parents, Michael and Irene Kaminski, always supported my academic pursuits, from my undergraduate days at Rosary College to my Ph.D. years at the University of Illinois. My father was the one who first introduced me to the Philippines with stories of the time he spent there with the U.S. Army after World War II. Michael Kaminski died in 2009, very unexpectedly, and his death has left a huge hole in our family and in our hearts. This book is for him. If he were here, he would hold this book in one hand, a shot glass filled with Crown Royal in the other, and he would toast, "Mabuhay."

Introduction

IT IS A PICTURE, taken by a news photographer in a period of calm during the vicious battle for Manila in late February 1945, that poses the central question of this biography: What was she doing there anyway?

In the photo, forty-eight-year-old Ethel Thomas Herold stands next to her husband, Elmer, turned slightly toward him, her hands clasped behind her back, her bespectacled eyes steady on the camera. She wears a pale sleeveless dress, firmly belted at the waist, tattered oxfords on her feet. There is a scarf over her graying hair, and its tied ends appear to be fluttering in a faint breeze, the same breeze that probably caused the skirt of her dress to blow against her body, emphasizing her emaciated legs. Elmer Herold, three years older than his wife, wears only a pair of shorts, also securely belted, and a pair of work boots. His ribs are a faint outline on his bare torso. He stands erect, though, his arms straight at his side, his eyes squarely meeting the camera lens. Behind them are piles of rubble and two rows of bombed-out buildings, stark reminders of the recent battle.

What was she doing there, this middle-aged American woman, caught up in one of the fiercest battles of World War II? The answer is that Ethel Thomas Herold was a citizen of empire. Throughout her life, imperialism and war shaped her definitions of patriotism and citizenship, for as Robert Westbrook has observed, "There is nothing like a war to concentrate the minds of citizens on the meaning of patriotism, national identity, and political obligation."[1] Exploring the life of Ethel Thomas Herold allows a unique opportunity to apply a gendered analysis to these shifting, contested meanings not just in one war but in the several American wars spanning the first half of the twentieth century, and it also demonstrates how imperialism could be used to define citizenship and express patriotism.

By the time the photographer from the *Denver Post* snapped the picture, Ethel and Elmer Herold had lived in the Philippines for over twenty years, working and raising their two children there. For Ethel, a "new woman" of the early twentieth century—college educated, community involved, and politically aware—the decision to move to the islands in 1922 was the result of lessons she had taken away from the Great War and of the American government's rhetoric of protecting and spreading democracy. She concluded that living and teaching in the Philippines represented the best way she could exercise her responsibilities as an American citizen and express her patriotism for the country she loved.

That an American citizen could relocate to the Philippines with relative ease stemmed from the conclusion of the Spanish-American and Philippine-American wars at the turn of the twentieth century, both violent demonstrations of the United States' imperialist agenda. President William McKinley justified the American war with Spain as necessary for ending Spanish colonialism in Cuba and the Philippines. When the Filipinos realized that the Americans intended to swap Spain's dominance for their own, many of them forcibly resisted in an "insurrection" that cost tens of thousands of lives. McKinley defended this warfare by claiming that the Filipinos, whether they wanted it or not, needed American guidance to establish democracy, an assertion that masked deeper U.S. needs for economic security and dominance in the Pacific. Still, thousands of Americans settled in the Philippines over the next decades to work for the government, military, and a variety of business ventures, all part of a multifaceted "Americanization" program supported by the United States government.

One of these early participants was Bart Thomas, Ethel Thomas Herold's eldest brother, who went to the Philippines as a public school teacher in 1901, part of a group known as, coincidentally, the "Thomasites," named for the ship that carried them. Though Ethel was only five years old when Bart left home, his absence during her childhood made an indelible impression on her and helped form her definitions of citizenship and patriotism. Ethel described this career choice as Bart "doing a patriotic thing," and she would later consider her own subsequent actions in the same light. Yet, according to Lori Ginzberg, patriotism has often been used as a rationale for the exercise of power and has "proven especially effective at shoring up the racial and gender hierarchies with the moral authority" it requires. Throughout her life, whether living in the Philippines or in the United States, Ethel would use patriotism and her perceived superiority of American citizenship to explain and defend her actions.[2]

Ethel Thomas Herold was born in 1896 in southwestern Wisconsin on the Thomas family's Willow Wood farm. Her birth on American soil made her by law a United States citizen; yet the fact of her gender complicated the meaning of that citizenship. Linda Kerber has acknowledged the important link between citizenship and gender, emphasizing that women's "relationship to the state has been different in substantial and important respects from that of men."[3] That difference can be traced to prescribed gender roles, with men's participation in the public world of politics and the military constituting a more obvious, concrete claim to citizenship than the domestic, family-oriented world of women. But the very creation of the United States caused some women to seriously consider issues of liberty and equality and to apply them to women, a signal that gender roles are fluid rather than fixed.

At some level, Ethel Thomas Herold understood that gender differences existed, though she rarely acknowledged them. Growing up with three older brothers who doted on her, she seemed to take for granted camaraderie and equality with men throughout her life, and this extended to her beliefs about citizenship and patriotism. Though she would have denied the linkage, her long life, which spanned most of the twentieth century, provides ample evidence that gender did in fact shape citizenship and patriotism. For example, the Spanish-American and Philippine-American wars that influenced her childhood were marked by a vigorous masculinity and a military participation exclusive to men. But at the same time, young Ethel Thomas learned the power of women's organizations from her mother and other local women in southwestern Wisconsin. Her association with the Woman's Relief Corps in her hometown of Potosi provided an education in the politicization of benevolent work and in female patriotic expression. This experience with women's organizations also helped lay the foundation for Ethel's support of imperialism for, as Vicente Rafael has shown, women who approved of colonization viewed it as a "logical extension" of domestic reform. And Ethel's work with the Equal Suffrage Club at Lawrence College in Appleton, Wisconsin, introduced her to debates linking citizenship, suffrage, and imperialism.[4]

As a young single woman during the years of the Great War, Ethel Thomas honed her notions of patriotism while majoring in history at Lawrence College and subsequently teaching high school. She utilized a history curriculum for her students that supported American war aims, and she occupied much of her spare time with volunteer work for the Red Cross and the local chapter of the Food Administration. The fact that she was a woman made her, in the eyes of the government and her neighbors, particularly qualified for this work, and this same fact would not have protected her from charges of disloyalty had she declined to participate. But she probably would not have declined because wartime propaganda, with its focus on the virtues of democracy and the duty of American citizens to spread that democracy, seemed to affirm the ideas and values she had been exposed to since childhood.

Her wholehearted support for the war effort also likely had to do with her wholehearted love for her Lawrence College sweetheart, Elmer Herold, who joined the army in April 1917 and served with the Tank Corps in France. In his 1890 poem "The Ballad of the King's Jest," Rudyard Kipling wrote, "Two things greater than all things are, / The first is Love, and the second War." He could have been describing Ethel Thomas Herold's life, which was as much a love story as a tale about imperialism and war. Her love for Elmer prompted her home-front activities during the Great War, and then, during World War II, it led her into the most dangerous situation of her life.

In 1920 Ethel and Elmer were married. Craving adventure, rejecting the ennui of the Lost Generation, and looking for a way to demonstrate the lessons they had learned from the war, the young couple moved to the Philippines in 1922. There they helped promote American democratic ideals by teaching in the public school system. Ethel resigned her teaching position in 1927 to start a family, and the couple settled in the northern Luzon city of Baguio, where Elmer worked for the Heald Lumber Company. While Ethel raised the children, she continued to support American imperialism through colonial domesticity that encompassed a variety of female social and cultural activities promoting American power and superiority. She thrived in this environment. Her American citizenship, along with her race and class standing, conferred a privileged position, which she enjoyed without guilt because she believed she was "doing a patriotic thing."[5]

Ethel's commitment to Americanizing the Philippines kept her in Baguio with Elmer and their two children through the 1930s, despite a worsening world situation that threatened the freedom of the United States and its global interests. She believed it would be disloyal to America's colonial plan to abandon the islands and considered it unpatriotic to even think that the Japanese could defeat the U.S. military. Besides, Ethel knew that her husband would not leave his job as a lumber mill manager, and she loved him too much to be separated from him.

When the Japanese attacked the Philippines on December 8, 1941, the Herolds were stranded there, along with thousands of other Allied nationals. Viewing them as a security threat and as possible bargaining chips, the Japanese rounded up and interned these civilians for the duration of the war. Ethel's comfortable expatriate life was turned upside down: the colonial elite were now powerless prisoners. For the first time in her life, American citizenship brought danger, hardship, and deprivation, robbing her of all the privileges she had once enjoyed. And during a time when most American women stateside could display their patriotism by taking a war job, buying war bonds, or even enlisting in the military, Ethel Herold had to express hers in whatever way possible in a prison setting—usually through the most mundane daily tasks, which could nevertheless provoke retribution from her Japanese captors.

The American military liberated the Philippines in 1945, and motivated by a sense of duty to help the people who had supported them during the war, Ethel and Elmer Herold decided to continue their postwar life in Baguio. In 1946, the Philippines finally achieved its long-promised independence, and subsequently Ethel became a stranger in a place she had called home for more than twenty years. Though her race, class, and American citizenship still afforded her some privileges, she watched with a mixture of frustration and sadness as Filipinos finally took over their own government, military, and businesses. Faced with threats of communist encroachment and with strong decolonization movements, she increasingly found the answer to Cold War problems in the conservative wing of the Republican Party, which she viewed as the protector of American heritage. From late middle age through her twilight years, Ethel Herold grappled with the consequences of American imperialism and of "doing a patriotic thing."

Citizenship and Patriotism in American History

This book explores the historical forces that shaped one twentieth-century American woman's perception of the obligations of citizenship and the meaning of patriotism. The biographical approach provides a unique opportunity to examine the relationship between citizenship, patriotism, and gender over an extended period of time, stretching from the Spanish-American War through the Cold War.

Other scholars have also recently turned their attention to issues of citizenship and patriotism. Linda Kerber, for example, has used selected court cases from the Revolution to the Vietnam era to explore the connections between citizenship and gender. Rogers Smith has examined citizenship laws from the colonial through the progressive periods to show how citizenship has been debated in the United States, and John Bodnar brought together a series of essays on patriotism covering about two hundred years of American history.[6] These books provide key theories for determining Ethel Thomas Herold's views on citizenship and patriotism, though as a unique individual she does not neatly personify any one theory.

According to T. H. Marshall, for many American women at the turn of the twentieth century, citizenship contained "civic, political, and social" components that propelled them to work for equal participation in suffrage, education, careers, and professional organizations. Francesca Morgan's study of American women involved in organizations such as the Daughters of the American Revolution and the Woman's Relief Corps in the late nineteenth and early twentieth centuries illustrates the intersection of citizenship, patriotism, and nationalism with a "women-centered nationalism."[7]

Though not technically women centered, Ethel Thomas Herold believed in gender equality and she understood the power of women to effect change. But she was also influenced more generally by what Rogers Smith has described as "centrist versions of progressivism"—new ideas about civic identity that "held that the U.S. should be a modern democratically and scientifically guided nation that was also culturally ordered, unified, and civilized." Centrists promoted U.S. leadership at home and abroad, both of which rested on racial hierarchies, though for Ethel Herold class sometimes trumped race.[8]

The Spanish-American and Philippine-American wars allowed the United States to put these progressive ideas into practice, which also illustrates how war has shaped meanings of citizenship and patriotism. Kristin Hoganson and Gail Bederman have considered the gendered aspects of these wars, with an emphasis on masculinity and its connection to civic identity. Rogers Smith has explored the debates over imperialism in the United States and their role in shaping meanings of citizenship, and Hoganson, Allison Sneider, and Louise Michelle Newman have linked the ideology and tactics of the woman suffrage movement with citizenship and imperialism. *Citizen of Empire* offers a focused examination of one woman's beliefs about the relationship between being a patriotic American citizen and supporting Philippine colonization. Ethel Thomas Herold represented one of the people Sneider writes about—that is, she tended to "hold divergent and contradictory opinions, and advocate inharmonious policies," especially the simultaneous embrace of imperialism and democratic rights.[9]

The Great War firmed up Ethel Thomas's ideas on patriotism and citizenship during the 1910s. Examining patriotic cultures, Cecelia O'Leary has shown that from the end of the Civil War until World War I, Americans debated meanings of "loyal" and "disloyal." Christopher Capozzola argues that World War I created the "modern American citizen," a model whereby both men and women met their political obligations by working with voluntary associations. Women's long history of involvement in such organizations, combined with an active suffrage movement, meant that their participation (or lack of it) would reflect on their standing as citizens. Indeed, Kathleen Kennedy has shown that American women's words and actions were scrutinized just as closely as men's to determine the extent of their loyalty during the war. And some women, according to Kimberly Jensen, claimed complete citizenship by taking up arms in the First World War.[10] Ethel Thomas never seemed to doubt the completeness of her citizenship; nevertheless, she engaged in paid wage labor and voluntary work to demonstrate her loyalty to the U.S. war effort.

During World War II, Robert Westbrook argues, liberal political theory shaped Americans' notions of wartime obligations, especially as they considered themselves citizens of a combined "state of families." The United States government urged its people to accept that they were fighting to protect human rights and the private spheres of home and family. The war against Japan also required Americans to grapple with an understanding of their enemy's alien political culture. And even at a time when total mobilization was required for the massive war effort, Marilyn Hegarty has shown that though women served their country, they were not necessarily credited with meeting wartime needs. While interned in the Philippines during the war, Ethel Herold became part of a community of families struggling for their human rights even as they fought to survive and somehow aid the war effort. She and the other Allied nationals countered Japan's "alien" political culture with the creation of their own version of a democratic government to organize the internees.[11]

According to Wendy Kozol, the association of women with domesticity persisted into the Cold War period, allowing women to express their patriotism through the various ways in which they cared for their homes. Emphasizing women's roles as active citizens rather than as symbolic subjects, Helen Laville shows that women expanded their domesticity through a range of organizations that permitted them to make contributions to international relations in the postwar period. As an expatriate in the newly independent Philippines, Ethel Herold was very conscious that her domestic duties, as well as her community activities, could be considered a reflection of her U.S. citizenship. Her work with the Monday Afternoon Club represented an attempt to help shape the postwar relationship between the United States and the Philippines.[12]

Living in retirement in Wisconsin, Ethel became involved in Republican Party politics as one of thousands of grassroots activists who, according to scholars such as Kim Phillips-Fein, Lisa McGirr, and Catherine Rymph, were instrumental to the growing influence of the party's conservative wing. Ethel embraced the free-market and small-government ideologies of Republican conservatism and supported its anticommunism agenda. She worked along with other conservative women to call attention to the evils of communism, which she viewed as a dire threat to the democracy she had championed her entire life. As Mary Brennan points out, these anticommunist women "challenged existing assumptions about women as political players" and, as I contend, further solidified their positions as political citizens.[13]

History and Biography

Citizen of Empire is part of a growing number of historical studies that show how the exploration of an "ordinary" person's life can serve as an effective window on important historical events. Because of its emphasis on imperialism and war, this biography is most closely related to Robert Bickers's *Empire Made Me* and Linda Colley's *The Ordeal of Elizabeth Marsh.* The life of Englishman Richard Maurice Tinkler allows Bickers to explore the experiences of average, even obscure, Englishmen in colonial Shanghai. Working first as a policeman, then at other, even less prestigious jobs, Tinkler existed on the margins of Britain's empire but with more freedom and choices than he would have had in England. Bickers describes his work as "a biography of a nobody which offers a window into an otherwise closed world." Ethel Thomas Herold was not exactly a nobody like Tinkler, but her experiences nevertheless help open up that still relatively closed world of women's participation in U.S. imperialism. Colley's book traces the "imperial careering" of Elizabeth Marsh, who traveled across the British empire in the eighteenth century, creating a story that is "an argument for re-casting and re-evaluating biography as a way of deepening our understanding of the global past."[14]

Recently, scholars have begun analyzing the attitudes and actions of people like Richard Tinkler and Elizabeth Marsh through the lens of transnationalism, which deemphasizes the importance of nation states and instead highlights the complexities involved with boundary crossings and international movement. Transnationalist history promotes a global consciousness and challenges conceptions of exceptionalism. David Thelen has described it as a way of observing "how people, moving through time and space according to rhythms and relationships of their own, drew from, ignored, constructed, transformed, and deified claims of the nation-state."[15] Ethel Thomas Herold, though she chose to spend most of her adult life outside of the United States, never wavered in her belief in the superiority of the country of her birth. She supported imperialism and believed in the benefits of Americanization. This was why she went to the Philippines; yet her years there subsequently affected the ways in which she viewed the place of the United States in the world and her place in the United States.

In researching and writing this biography of an "ordinary" person, I have encountered a few challenges. The pertinent documents of Ethel Thomas Herold's life are sufficient but not extensive. Ethel was a prodigious letter writer, but her correspondence prior to World War II has vanished. She kept a diary of, then wrote a book-length account about, her first two years in the Philippines. Those also have not survived. Her fragmented World War II diary is extant, as well as a typed, revised version, plus her five-hundred-page autobiography that she titled "Memory Quiz," written to ease her grief following Elmer's death in 1971. The Herolds' daughter, Elizabeth (Betsy) Herold Heimke, saved all of the letters her mother sent her after the war, from the time Ethel and Elmer returned to the Philippines through their return to southwestern Wisconsin and into Ethel's twilight years in a retirement home. Since these letters served as substitutes for face-to-face conversations, she wrote in much detail about everything—her observations, hopes, beliefs, and activities.

As sources, autobiographies are problematic, of course, because of the issue of memory. In Ethel Herold's case, her memory of events proved very accurate, though how her feelings and viewpoints changed over time can only be intuited. Self-representation is also an issue. To a large degree, Ethel created a version of herself that was superpatriotic and nearly faultless. This biography does not seek to prove any "truth" of her life or promote any certain "correct" form of patriotism but rather to understand and historically contextualize how and why she made her choices. For the early years of her life, when she was relatively silent about issues of patriotism and citizenship, I have interpreted the events she chose to remember through existing scholarship on women in the early twentieth century. Though I believe that my inferences are sound, I realize that other scholars might draw different conclusions.

While Ethel Thomas Herold was a prolific writer, her husband was steadfastly silent. Elmer left the family correspondence to Ethel, only rarely adding a line or two of his own, much less writing a complete letter. Thus, the man who was the love of Ethel's life and her closest companion for more than fifty years remains a quiet, stoic figure in this story. We see him only through her eyes and are deprived of his view of her. But even this one-sided picture shows that love motivated Ethel Thomas Herold, as much as or at times even more than, patriotism.

Ethel held strong opinions, which she stated unhesitatingly. As fascinating as her own writing is, it would be historically irresponsible to portray her life solely through her own extant documents. Contemporary newspapers prove particularly enlightening. Though Ethel never achieved any national prominence, she was not invisible in her day. The newspapers of Grant County, Wisconsin, regularly reported on the doings of the Thomas family in the late nineteenth and early twentieth centuries. The daily paper in Appleton, Wisconsin, covered events at Lawrence College. Ethel and Elmer Herold were well known enough in Baguio's American community that stories of their business and community endeavors, as well as their social life, routinely appeared in the Manila and Baguio papers. In addition to these newspapers, I combed the archives of Lawrence College, read through the papers and published memoirs of various Americans, both men and women, who lived in the Philippines, and consulted several collections in the National Archives and the Library of Congress.

Structure of the Book

This biography is divided into six chronological chapters. The first, which traces the influences of Ethel Thomas's beliefs about citizenship and patriotism, begins with her early life in southwestern Wisconsin and ends with her graduation from Lawrence College. The second examines both her paid wage labor and voluntarist activities during the Great War, exploring how women pushed for a fuller citizenship in wartime and how their actions expressed patriotism. In the third chapter, Ethel Herold's story moves to the Philippines to show how she participated in the Americanization of the islands, first through public school teaching and then through cultural work, to express her loyalty as an American citizen. The next chapter illustrates how war and an enemy occupation made American citizenship a dangerous thing for Ethel and the extent to which her patriotism was tested. Chapter five concerns the meaning of citizenship in a newly decolonized country and explores how Ethel reconciled her loyalty to the United States with her gratitude to the Filipinos who, despite their own suffering during the war, had further risked their own safety to help the Americans. The last chapter brings the story full circle, with the Herolds back in Wisconsin after Elmer's retirement and both actively participating in local Republican Party politics.

Throughout these pages I often identify Ethel Thomas Herold by both first and last names: Ethel Thomas in the first two chapters, Ethel Herold in the remainder, and Ethel Thomas Herold when referring to her entire life span. To avoid reader fatigue, I also refer to her as Ethel (and likewise refer to her husband as Elmer), and I do not believe using her first name diminishes or trivializes her in any way. Besides avoiding repetition and clearly distinguishing between the two Herolds who lived together for just over fifty years, this periodic first-name approach better conveys the mood I want to create for this biography, an up-close and personal one. Radical feminists argued in the 1960s that the personal is political, and Linda Kerber has noted that "it is in citizenship that the personal and political come together."[16] This is abundantly clear in the life of Ethel Thomas Herold.

Chapter One

The Formative Years of a Female Citizen

THIS WAS HER FIRST clear childhood memory: "All the family standing around in the kitchen, everyone crying. Pretty soon my oldest brother, Bart, stooped down, put his arms around me, kissed me goodbye, and said he was going way off to the Philippine Islands. I hated to see my brother go away, so I cried too."[1]

It was the summer of 1901. The whole family at that time included Ethel's parents, Elizabeth and Clem Thomas, and their five children: Bart, freshly graduated from normal school and about to embark on a teaching career in the Philippines; Edna, who with her new high school diploma would take up a teaching position at the grade school in nearby Elm Dale in the fall; the middle sons, Fred and Roscoe, already straining against their rural life; and the baby of the family, Ethel. That day, five-year-old Ethel Thomas confronted the reality that the world was much larger than her family's Willow Wood farm in southwestern Wisconsin. Despite the fear and uncertainty undoubtedly present during that farewell scene in the Thomas kitchen, a touch of excitement comes through in Ethel's recollection of the event. Even at that young age, at some level she apparently understood the importance of Bart's work.

The lessons that Ethel Thomas learned as a child, both from her family and from the community at large, formed the core of her beliefs concerning female citizenship and patriotism that influenced the choices she would make as an adult, especially her active support of American imperialism. In writing about her early years, she rarely made these conscious connections, so the links here rely on drawing conclusions from secondary sources and from what Ethel chose to include in her autobiography about those years. This chapter examines three things from childhood and her young adult years that seemed to have had the biggest impact on shaping her definitions of citizenship and patriotism: Bart Thomas's teaching career in the Philippines, local women's participation in benevolent associations, and her own experiences as a coed at Lawrence College. All of these showed young Ethel Thomas how women infused their various social and cultural projects with the political as they increasingly staked their places in the public world.

Many of Ethel Thomas Herold's beliefs were rooted in the definition of a "nationalist" as someone whose life "was bound up with the destiny of the United States and who worked to create a transcendental culture in which all other loyalties and identities were subsumed into one national identity." Though the terms nationalist and nationalism had become popular by the beginning of World War I, and though she grew up in a period of national unity fostered by the Spanish-American War, Ethel typically described herself as a "patriot." In this conception of patriotism, one demonstrates loyalty to family and friends as well as to country but with the understanding that the welfare of those people is contingent upon the preservation and expansion of the United States.[2]

Patriotism and loyalty to the United States ultimately drove Ethel's interest in applying for and accepting a job with the Philippine public schools—her contribution to that transcendental culture. Her work as a school teacher also partially reflects what can be described as gendered cultural uplift, part of a "women-centered nationalism" that also highlighted patriotism.[3] Although Ethel's actions promoted women's cultural authority, she did not acknowledge them as women centered since she did not express a belief that women possessed an inherent moral superiority over men. Indeed, throughout her whole life, she unapologetically looked to men for guidance and as role models, even as she developed her own strong and forceful personality and even as she assumed equality between men and women.

The Family, Politics, and the Spanish-American War

The youngest of the Thomas siblings, Ethel was close to both of her parents but especially to her mother. Elizabeth, usually called Liz or Lizzie, instilled in all of her children a love of education, respect for hard work, and a desire to make a contribution to the community. Liz had been born on August 14, 1859, in Beetown, Wisconsin, a settlement founded by a group of ex-slaves and whites in 1855 in the midst of a national debate over slavery. Her father, James Red, "a miner always looking for riches he never found," farmed in Beetown until the late 1870s, when the family headed for a small mining town called Webb City near Joplin, Missouri. There, Liz met her future husband, Edward Clement Thomas, originally from British Hollow, Wisconsin, who ran a small store for the Webb City miners. The couple married on August 18, 1879, just after Lizzie's twentieth birthday.[4]

The newlyweds settled into a cozy working relationship in Clem's store, and they prospered. But in 1883 Clem's father, James Thomas, now in his early seventies, begged his son to come home so that he could help run the family farm. "Filial love meant something in those days," his granddaughter Ethel later pointed out. So, reluctantly but dutifully, Clem and Lizzie Thomas, along with their toddler son, Bart, moved to the family farm, known as Willow Wood, in southwestern Wisconsin. With its gentle rolling hills, fertile land, and mineral wealth, this part of Wisconsin was heading into a boomlet in the 1880s. Farmers grew corn and wheat, and raised cattle and hogs. Miners, who gave the state its badger nickname, dug iron and other metals out of the hillsides. The nearby Mississippi River and a railroad line facilitated the movement of these items—including beer from the well-known Potosi Brewery—to market and kept the area's residents in easy reach of both Iowa and the rest of the state of Wisconsin.[5]

James and Elizabeth Thomas, grateful for their son's help, built a house for Clem and Liz, which quickly filled up with five children: Bartlett Edward (already born in 1881), Edna Elizabeth (1883), Fred Alfred (1885), Roscoe Conkling (1888), and finally, on March 25, 1896, Ethel Clementine. From the beginning of her life, Ethel Thomas was not only surrounded by a large family but also by politics. One of her brothers was named for a well-known Republican politician of the era, a clear indication of the family's party loyalty. Her father's several elections to positions of supervisor and as a justice for Potosi signaled that the Thomases believed in active political involvement whenever possible.[6]

The national and international political events that filtered into this small corner of Wisconsin profoundly affected Ethel Thomas's life. She was two years old when the United States went to war with Spain, ostensibly to free Cuba and the Philippine Islands from

Spanish colonial rule. This is the version of the Spanish-American War that Ethel would come to embrace and go on to support by living and working in the Philippines for nearly forty years. She believed in American exceptionalism, the idea that the United States was on a well-intentioned and benevolent mission to spread democracy around the world. She trusted wartime propaganda that portrayed the United States as a "generous liberator, spreading democracy as it defends civilization." Ethel Thomas Herold spent her whole adult life, in wartime as well as peacetime, striving as a loyal citizen to uphold that image. For her, no need or interest motivating U.S. foreign policy was higher than that of ideology. Ethel would always prefer to believe that her various actions proved she willingly answered "the patriotic call" from her government.[7]

Though at the time Ethel Thomas was too young to comprehend the complexities of the Spanish-American War and its immediate aftermath, her family and neighbors routinely digested articles about political and military developments from the three weekly Grant County, Wisconsin, newspapers. Ethel's family—with brothers not quite old enough to join the military and a father who served in local government—likely discussed these events. This was a climate in which American citizens revived their sense of national unity by emphasizing their "American-ness" against the Spanish and even the Filipinos. Many of Ethel's early memories were probably stamped with this link between war and national unity, and being part of an imperial power would always affect the way she viewed what it meant to be an American.[8]

Between all of the readily available information about the war and the Thomas family's predilection for political activity, it is not surprising that Ethel's eldest brother, Bart, chose to take a teaching position in the Philippines. The challenges of stabilizing the fledgling colony in the face of Filipino resistance and of molding the Philippines into America's image required bold, masculine men. Bart Thomas, tall and fit from his years of working on the family farm and armed with a teaching degree from a normal school, decided to answer his government's call for teachers to work in the Philippines.[9]

As the United States took possession of the islands, Congress considered the most effective method for administering them. In 1901, it ultimately decided to allow the executive branch, rather than Congress, the power to run the Philippines, although the president was required to update Congress on events there, and Congress could repeal his decisions. President William McKinley chose William Howard Taft, a federal circuit judge from Cincinnati, Ohio, to supervise the establishment of a civilian government. Though Taft had opposed U.S. acquisition of the Philippines, he viewed this appointment (first as a commissioner, then as governor) as a way of making his mark, as a way of bringing democracy to the Filipinos.[10]

Once in the Philippines, Taft proceeded to establish a free public school system that would "fit the people for the duties of citizenship and for the ordinary activities of a civilized community." This was not an educational method exclusive to the imperial relationship. At the end of the nineteenth century, progressive reformers in the United States realized that children represented a "captive public" when they attended school, facilitating good-citizenship lessons. This approach, which intensified during the First World War to produce "100 percent Americans," seemed to American officials the best teaching method for Filipino children, who, according to the dictates of U.S. imperialism, required instruction in the benefits of democracy and capitalism.[11]

The Bureau of Public Instruction—later renamed the Bureau of Education—created public primary and secondary schools in the Philippines. The bureau received authorization to recruit up to one thousand American teachers to staff some of these schools. Considered "master teachers" ostensibly because of their schooling in the United States and because they knew English, these Americans taught in coed classrooms that had been purged of the Catholic crucifixes, religious statues, and pictures that the islands' Spanish colonizers had introduced. Within about twenty years, 12 percent of the islands' 1.2 million inhabitants attended public schools.[12]

Fred W. Atkinson, the first U.S. superintendent of Filipino schools, oversaw recruitment of American teachers. The successful applicant had to possess a college or normal school degree, plus several years of teaching experience. Or, subject to Atkinson's approval, university presidents and state departments of education could appoint between three and six teachers each. Atkinson likely approved Bart Thomas's application because, although Bart had the required degree, he did not have the requisite experience. A Grant County newspaper article also hinted that political clout played a part in Bart's appointment. It identified Bart's father, Clem Thomas, as "chairman of the town board" and queried, "Who says Republics [*sic*] are ungrateful[?]" Yet the article contained no criticism of the program or of the American occupation of the Philippines.[13]

Bart Thomas and more than five hundred others departed from San Francisco on July 23, 1901, on the *U.S.S. Thomas,* a military transport that earned these teachers the "Thomasite" nickname. At a time when close to three-fourths of teachers in the United States were women, men comprised two-thirds of the teachers aboard the ship, a reflection of the physical dangers still present for Americans in the Philippines. Her brother "was doing a patriotic thing," Ethel Thomas pointed out years later, in signing on to teach under those conditions. But Bart also considered the job a "paid adventure." His transportation costs were free, he received half salary during his travel, and he collected a thousand-dollar salary in gold the first year, payable in monthly installments, with promises of annual increases. Bart Thomas's patriotic service was expected for a term of three years, and except for one home leave, he taught in the Philippines until 1910.[14]

During that time, teaching jobs in the Philippine public schools had come under the jurisdiction of the civil service. Prospective teachers from the United States first applied through the U.S. Bureau of Insular Affairs, which was responsible for administrative matters pertaining to the islands, and then through the Philippine Bureau of Education. Exams were rigorous, convering subjects that ranged from political and physical geography to history to composition. Applications for and promotions in civil service positions were considered fair and unbiased since they relied on examinations, but because of imperial administration and contemporary racial attitudes, there was little real equality between American and Filipino public school teachers. Bart Thomas's salary, for instance, represented five or six times what a Filipino teacher earned.[15]

Yet Americans insisted that the disparity had to do with education and ability, not with race. Because the American teachers arrived with college or normal school degrees, so the argument went, they warranted higher salaries. American teachers also considered themselves more professional, claiming that Filipino teachers were frequently idle and even drunk at times. Finally, the American teachers' jobs required supervisory skills. Not only did they teach Filipino students and train Filipino teachers, but they usually had administrative responsibility for the schools, based on the assumption that Filipinos were not capable. The Bureau of Education, then, even in its cultural work, reinforced the racism of empire.[16]

The presence of the American teachers was a constant reminder that because of U.S. imperialism, Filipinos were second-class citizens in their own country. The Spanish-American War ignited debates in the United States about the status of the people who came under their jurisdiction as a result of the war. Bart Thomas's career choice strongly indicates that Ethel Thomas and her family were in the imperialist camp, which relied on aspects of liberalism, republicanism, and racism to argue that these "lucky new subjects" required education in enlightened civilization and self-governance. The new subjects would remain so since Filipinos were viewed as too "racially distinct, inferior, and troublesome" to become U.S. citizens. This did not represent a new interpretation of citizenship. The U.S. government already prevented some immigrant groups from becoming naturalized citizens because of race, and African Americans, Native Americans, and women did not enjoy equal citizenship rights with native-born white men.[17]

After about nine years in the Philippines, Bart Thomas returned to the United States. He arrived for an extended visit in Potosi during the summer of 1910 along with his wife, Florence, whom he had married on his 1904 home leave, and their three sons. His presence reinforced Ethel Thomas's interest in the islands and gave her valuable insight into relations with people of different cultures. The fourteen-year-old girl spent hours listening to Bart tell stories of the Philippines, and she became fascinated with the natural history of the islands and the different groups of people that populated them.

Ethel's appreciation for and understanding of the Philippine Islands stemmed not only from the stories Bart told, but also from the items he gave to family members. In 1907, for instance, when Bart and Florence Thomas were living in the Cagayan Province of the Philippines, Bart had sent a birthday gift to his father, a walking cane of Palayon wood with his birth date engraved on it. Tucked in the package was a dress of Chinese silk for Ethel.[18]

These gifts must have struck Ethel as wonderfully exotic, perhaps further spurring her interest in Asia. During the early twentieth century, many white women in the United States, especially wealthy ones, began collecting Asian art and artifacts. "Oriental stores," which first cropped up before the end of the previous century, became increasingly popular, spreading Asian goods among the American middle class. But these particular items brought imperialism directly into the Thomas household, making it a domestic contact zone with the Philippines. The Chinese silk dress set Ethel Thomas apart from other Potosians and proclaimed her family's connection with U.S. colonization.[19]

That summer of 1910, when Bart returned for his visit, Ethel witnessed the complex interactions of two groups of people with very different ethnic backgrounds and different citizenship status. This was a rare opportunity because, for the first twenty-five years of her life, she lived among and associated almost exclusively with white, middling-class Wisconsinites. In 1910, however, the Burlington Railroad Company hired approximately three hundred Mexican workers to install a double track through Potosi, along the Mississippi River. Ethel Thomas remembered that the townspeople were "bewildered" by these foreign men who did not speak English. Their presence, while not entirely unwelcome, provoked some tension that Ethel put down to the language barrier rather than to overall ethnic differences. One day Bart Thomas happened into the post office when a group of railroad workers trying to send home money orders were met with a clerk who could not understand them. Bart had learned Spanish in the Philippines, so he intervened, smoothly directing the purchasing and sending of the money orders.[20]

His assistance was not a onetime event. Realizing that he could be useful, Bart regularly showed up at the post office on the workers' paydays, freely offering his translating skills. The men became so comfortable with Bart that they sometimes appeared at the Thomas house to ask him for help in writing letters home. His language abilities then came in handy during a violent situation that developed one August evening at the Potosi railroad station. A group of laborers, garrulous with drink, descended on the building, shouting and waving knives at the station agent. The agent, who did not understand Spanish, jumped in his car and fetched Bart. Back at the station, confronted by angry men, Bart learned that one of the Mexican workers, Erculano Martinez, had stabbed and killed another, Victriano Fuentes, and that the men wanted help in tracking the culprit through the cornfields at the river.[21]

Bart served as interpreter for the Mexican workers at Martinez's preliminary hearing, a role he continued when the trial convened in the county seat of Lancaster in October. It took two days for the jury to convict Martinez, whom one newspaper had described as looking "like a man of depraved, criminal instincts," of second-degree murder. The defendant maintained his innocence, at one point leaning toward Bart Thomas "in a cunning confidential manner and repeated in an almost inaudible tone" that one of his companions committed the crime. The judge sentenced Martinez to twenty years of hard labor at the state penitentiary.[22]

Since this incident remained sharp within Ethel Thomas Herold's mind for more than sixty years, the Martinez case likely affected how she perceived interactions between whites and nonwhites, citizens and aliens. The Mexican railroad workers had caused a stir in Potosi. Though the town was no stranger to laborers, its residents did not regularly encounter people who were not white, Anglo-Saxon Protestants. Ethel Thomas viewed the men as hardworking but also as different, even slightly inferior because of their ethnicity, their class, and especially their inability to speak English. They required help from her brother Bart, who out of a sense of duty gave it. That Ethel (and the newspaper reports) always referred to the men as Mexican indicates that she perhaps made a link between ethnicity and citizenship—that dark-skinned men who did not speak English were unlikely to be citizens of the United States.

Small-Town Life and the Influence of Organized Women's Activities

Politics and community activities shaped young Ethel Thomas's life, and they became more pronounced after the family moved from the Willow Wood farm to Potosi. Bart Thomas's departure for the Philippines in 1901, along with the realization that his other two sons would reject agricultural careers, prompted Clem Thomas to give up farming. In 1904 he became a rural mail carrier, earning approximately fifty dollars per month plus fifteen days of paid vacation every year, with a government pension to look forward to in retirement. While his age and physical condition played a large part in that decision, he may have also been thinking about finding a job that could raise the status of his family. A government job and the purchase of one of the largest houses in Potosi in 1906 helped elevate the Thomases' status in the community and gave Ethel her first taste of life away from Willow Wood.[23]

At the beginning of the twentieth century, Potosi had a robust population of 1,568. A long, narrow town built in a ravine near the Mississippi River, it lay about twenty miles slightly north of Dubuque, Iowa. Gas street lamps illuminated the village at night until electricity arrived in 1916. In 1906, the town boasted a lumber company, a state bank, the brewery, and a steamboat company, plus a lead and zinc mining company. Additional mines opened throughout the area over the next couple of years, and leasing his farmland to a mining company proved lucrative enough for Clem Thomas not only to purchase a nice home but also to put some money aside for his youngest daughter's college education.[24]

Benefits abounded for Ethel Thomas in Potosi. She attended the town school located right across the street from her new home, learned how to swim in the summer, went sleigh riding and skating in the winter, and took music lessons from a local instructor. Anna Bonn, a farm neighbor who forged a close relationship with Ethel, encouraged the young girl to play the organ and to sing. Mrs. Bonn, as Ethel always called her, also reinforced what the young girl had learned from her mother about community involvement and patriotism. This neighbor tapped Ethel to help with her annual winter dinner, which celebrated the sacrifices of the veterans of the Civil War and the achievements of the Woman's Relief Corps (WRC).[25]

It is not clear how deeply involved Ethel Thomas was in other WRC activities besides the annual dinner, but her association with the group indicates that from an early age she learned about the link between charitable endeavors, patriotism, and good citizenship. Formed in 1883, the WRC attracted both female relatives of Union veterans and women who had worked for the North on their own. However, in an effort to be democratic, the organization did not restrict its membership to those women. Although local chapters cropped up across the country, the WRC had its strongest presence in New England and the upper Midwest. It is not surprising to find Wisconsin included there, given the state's claim as the birthplace of the Republican Party and its strong antebellum abolitionist views.[26]

WRC members focused their efforts on promoting Union patriotism by helping needy Union veterans, honoring their dead, promoting the celebration of Memorial Day, and creating patriotic rituals such as putting American flags in schools and requiring students to recite a pledge of allegiance to the flag. All of these activities illustrate that WRC members were determined to be patriotic. These women tried to downplay old sectional political issues, instead focusing on how a Union victory ultimately helped foster a national patriotism, albeit one based on race—a clear sign of just what the Civil War did and did not change.[27]

All of this may have seemed like ancient history to a girl whose own life had not been personally touched by the Civil War, but Ethel Thomas apparently absorbed some of the WRC members' conversations about the importance of being a patriotic woman. This became a lifelong objective for her. In addition to honoring the past, many members of the WRC involved themselves in contemporary matters, including a variety of women's rights issues, woman suffrage, and racial equality. Indeed, an official aim of the WRC was to "maintain true allegiance to the United States of America; to inculcate lessons of patriotism and love of country among our children in the communities in which we live; and to encourage the spread of universal liberty and equal rights to all." In attempting to meet that goal, WRC members increasingly challenged the prevailing assumption that women lacked a political presence in American society, and their activities serve as reminders of the close relationship between politics and women's cultural activities.[28]

The Spanish-American War and the Philippine-American War provided WRC women with additional opportunities to prove their patriotism even though they still lacked equal political rights with men. But as club women built monuments to the latest veterans, supported educational efforts designed to raise patriotic boys, and rejected criticisms of President McKinley's handling of the wars, they sparked an internal debate about how publicly women should demonstrate their patriotism. While the WRC declined to approve of women marching in Grand Army of the Republic parades, it sanctioned women providing patriotic information to school children. Overall, for the WRC, patriotism required a belief in national unity and allegiance to the federal government.[29]

While Anna Bonn involved Ethel Thomas in one of the more politically oriented female organizations, Liz Thomas served as her daughter's primary role model for community benevolent activity. Yet even this did not lack political components. Since at least the nineteenth century, American women used voluntary associations to expand the definition of "woman's place" to give it a decidedly public component. Hundreds, even thousands, of these organized women's groups in the United States addressed issues ranging from soldiers' aid to temperance to poverty relief to woman suffrage. Women's involvement in these groups challenged assumptions that a woman's duties should keep her in the home.[30]

Moreover, participants in the women's club movement engaged in important cultural work as the United States extended its national borders, so their work was affected and informed by debates over definitions of the nation and cultural standards, as well as changes in economics and politics. Many American women belonged to more than one organization or club, an indication of both their wide variety of interests and an interconnectedness among those interests. The cultural work accomplished by these women's clubs also helped promote American nationalism and patriotism by encouraging women to raise their children to be good citizens. Thus, American women who supported U.S. colonization in the Philippines viewed it as a "logical extension" of their domestic benevolent work.[31]

Like thousands of other American women, Liz Thomas belonged to and was active in several local southwestern Wisconsin organizations. She joined the women's auxiliary of the Modern Woodmen of America, a fraternal benefit society in which her husband, Clem, had membership. Most of their activities involved raising money for the less fortunate in their corner of the state; a poverty supper, for instance, attracted "goodly attendance, much fun and enjoyment" in the spring of 1901. Moving to Potosi in the first decade of the twentieth century afforded the Thomas women additional opportunities to participate more often in female organizations. Liz Thomas, a staunch Methodist who attended church every Sunday and scrupulously kept the Sabbath holy, also belonged to the church-affiliated Woman's Home Band and the Ladies' Aid Society. She took her turn hosting these meetings in her home, with Ethel assisting, providing the young girl with a bird's-eye view of women's organizational abilities.[32]

Throughout her entire adult life, Ethel Thomas would emulate her mother's penchant for joining women's groups. She would never, however, match her mother's style of religious devotion, gravitating toward membership in secular organizations like the WRC rather than those sponsored by individual churches or denominations. Given this, Ethel's choice of college seems inconsistent with her secular preferences but not with her class aspirations.

Higher Education and the "New Woman"

As Ethel Thomas prepared to graduate from high school in the spring of 1913, Liz insisted that her daughter go on to college, so that wherever life took her, the degree would provide three things: self-confidence, the ability to earn a good living, and independence. After college, Liz expected Ethel to work five years in her career before marrying. In the 1910s, this represented a very modern, progressive interpretation of women's roles: that educated young women could somehow combine marriage and career, ideally in succession rather than simultaneously. It also represented the fact that club women embraced the "new woman" of the early twentieth century and charged her with the duty of training her children to value citizenship. Liz Thomas raised all of her children, sons and daughters, to be useful citizens in their communities.[33]

As a college student, Ethel Thomas would become one of more than 140,000 American women (mostly white, Protestant, and middle class) who attended college in the early 1910s.[34] For the young new woman of this era, such education was the necessary basis for the business or professional career she intended to pursue. Moreover, this new woman could choose to delay marriage—if she married at all—to accommodate such a career. If and when she married, she gave birth to fewer children than non-college-educated women and spent her time pursuing charitable and/or civic activities. This perfectly describes Ethel Thomas Herold, who would become a teacher, marry at twenty-four, have the first of her two children at thirty-one, and organize one of the most active charities in the Philippines.

During the decade in which Ethel Thomas attended college, the number of American women enrolled in institutions of higher education rose from 140,000 in 1910 to 283,000 in 1920, with women by then making up just over 47 percent of all enrolled students. Like most of her female counterparts, Ethel came from the capacious middle class, and her parents made sacrifices for her to attend college, though the fact that she had been raised on a farm did not make her particularly unique. Alice Freeman Palmer, Carrie Chapman Catt, and Anna Howard Shaw, all well-known suffragists, had similar backgrounds, though the latter two women had to overcome objections from their fathers. Ethel Thomas was fortunate in that both of her parents supported her aspirations for a college degree.[35]

Higher-education curriculums underwent changes between 1870 and 1915 as classical courses such as mathematics, philosophy, and science competed with modern ones such as engineering and home economics. Debates over which were proper for young men and young women continued throughout this time period, and they were not restricted to higher education administrators. The lengthy discussions Ethel Thomas had with her mother prior to attending college reflect this. Liz Thomas wanted a feminized education for her daughter, one focusing, perhaps, on literature, but Ethel, eager for a modern college education, rejected her mother's old-fashioned approach. Not only did she want to teach in high school at a time when most women pursuing careers in education taught at the grade school level, but she also wanted to teach the subject that most interested her: history. In the early twentieth century, that was considered a subject for men; yet Ethel Thomas decided to challenge this stereotype. Growing up with three older brothers who doted on her, she was accustomed to being around men and even holding her own with them.[36]

When it finally came time to decide on a school, Ethel Thomas followed her high school principal's recommendation and chose Lawrence College in Appleton. Amos A. Lawrence, a Boston merchant, had founded the college in 1847 as a liberal arts institution. Bolstered by the strong religious faith of the Methodist church, the college was coeducational and racially integrated from its inception. By the time Ethel matriculated, Lawrence had three divisions: College of Liberal Arts, Conservatory of Music, and Department of Art, and employed forty-four teachers, many of them professors with PhDs. In addition to rigorous classes, students could participate in any of the college's four literary societies, four sororities and four fraternities, glee club and choral union, orchestra and brass band, YWCA, and various Bible study groups.[37]

Ethel Thomas's tepid interest in religion makes her choice of Lawrence College an interesting one. It may have represented some kind of compromise between the somewhat pampered baby of the family and her parents. Lawrence was located clear across the state of Wisconsin, ensuring that visits home to Potosi would be restricted to major holidays and semester breaks. Perhaps Liz Thomas was convinced that the religious nature of the institution would make up for the fact that her daughter would be so far away. And perhaps Ethel decided she could cope with the religious aspects because Lawrence was such a prestigious private college. Class conscious all of her life, Ethel Thomas understood that a degree from the right school could open many doors. And for her more immediate plans, a bachelor's degree from this four-year college would qualify her to teach a specialized subject in a Wisconsin public high school.

In the fall of 1913, Ethel Thomas was one of 190 incoming freshmen—the largest such class to date at Lawrence—and one of 600 students on the campus that academic year. She roomed with nine other freshmen and two juniors in the Ormsby Hall Annex, and she learned the campus layout as she made her way to her English, history, art, public speaking, and German classes. Like the other freshman coeds, she would have worn a "uniform" consisting of a long dark skirt, a white blouse of crepe de chine or georgette, and the green cap that marked her as a first-year student. In addition to her academic courses, Ethel embarked on extracurricular activities, of which the Choral Club proved to be her favorite. Indeed, she would find solace and inspiration in singing throughout her life.[38]

Ethel also enrolled in Lawrence's prestigious music conservatory, and in the fall of 1914, she began private voice lessons, paid for with money borrowed from her Potosi neighbor Anna Bonn. She joined the Girls' Glee Club, which gave her the opportunity to travel around Wisconsin performing in a series of small towns. Ethel embraced the sorority system as well, joining Delta Delta Sigma. Always aware that she was a small-town girl with farming roots, she viewed her Delta membership as a way of fitting into life at Lawrence and elevating her status. Although she was part of the second generation of college women who joined sororities, her interest in them did not represent the norm. While most sorority women prized social activity over academics, Ethel never lost sight of the fact that education and scholarly achievement came first.[39]

Religion played a minor role in Ethel Thomas's college experience, just as it had earlier in her life. As a child, she had attended the local Methodist church with her family every Sunday but chafed under her mother's ban on dancing and card playing. Ethel took every opportunity, usually assisted by her older brothers, to violate those religious rules; yet she maintained the ritual of church attendance. Lawrence College students had compulsory chapel before morning classes, and Ethel's attendance stemmed more from a sense of duty than conviction. When she had the choice of joining a religiously based extracurricular activity, she opted for the College Girl Sunday Class at the local Congregational Church. She may have viewed this in class terms, considering the Congregational Church to be more upper-class than the Methodist. Ethel's participation in the various activities of the College Girl Sunday Class seemed in fact perfunctory, designed to meet obligations and extend her social networks rather than to express a deep faith. She tended to keep religious beliefs private instead of displaying them through public behavior.[40]

Ethel Thomas joined academic clubs and held class office, activities that honed her special interests and familiarized her with organizational structures and rules. She was not content to simply join clubs and societies; instead she felt that she had to hold office, to direct, to do real work. During her senior year alone, she served as class vice president, president of the History Club, social secretary of the YWCA, and secretary-treasurer of the Equal Suffrage Club. As with many other new women, suffrage loomed large in Ethel's life. But for her, unlike for most suffragists, the right to vote took on a secondary importance, as she used the suffrage movement to sharpen her ideas on citizenship and imperialism.

The Suffrage Campaign

In her sophomore year, Ethel Thomas declared a history major in preparation for her career as a high school teacher. Part of the major required courses in politics, so Ethel and her friend Janet Strathearn had signed up for a course in American politics with Professor Charles Atkinson. Jan, from Kaukauna, Wisconsin, shared dormitory space at the Ormsby Hall Annex with Ethel, and the two also shared a heritage of women's voluntarism. Jan Strathearn's mother served as president of the Wisconsin State Federation of Women's Clubs and participated in a wide array of religious and community activities. As interested in political science and history as Ethel was, Jan seemed destined to follow in her own mother's footsteps.

When the two female sophomores—the first women ever to take Atkinson's class—entered a room of seventy young men, the professor ordered, "Gentlemen, arise, ladies are entering the room." Frustrated and chagrined by this kind of attention, Ethel Thomas and Jan Strathearn vowed to always do their best in class, to prove to Atkinson and the male students that they had a rightful place there. Ethel prepared well for class, and by the end of the semester she realized that she had gotten "a tremendous lot" out of the course. That "tremendous lot" likely included formulating ideas about women's roles in politics and about the links between gender, citizenship, and voting. Ethel's ideas mostly resembled those of nineteenth-century suffragists who managed to reconcile classical liberal and republican traditions with beliefs in "natural" gender and racial hierarchies.[41]

During her junior year at Lawrence College, Professor Atkinson pushed Ethel to act on her newly developing political ideas. Carrie Chapman Catt, president of the National American Woman Suffrage Association (NAWSA), had sent out hundreds of letters to encourage the organization of woman suffrage clubs on every campus in the country. One of those letters had been addressed to Professor Atkinson. Catt, born in Ripon, Wisconsin in 1859, had resumed the NAWSA presidency in 1915 and guided the group through its final, successful push for woman suffrage with her "Winning Plan," a combination of state campaigns supported by a drive for a constitutional amendment. Campus involvement figured prominently in that plan.[42]

Since Ethel Thomas and Jan Strathearn were the only two female students in his class, Professor Atkinson directed them to organize a woman suffrage club in the spring of 1916. Louise Dudley, a young English professor, agreed to serve as advisor to the club, and Catt and NAWSA provided materials for monthly meetings. Ethel endured a lot of teasing from the men at Lawrence, including her steady boyfriend, Elmer Herold, and faced quite a bit of apathy from the women. Though perhaps disappointing, this response was not unusual. Campus suffrage clubs had just begun to thrive; yet they continued to generate much controversy as college students, like their counterparts in other women's organizations, debated the proper roles of women as well as the duties of citizenship.[43]

The link between citizenship and voting rights was not an absolute in the Jim Crow era. Despite post-Civil War constitutional amendments giving them the right to do so, most African American men still could not vote in the early twentieth century. Though the woman suffrage movement promoted "Votes for Women," Jim Crow was not genderless; therefore, African American women would also find themselves disenfranchised because of racial discrimination. Still, suffrage supporters optimistically viewed having the vote as a key component toward women gaining equality with men.

Yet the vote would not automatically "liberate" women from traditional gender roles, nor would all women embrace that particular goal. Women who regularly attended Christian churches did not constitute a core community for the suffrage movement because they worried that the vote would interfere with the ideology of separate spheres for men and women. Many club women sought a kind of balance by embracing the "new woman" even as they tried to smooth out any hint of radicalism by tying it to the duties of motherhood. A new woman could express her political views and even take part in politics by raising her children to be good citizens. Such activities drew on the heritage of the Revolution-era "Republican Mother" and did not require women to shift their primary identity from a private domestic one to a public one.[44]

The suffrage debate was also caught up in and fed off of the national debate over imperialism. Though these arguments had developed at the beginning of the century when Ethel Thomas was still a child, it is likely that she was first exposed to them as she immersed herself in the literature of the suffrage movement. She remembered that she and Jan Strathearn "struggled along" with the Equal Suffrage Club meetings during their junior year, issuing reports on why women deserved the right to vote. Ethel's research for those reports would have revealed that suffragist arguments included debates about political and citizenship rights for potential new citizens, people living in the path of the United States' expansion.[45]

Suffragists were divided over the issue of American imperialism in the Pacific, especially as they were unsure of how this would translate into rights for women. Middle-class white women tended to ally with middle-class white men who held the political power. And as the majority of politically powerful white men chose to support imperialism, suffragists realized that by supporting this particular national policy they could show themselves to be loyal citizens worthy of the right to vote.[46]

Given Ethel Thomas's family connection with imperialism in the Philippines and the patriotism that had been instilled in her as a child, this discussion would have fascinated her. She may have sided with such women as the late Susan B. Anthony—Quaker, pacifist, and early suffragist—who conceded that the Spanish-American War would at least bring freedom to large groups of people. Moreover, when Filipinos resisted the American occupation, Anthony did not equate their actions with those of freedom fighters. Instead, she saw it as a race war that, if it resulted in a Filipino victory, would lead to the "murder and pillage [of] every white person on the island"; and she criticized anti-imperialists as "treasonous because they were inciting the Filipinos to mutiny." Anthony's arguments for supporting imperialism would have struck a chord with Ethel Thomas, especially the linkage of anti-imperialism with treason. A patriotic citizen, Ethel might reason, should support continuing U.S. intervention in the Philippines.[47]

These issues, rather than suffrage itself, probably seemed more important to Ethel Thomas, who later admitted that her own commitment to woman suffrage was only lukewarm. She worked diligently for the club mostly because she feared that Professor Atkinson would fail her if the campus's Equal Suffrage League proved unsuccessful. The professor apparently believed that practical experience in a political campaign would enhance his students' book learning of American politics. The fact that Ethel confessed that she and Jan Strathearn found their History Club much more interesting because of the "men members who added spice to the topics of discussion" illustrates the variety of women and their motivations for supporting the suffrage movement. It seems that Ethel Thomas had only a rather detached, intellectual interest in suffrage and that, as a young single woman, she preferred to spend her spare time in the company of young men.[48]

Though Ethel did not view the suffrage club as one of her most interesting extracurricular activities, she nevertheless served as its secretary-treasurer while Jan Strathearn was elected president. The Lawrence College newspaper indicated strong support on campus for woman suffrage, at one point running the encouraging headline "Stand Up for Women's Rights." A subsequent editorial advised, "Whether or not we are believers in equal suffrage, we all agree that the question is vital—one that we cannot avoid. It is therefore necessary that we deal with this subject as intelligently as possible; the suffrage club opens the way for both men and women."[49]

The excitement over the organization of the club intensified with the announcement that the famous British suffragist Emmeline Pankhurst would speak at the Congregational Church in Appleton on May 11, 1916. As officers of the sponsoring Equal Suffrage League, Ethel Thomas and Jan Strathearn handled all of the "errands" involved with Pankhurst's appearance: confirming the lecture location, printing publicity posters, and printing and selling tickets. Since the club was short of funds, the two officers paid the printing costs, expecting to recoup the money with ticket sales—after deducting Pankhurst's speaking fee.[50]

Emmeline Pankhurst's stop in Appleton was part of her seven-month lecture tour throughout the United States and Canada to secure donations to help starving and homeless Serbians, mostly women and children, who were suffering from their country's attempt to prevent the Germans from moving across the rest of eastern Europe. Pankhurst spoke in different locations across North America, including at a tea given by the Equal Franchise Society in Philadelphia and at a gathering of female students at Bryn Mawr College. Her public speeches showed, however, that this militant English suffragist had been "overshadowed by the militant patriot," which made a strong impression on Ethel Thomas. The war aims of the Allied countries in the Great War seemed more immediately important than woman suffrage.[51]

Though early ticket sales (twenty-five cents per person) were disappointing, last-minute publicity turned the event into a success. The night before Emmeline Pankhurst's lecture, both of the Appleton newspapers "came out with tall headlines" announcing the British suffragist's appearance at the Congregational Church. The *Lawrentian* ran it as a front-page headline: "Famous Suffragette to Speak Here." The newspaper promotion, Ethel remembered, "really awakened most of Appleton, as well as the apathetic Lawrence students, including the men. Elmer's fraternity even came like a phalanx. Jan and I and the other club members were almost overwhelmed as the crowd came in."[52]

Emmeline Pankhurst's speech, titled "Why the English Suffragettes Ceased to be Militant at the Outbreak of the War," struck Ethel as very persuasive, and she believed that the "delightfully firm speech would have made anyone vote favorable for woman suffrage." Printing the text of the speech the following week, the college paper lauded Pankhurst for placing "duty to country ahead of that of woman's rights," diplomatically concluding, "Whether one sympathizes with Mrs. Pankhurst or not, one must admit that she is a finished speaker, and her address last night [*sic*] will be remembered for years to come by those who were fortunate enough to get inside the door."[53]

Ethel Thomas admitted that she was so busy counting the money from the ticket sales that she did not have the opportunity to listen carefully to the lecture. Still, she heard enough to be persuaded by Emmeline Pankhurst's argument that in wartime, loyal citizens should set aside all other issues and concentrate on achieving the military victory. Though this very issue would plague the American woman suffrage movement in little more than a year, Ethel's reaction to the speech indicates that Pankhurst helped her to make up her mind that duty to country was always paramount. And in wartime, that duty, as Ethel saw it, was to follow the government's lead. [54]

Emmeline Pankhurst's lecture was only one of the big suffrage events that spring. Professor Atkinson, a Wisconsin delegate to the Republican convention, reminded the members of the suffrage club that the convention was going to be held in Chicago in June. As a delegate, he had the option to invite visitors. Carrie Chapman Catt planned a huge suffrage parade to coincide with the convention to garner Republican support, and the club chose Ethel Thomas and Jan Strathearn to accompany Atkinson. Louise Dudley, the club's faculty sponsor, served as chaperone for the two young women. The trio went to the Congress Hotel in Chicago, where they listened in on the conversations of convention delegates as they discussed the split in the Republican Party that caused the creation of the Progressive Party, led by former president Theodore Roosevelt. The women also went to the convention itself, held in the Coliseum, which Ethel found to be an "eye-opener": seeing a political party in action.[55]

In the midst of two days of steady rain, on Wednesday, June 7, 1916, at 4:00 o'clock in the afternoon, the suffragists held their parade. Lawrence College's representatives from the Equal Suffrage League joined with Republican women from every state in the union on the dirty city streets wearing long white dresses, white straw hats trimmed with yellow bands, and sashes of yellow and white bearing the slogan "Votes for Women." Some five thousand suffragists gathered in Grant Park, just behind the majestic Art Institute, and marched four abreast down Michigan Avenue, escorted by mounted police. Inside convention headquarters at the Coliseum, they settled in to listen to Carrie Chapman Catt read the party's plank on woman suffrage. An "exploding" yes vote affirmed the party's position.[56]

Ethel Thomas maintained an interest in suffrage into the next academic year. In the fall, the Equal Suffrage League spent the last of the Pankhurst money on a grand spread to celebrate the Democratic Party's adoption of a woman suffrage platform. Although a supporter of Republican Charles Evans Hughes, Ethel took the Democrats' action as a sign of victory for the suffrage effort, concluding that "there was no further need for us to carry on, we thought we had done our duty."[57]

Those were the key words—"we had done our duty"—that summed up Ethel Thomas's suffrage activities. Though she supported women's right to vote, she never considered herself a feminist, and gender never prominently figured into how she viewed her place in society. She accomplished everything she reasonably hoped to on behalf of suffrage, including impressing her political science professor. By the late fall of 1916, larger international issues had the potential for a negative impact on Ethel Thomas's life. The war in Europe had been raging for more than two years, and although President Woodrow Wilson had won reelection by emphasizing his ability to keep the United States out of that fight, it was becoming clear that he would not be able to do so for much longer. A war declaration would take Elmer Herold away from her.

Romance at Lawrence College

Dedicated though Ethel Thomas was to receiving one of the finest college educations available in Wisconsin—along with a healthy dose of extracurricular activities—she also pursued romance. After all, her education and subsequent career were not intended as substitutes for marriage but only as a temporary and useful delay. Coeducational institutions of higher learning proved to be logical places for forging romantic attachments. As a new woman of the twentieth century, it is likely that Ethel hoped to find a young man who supported her plan to have a career prior to marriage and who shared her political beliefs. In an extraordinary stroke of luck, she found him almost immediately.

In the first month of her freshman year, while planning for the class contests and class elections of All-College Day, Ethel met Elmer Herold, a tall, handsome, dark-haired first-year student from Prairie du Chien, a town about forty miles north of Potosi in Crawford County, Wisconsin. Born in 1893 to John and Nellie Herold, with two older brothers and one younger, plus a little sister, Elmer did not graduate from high school until the spring of 1913. The delay in his secondary education may have occurred because of finances. He probably worked in his older brother Pearl's store to help out the family and to save money to attend Lawrence College, in preparation for becoming an engineer.[58]

Fate, in the form of a giant coffee pot, brought Ethel Thomas and Elmer Herold together. The two freshmen were assigned to the coffee-making detail for All-College Day even though Ethel "knew plenty of nothing" about making coffee for so many people. But Elmer told her that his father had been in the hotel business, so he felt confident about his ability to make coffee for close to two hundred freshmen. All-College Day represented the friendly, historic rivalry between sophomores and freshmen and provided a series of contests—football, tug of war, soccer, flag rush—that would decide supremacy. Ethel enjoyed watching the various competitions and then observed that the coffee "was all drunk, so I guess it was all right." At the end of the day, Elmer (or Mr. Herold, as Ethel called him then, with Elmer addressing her as Miss Thomas) found a way to sit with Ethel on the bus ride back to Lawrence College. Impressed that he did not try to kiss her goodnight, Ethel accepted his invitation to a movie for the following Saturday night.[59]

Dating represented a modern form of courtship, the word itself frequently used by college coeds in the 1910s. A variety of factors had converged to make dating a more practical form of courtship, at least from the perspective of the two parties involved. Urbanization, industrialization, immigration, progressive reform, and women's rights all heralded a new era in the United States. Along with the new century came expectations for new, more egalitarian relationships between government and citizen, boss and worker, men and women. Among the working classes, those urban dwellers who were still relative newcomers to America, it was rare to find a chaperoned place, like the front parlor of a home, in which courting couples could meet. Among the middle and upper classes, increasing numbers of young adults went off to college, where dormitories were not suitable for courtship calls. Young couples, who chose each other, began to go out: to dance halls, restaurants, and movie theaters.[60]

While she judged her first date with Elmer Herold a success, Ethel Thomas had no flowery, romantic recollections of it. Instead she proclaimed it "all right," her favorite phrase of understatement. Elmer probably took her to either the Bijou or the Mer Mac, the two theaters located closest to the college campus, where the popular films of that fall included *Broken Threads United, The Call,* and *The Fifth String.* Elmer gave Ethel no reason to feel overly romantic about the date or their relationship, telling her up front that since he was working his way through school he had very little money to spend. He worked as a window washer and also hoped to land a restaurant job waiting tables on Saturday nights, the crucial date night of the week. At the conclusion of that first date, he remained true to his manners from the evening of All-College Day and did not try to kiss Ethel goodnight. All of this probably made him only more attractive; he was good-looking, smart, ambitious, and not put off by an independent modern woman.[61]

During Christmas vacation of 1913, the first time they were apart, Ethel and Elmer exchanged letters in which they began to address each other by their first names. Her parents were not pleased. Clem Thomas admonished his daughter, "Now remember we are not sending you to college to marry some damn fool," while Lizzie reminded her that she had to wait five years after college to get married. When Ethel returned to Potosi for the summer, Elmer took off for Iron Wood, Michigan, to take a job in a creamery so that he could earn money toward the next year's tuition. Again, they kept in touch by letters that arrived so frequently that Ethel had to dodge questions from her parents about the seriousness of her attachment.[62]

Upon returning to Lawrence in the fall of 1914 for her sophomore year, Ethel was "surprised how glad Elmer and I were to see each other again." By the spring semester, the young couple dated frequently, but their relationship did not turn serious until their junior year. Foregoing their usual Saturday night movie one fall evening in

1915, the pair took a long walk, talking earnestly about their future. Money and careers figured prominently. Ethel reminded Elmer that she had promised her mother that she would teach school for five years after graduation and that she owed Anna Bonn money for her voice lessons. Elmer, the only one in his family to go to college, had to earn his own way so as not to place a heavy economic burden on his parents. Despite his various jobs, he had to borrow some money from his father, which he expected to pay back as soon as possible. But he did not intend to end his education with a degree from Lawrence; he planned to go on to engineering school in Cleveland, Ohio.[63]

Ethel Thomas and Elmer Herold realized that it would be years before they could get married, if, in fact, that was what they wanted. As much as they enjoyed each other's company, they both knew that they were novices at male-female relationships, so they agreed that they should each date other people. In the spring of 1916, however, after some months of playing the field, Ethel finally realized that Elmer was the one for her, but she had no idea whether he felt the same. Dateless one Saturday night, she remained in Ormsby Hall, writing a letter, cleaning, and mending. As she topped off her quiet evening with a long soak in a hot bathtub, two young women came into the bathroom gossiping. Ethel recognized their voices, and apparently they were unaware that she was in the room. One of the girls, who was "very pretty, had lots of money and flashy clothes," described Elmer Herold as "the grandest man I have dated on this campus" and concluded that she "really could go for that man."[64]

Ethel Thomas agonized that whole evening. Had she lost Elmer? Was there anything she could do about it? By morning she had decided on a course of action. She called Elmer's fraternity house as early as she dared, and when he answered the phone, she asked him if he would like to help her study Spanish that evening. He said he would. The couple "did powerful little Spanish" that Sunday evening and reached a "powerfully good understanding" just short of becoming formally engaged.[65]

The way this episode played out suggests that although they had both agreed to date other people, Elmer Herold had already made up his mind about Ethel Thomas and only perfunctorily dated other women. As soon as she finished playing the field, so did he. Elmer may have already determined that the best way to end up with Ethel was to encourage her to date other men, giving her enough time to conclude that she wanted an exclusive relationship with him. Under ordinary circumstances, their steady dating would have led to a formal engagement and then to marriage, but these were not ordinary times. War was already raging in Europe, and the United States would soon be drawn into the conflict, pulling Ethel away from Elmer so that they could both do their patriotic duty.

Chapter Two

Citizenship and Patriotism during the Great War

AFTER COMPLETING a successful, enjoyable freshman year at Lawrence College, Ethel Thomas returned home to Potosi for the summer of 1914. Though she described her hometown as "its usual quiet self," she realized, given the world situation, that this calm might not last much longer. Her brother Bart's teaching career in the Philippines had educated her about American interests in Asia; now deteriorating relationships in Europe would reveal to her American entanglements across the Atlantic Ocean. Keenly aware of the connection between history and current events, Ethel Thomas avidly followed European news, hoping for a peaceful settlement but bracing for the worst.[1]

Near the end of June 1914, the archduke of Austria, Franz Ferdinand, was assassinated in Sarajevo, an act of violence that led, over the course of the summer, to a world war that would last for more than four bloody years. Ethel Thomas's experiences during those war years, both as a home-front volunteer worker and as a history teacher in a public high school, provide opportunities to examine the relationship between gender and citizenship and the contest among Americans over the meaning of patriotism. She believed in American war aims and soaked up the government's propaganda. She agreed that U.S. intervention was necessary to protect democracy at home and to ensure its dissemination around the world, that loyal citizens would support this monumental effort. As Ethel volunteered for wartime support work and entered the paid labor force, she endured home-front deprivations, worried about Elmer Herold's safety, and bore witness to the ravages of the Spanish influenza pandemic. These experiences defined loyalty, patriotism, and citizenship for her. When combined with the events of her teaching career, these perceptions of her citizenship would draw her to the Philippines just a few years after the end of the Great War.

While Europe Was at War

President Woodrow Wilson instructed Americans to remain neutral in thought and deed even as the United States offered to serve as a mediator between the belligerent European powers. But throughout the long month of August 1914, despite the president's pronouncement, some Americans began to choose sides, favoring either the Allies or the Central Powers, often according to their own ethnic heritage. While some American men volunteered for the British army or the French Foreign Legion, American women became involved in war-relief work, typically through local chapters of the Red Cross. This gave them the opportunity to turn the most ordinary, domestic work like knitting socks into a political statement.[2]

The Thomas family was among those Americans who took sides early on in the conflict. Their sympathy for the Allies—especially the French and the British—likely had dual origins. The Thomases' history of active political involvement probably led them to want to help protect the democratic-style governments of other countries, which would soon become one of President Wilson's war aims. And as for ethnic loyalty, the Thomas family had originated in the British Isles, another reason for them to support the Allied countries. Reflecting the family's dedication to backing their ideas with action, Ethel Thomas and her mother, Liz, began knitting for the Red Cross that first summer of the war and continued for the duration. Liz Thomas even donated the use of her own sewing room at home for the Potosi Red Cross workers.

This kind of grassroots support was exactly what President Wilson had been hoping for. Despite his neutrality rhetoric, he in fact maneuvered American public opinion to support the British and French war effort; thus, even prior to the April 1917 American war declaration, its citizens were expected to show their loyalty by sanctioning this support. The most vocal nationalists claimed that true patriots backed federal government policies, especially those advising military preparedness. Although much of this preparedness focused on training young men for military service, the government did not ignore the potential contributions of women. All American citizens could participate in "vigilance" to promote loyalty, and women could undergo weapons training in case they were needed for homeland defense.[3]

American women who supported preparedness made it clear that they intended to help protect the United States from all domestic and foreign enemies. Many of them did so through their promotion of "patriotic motherhood," a continuation of the ideals espoused by nationalist women during the Spanish-American War years. Patriotic motherhood acknowledged women's continued importance in the domestic realm to raise good citizens, as well as their more overt political activities to alert everyone to the dangers of an undefended country. The key to peace and prosperity, then, rested with a government and population capable and willing to fight. Though unable to contribute directly to patriotic motherhood, Ethel Thomas would use her position as a schoolteacher in Lancaster, Wisconsin, to inculcate students with lessons in patriotism and good citizenship.[4]

As the United States headed into the war, it became clear that patriotic mothers raised their sons to believe that good citizens became soldiers when their country called, a direct link between gender and citizenship. But the martial elements of citizenship never completely excluded women. During the Revolution and the Civil War, some women laid claim to citizenship by taking up arms to defend their communities and their families and to show their commitment to a cause. This continued during the Great War when female nurses and doctors, as well as women involved in home-front defense, attempted to carve out a place for themselves in the military, thereby creating a definition of full female citizenship. In a variety of ways, therefore, the war gave American women the opportunity to justify their claim to citizenship. There is little evidence, however, that Ethel Thomas felt the need to secure a position with the military to solidify her citizenship or that she felt the need to prove her citizenship.[5]

In an increasingly tense international situation, though, the U.S. government concentrated on young men and the military. In June 1916, the month Ethel Thomas completed her junior year at Lawrence College, Congress passed the National Defense Act, which provided for voluntary enlistment rather than national conscription. It authorized an increase in the regular army and the state militias and also called for the training of new officers through establishment of the Reserve Officers' Training Corps. Along with the strengthening of the Plattsburg summer camp programs, this guaranteed that fresh, eager, intelligent young men would be available if the time came to fight. No better pool of candidates could be found than those at

American colleges and universities, and Elmer Herold was part of this pool.[6]

That summer of 1916, while Ethel Thomas was once again back in Potosi, her mother read from the newspaper every morning, noting the latest on submarine warfare, and local women continued to arrive at the Thomas home to knit and roll Red Cross bandages. Ethel and her parents also discussed the upcoming presidential election. As Republicans, the Thomases supported former New York governor and Supreme Court justice Charles Evans Hughes, but of course only Clem Thomas could cast a ballot. This led to lively arguments on the topic of woman suffrage for, as Ethel recalled, "papa opposed woman suffrage—to be sure mamma did not." The suffrage campaign must have been fresh in Ethel Thomas's mind, with the recent visit to Appleton by Emmeline Pankhurst and Ethel's attendance at the Republican Party convention and suffrage parade in Chicago. Yet, in the face of the European war, it was not a high priority for her because she had apparently accepted Pankhurst's argument that in wartime loyal citizens should devote all of their energies to the war effort.[7]

The 1916 election proved crucial not only to the fate of woman suffrage but also to the continued neutrality of the United States. Democrat Woodrow Wilson ran for reelection, capitalizing on the fact that he had kept the country out of war. His critics found his policy on neutrality inconsistent and wondered how long it could continue, and some hawks agitated for war. Republican Charles Evans Hughes also preferred that the United States stay out of the war, but fearing that it would not be possible, he proposed a plan for preparedness. The Thomas family supported Hughes's plan, all the while hoping that war could be averted. Yet Ethel Thomas, largely influenced by Republican arguments, had already acknowledged the connection between patriotism and preparedness and militarism.

When she returned to Lawrence College in the fall of 1916 for her senior year, the Appleton newspaper was full of stories about the war and the upcoming presidential election. In November, 61.6 percent of registered voters turned out on Election Day, indicating the importance of the issues at stake. Charles Evans Hughes carried the Northeast and the Midwest, including Wisconsin, but his 254 electoral votes were not enough to win. Wilson eked out a victory, carrying 49.4 percent of the popular vote over Hughes's 46.2 percent and revealing critical divisions among Americans over the issue of the war. Women as well as men held differing opinions on the topic. Though Ethel Thomas represented the nationalist women who tied preparedness with patriotism, many others, especially those associated with the women's rights movement, connected women's citizenship to pacifism.[8]

Despite this public debate over the relationship between gender and citizenship, Ethel did not consciously acknowledge the gender component. Considering her formative years, this is not surprising. Her parents expected the same things from their sons and daughters: hard work and contributions to society. Ethel enjoyed the company of men, and though she recognized differences between men and women, she did not debate issues of gender inequality but rather presumed equality. In this, she represented the conservative women of the era who believed in a patriotism that required men and women to play equal parts in American society. To such women, this was the only way to build a strong country. Ethel Thomas seemed to view citizenship as her birthright and considered loyalty the highest form of patriotism. Preparedness represented a practical fallback option: if negotiations failed, her country would be ready to defend itself.[9]

The longer the war dragged on in Europe, the likelier it appeared that the United States would be drawn into it. Despite President Wilson's commitment to neutrality and to a negotiated settlement between the belligerent powers, American relations with Germany worsened. By the beginning of 1917, unrestricted submarine warfare and diplomatic intrigues in Mexico led the president to abandon his initial stance. On Monday evening, April 2, 1917, Wilson delivered a war message to Congress; four days later it obliged him with a declaration of war against Germany.[10]

Home Front Support

Ethel Thomas had believed Woodrow Wilson's 1916 campaign pledge about keeping the country out of war and hoped peace would continue, so it was with some "shock" that she digested the news that war had been declared. Even though she had supported Hughes and preparedness, she was not a hawk; she apparently had great faith in diplomacy and negotiation and was surprised when Wilson opted for war. Nevertheless, it did not cross Ethel's mind to oppose the president's decision. She had already been doing her part for the Allies through Red Cross work in Potosi; now she would wholeheartedly support the Americans. To show their patriotism, two hundred of Lawrence College's female students, including Ethel, organized a Red Cross Association, meeting regularly in campus buildings to make bandages and other hospital supplies.[11]

Apparently, Ethel Thomas believed that as a citizen, her obligation was to support her government's decision to go to war, and in doing so she conflated government with country. She did not view the war declaration as a partisan issue. Though a staunch Republican, she would not refuse to support the war simply because a Democratic president had called for it. Ethel believed that the stakes were higher than any party squabbles, thereby allying herself with what has been identified as the "militaristic tradition" of patriotism: a "faith-like loyalty" to the United States as the highest form of allegiance."[12]

Demonstrating that allegiance, through both work and pageantry, became important measures of loyalty and patriotism, and Ethel Thomas was determined to measure up. The Monday after the war declaration, more than fifteen thousand people turned out to watch Appleton's Loyalty Day parade, including almost the entire Lawrence College student body, making it the "greatest demonstration of loyalty which this part of Wisconsin has ever seen." It is unlikely that Ethel skipped this extravaganza of public support for the war. Some five thousand people, including students and veterans of both the Civil War and the Spanish-American War, marched twenty-five blocks in the crisp April sunshine. The parade even included representatives from the campus German societies, evidence that ethnic hostilities did not immediately flare up in Appleton. Mounted police kept traffic in order but were not needed for crowd control as "a heavy pall of seriousness hung over the watchers."[13]

Most Lawrence students, faculty, and administrators eagerly supported the war. As tensions had grown between Germany and the United States in late March 1917, sixty male students organized a military company, committing to three drills per week and pledging to offer their services to the U.S. military in the event of war. Elmer Herold joined them. Such enthusiasm just prior to a formal declaration of war was typical on campuses across the country. Princeton University, for example, had to hold male students back from volunteering, with its president assuring them that they would have more access to military instruction as long as they remained on campus.[14]

Once Congress declared war, it was impossible to rein in the enthusiasm of these young men. Lawrence College president Samuel Plantz announced during morning chapel on April 17 that in light of the military's need for officers, any student who joined a training camp would be allowed to graduate with his regular class, with grades based on the fall semester's work and college credit given for military service. He also informed the students that athletic competitions had been cancelled and replaced by military drills, and he asked all campus organizations to curtail their social functions. Plantz expected them to set an example for "curbing extravagances," even to the extent of putting the dormitories on war rations.[15]

Preparedness, once a political debate, was now a necessity, as President Wilson considered the best way to staff both industrial and military positions. He swiftly settled on conscription as the best option. Despite some continued opposition, especially from the House of Representatives, where many congressmen from the South and the West opposed the draft, Selective Service sailed through Congress. Wilson signed it into law on May 18, 1917.[16]

Instituting the draft, compelling men to fight in a war whether they supported it or not, prompted Americans to consider the meaning of "obligation" to their country and their government. Americans' sense of obligation, which cut across party lines, was rooted in a republican political tradition that privileged the common good over that of the individual, hopes for a harmonious community, Christian beliefs regarding virtue, and paternalism. Normally, citizens fulfilled their obligations voluntarily, but the divisive nature of the war meant that the government had to educate its people about their obligations and compel them to fulfill them, creating a "culture of coercive voluntarism." Thus, President Wilson described Selective Service as "in no sense a conscription of the unwilling; it is rather, selection from a nation which has volunteered in mass."[17]

Elmer Herold, who apparently shared Ethel Thomas's views of loyalty and patriotism, never questioned this particular obligation to his country. Near the end of May 1917, he learned that a three-month training course for officers would be starting at Fort Sheridan in Illinois, so after passing the required physical and written exams, he reported there for training. Of his departure from Lawrence College, Ethel remembered, "Ormsby's front porch where Elmer kissed me goodbye was a hallowed spot." It turned out to be a temporary farewell because Elmer returned on leave about two weeks later, in time to surprise Ethel at his fraternity's spring formal. The next morning, they talked once again about their future, and Elmer asked Ethel if she would be waiting for him when he came back. That was Elmer's proposal, and Ethel said yes. She acknowledged that the promise she had made to her mother to work five years "did not matter to us then. Just as long as he got back alive and I was still waiting. We kissed each other more that day than all the other times put together. It was so wonderful to belong to each other. From out of his pocket, he drew his Phi Kap pin and with ceremony pinned it on me. However, we agreed not to tell the others now. I would conceal the pin for a proper occasion."[18]

Commencement for Ethel Thomas "lost its meaning" without Elmer Herold there to share it with her, and during the ceremony she must have been thinking about her next visit with him. He managed to convince Clem and Liz Thomas to let their daughter come home via Chicago so that she could meet him there. Elmer Herold made reservations at the Morrison Hotel, he with a room on the third floor and she with one on the sixth. After dinner and dancing, Elmer gave Ethel a goodnight kiss in front of her door before heading down to his room. "That was 1917 morality," she later observed. During breakfast the next morning, they "talked of the future and sweet nothings" until it was time to catch their trains. As they went their separate ways, they did not know when they would see each other again.[19]

"What a queer summer," Ethel Thomas thought of those months after her college graduation. She knew this was not going to be one of her "carefree quiet" vacations—those were gone, perhaps never to return again. When she came home to Potosi as a college graduate in June 1917, Grant County was already deep into wartime activities. Its nearly 40,000 residents prepared to purchase their first Liberty Bonds, and just over 3,000 young men registered for the draft, including 120 from Potosi. Two hundred and fifty women in the county seat of Lancaster joined the Red Cross, diligently sewing and attending first aid classes in the city hall. Potosi hosted a two-day celebration at the end of June in honor of veterans, and despite inclement weather, large crowds turned up for the festivities. Ethel participated in an afternoon program, singing the banjo song "Just Be Glad."[20]

Throughout the war, she tried to take a cue from that jaunty song and to never waver from her conviction that democracy and freedom, as well as true love, would prevail. So she rolled up her sleeves and went to work to help make that happen. All summer, Potosi women streamed into Liz Thomas's Red Cross sewing room, heeding the call from the state and county councils of defense to "co-operate in solving the very real war problems with which they are confronted." The State Council of Defense, founded in April, coordinated war activities in Wisconsin by organizing military, financial, industrial, and social resources. Civilians, especially women, could most effectively express their patriotism through Red Cross work, and President Wilson intended to use the organization to foster cohesiveness throughout the country. This was one of the earliest signs that the government recognized the value of women's contributions to the war effort. Women were valued for their work as industrial and agricultural workers during the war and also for the organizational skills they had developed in voluntary organizations. These women viewed their various services to the state as a key part of citizenship.[21]

Yet women were not left to their own devices in these organizations, despite generations of experience with benevolent and cultural societies. White women's nationalism became "masculinized" during the war to the extent that their volunteer efforts were put under the jurisdiction of the government and of the professions, both predominantly male. Finally, the United States government realized the importance of the concerns these women had about spreading patriotism and threw its own might behind efforts to create a state-based patriotism. When the government came to this conclusion, women's work on patriotic projects suddenly obtained a new vibrancy. Ethel Thomas would not have objected to the government taking control of these wartime support organizations. She would have viewed it as men and women working together toward a common goal that would benefit the country and the world.[22]

Indeed, women figured prominently in home-front support throughout the country, but their work did not completely reverse or challenge gender roles. Men usually organized women's activities and typically kept them separate from men's. The State Council of

Defense, for example, appointed Red Cross member Mrs. Henry H. Morgan of Madison to coordinate women's activities in Wisconsin. The council then assured the public that women were being tapped for their traditional domestic duties: "Every woman can render important service to the nation in the present emergency. She need not leave her home or abandon her home duties to help the armed forces. She can help to feed and clothe our armies and help to supply food to those beyond the seas by practicing effective thrift in her own household."[23]

Women's wartime contributions depended on voluntarism, which was depicted as consensual, unpaid work in organizations that fell just outside of direct government control. Because of their long association with benevolent work, middle-class American women, both black and white, were accustomed to donating their labor to the cause of improving their communities and even their country. And they were very conscious of this contribution and of its increased value in wartime. One clubwoman, Mrs. Coffin Van Renseelaer, bragged that women's voluntarism "is the means of saving millions of dollars" for the United States government.[24]

The Thomas family enthusiastically responded to the calls for voluntarism. Ethel Thomas and her mother barely had time to keep up with the war news in the paper during the summer of 1917 because they were so busy sewing and tending a war garden. American women, from the upper-class matron to the rural farmwife to the industrial working-class immigrant, took to their needles by the thousands during the war, knitting and sewing. The image of the knitting woman, in fact, became emblematic of the female citizen during World War I. Ethel Thomas chose to do her part by embracing such obligations.[25]

The Thomases planted a war garden on the hill behind their large stone house in Potosi. Apparently, Clem Thomas had initially resisted the idea, thinking that his wife and daughter would be planting the garden for family budgetary reasons. It wounded his pride to imagine that Liz could not purchase what the family needed at local stores. But when the women convinced him that the garden "was a matter of patriotism rather than economy," he enthusiastically took on his share of the work.[26]

Gardening also had a connection to Ethel Thomas's chosen career. Since 1914, the United States Bureau of Education had been developing programs on home and school gardening, a clear recognition of the importance of food production in wartime—even when the war was still restricted to Europe. This lead time facilitated production after the United States entered the war. By early 1918, P. P. Claxton, the commissioner of the Bureau of Education, had drafted a plan in which children aged nine through fifteen would cultivate gardens in their own backyards and even in nearby vacant lots. School teachers, Claxton proposed, would direct their work. Given this connection between food and education, it is not surprising that Ethel Thomas would find herself involved in these kinds of war-support efforts when she began teaching.[27]

As a first-year teacher at the Lancaster high school, Ethel earned an annual salary of $675 (with $28 a month going toward rent for a room in a local boarding house). This was near the bottom of reported average salaries for high school teachers in that time period. Many teachers scraped by on such wages because school districts resisted implementing raises and pressured teachers to stay on the job by legally enforcing employment contracts and by appealing to the teachers' sense of patriotism. Their services were in great demand during the months that the United States was at war. By the late spring of 1917, the Bureau of Education realized that elementary and secondary schools needed about 130,000 new teachers to replace those who had joined the military or had opted to take a job more directly related to the war. Colleges and universities would only be able to produce 35,000 trained teachers per year, which left about 100,000 positions open for poorly and/or hastily trained teachers, many of whom ended up in rural schools.[28]

Lancaster High School offered a curriculum that ranged from domestic science to English to German (which was banned, in a fit of patriotism, the following year) and Latin. The institution advertised itself as "A School of Ideas and Efficient Service," a motto entirely appropriate to Wisconsin's progressive bent. In those early months of the war, the school also proudly proclaimed itself "loyal to our government in every way possible," and the government viewed schools as an important component in cultivating the support of its citizens. Lancaster schools closed on the second day of classes for Grant County's special send-off of its first group of soldiers. Some ten thousand people came to town on September 18 to watch the mile-long street parade, listen to short speeches, take part in an evening dance, and watch the fireworks. A second farewell, equally elaborate but with a half-day holiday for school children, took place at the beginning of October.[29]

The war itself aided Ethel Thomas's teaching endeavors as she discovered ways of relating European events to almost any aspect of ancient, medieval, or modern history. She urged her students to keep a scrapbook of the war, and they used these for reference during their weekly current-events discussions. She may have drawn inspiration from an editorial in the *Weekly Teller* that urged more teaching of American history in schools, to "emphasize the study of American ideals and true American citizenship . . . [to] help instill patriotism." The editorial advised that history should be made popular by not teaching it simply through textbooks and recitations.[30]

The newspaper editorial and Ethel's own enthusiasm for combining history with current events echoed much of the federal government's proposed study plans for students from the elementary grades through college. The nation's schools were viewed as an integral part of the wartime propaganda machine. Although P. P. Claxton disagreed with school districts that eliminated German language and literature from their curriculums, the Bureau of Education cooperated with the Committee on Public Information (CPI) and its collaborative organization, the National Board for Historical Service, to distribute "war study courses." These courses taught school children about the benefits of democracy and capitalism, emphasized Americanization, and highlighted the evils of Germany. It was a curriculum that Ethel Thomas could patriotically embrace.[31]

Samuel B. Harding, a professor of European history from Indiana University, wrote the plan for high school students, *The Study of the Great War: A Topical Outline, with Extensive Quotations and Reading References.* The curriculum guide blamed Germany for the war, portraying the country as a militaristic, unchristian society. Harding included as causes of the war Germany's constitution, its profits from past wars, and the kaiser's demand for "a place in the sun." Though the plan appeared to be steeped in scholarly methodology—complete with numerous citations—much of Harding's information actually came from the CPI and the propaganda offices of the other Allied countries rather than from historical sources. Nevertheless, between 700,000 and 800,000 high school teachers and students out of a nationwide total of 20,650,000 received the study plan. Other "informational" pamphlets were available, too, including one titled *The War Message and Facts Behind It* and a collection of prose, poetry, and songs called *The Battle Line of Democracy.*[32]

Teaching provided Ethel Thomas with a way of expressing her patriotism in a manner consistent with the "new woman" model that had influenced her during her college years. It also allowed her to act as a patriotic mother by proxy, reinforcing what she assumed her students were learning from their own mothers. Teaching, therefore, with its promotion of American democracy, along with her various other volunteer activities, constituted Ethel's contribution to the state, her demonstration of citizenship. Other American women chose different ways to make their contributions, such as taking up factory work, joining auxiliary branches of the military, or shipping out to France as civilian employees of the American Expeditionary Force. All of these activities helped women lay claim to an equal position in American society.

When Ethel Thomas entered the paid work force in 1917, she did so at a time when patterns of women's work were in transition. Women had begun to move from blue-collar to pink-collar jobs, taking positions in offices and department stores. But there was no massive influx of women into the work force because of the war. The years 1910 to 1920 saw a 6.3 percent increase in working women. About 400,000 moved into semiskilled factory jobs and worked as common laborers, and over 750,000 took on office-related jobs such as clerks, typists, stenographers, and telephone operators. More than 500,000 women gave up jobs as servants, in-home pieceworkers, and laundresses to meet the needs of a wartime economy.[33]

As young American men heeded the military's call, working women responded to the needs of business and industry to keep the military supplied and the home front functioning smoothly. They viewed these job changes as exciting personal challenges that often netted them pay increases. This alteration in women's work reflected the continuation of a patriotic pattern begun at the birth of the United States when the Revolutionary War propelled colonial women to boycott British tea and cloth and to take charge of the family business while their husbands and sons went away to fight. Subsequently, the Civil War opened up nursing opportunities for young women as well as some positions in federal government offices.

In most cases, however, even in wartime, a woman's job choice was influenced and/or limited by class. During the Great War, women who switched from one type of factory job to another still tended to hail from the working classes. Even though a job transfer could be labeled patriotic because it usually involved moving into manufacturing war materials, Ethel Thomas never considered factory work. Her notions of patriotism did not stretch beyond her class assumptions: she was a college graduate whose parents lived in one of the finest homes in Potosi. Her father had moved beyond the physical labor of the fields; he became a mailman who took regular vacations and had a pension awaiting his retirement. Ethel's status and her accomplishments meant that she had a certain set of talents that she could apply to the war effort. Moreover, she was such a good teacher that the school hired her back for the 1918–19 year, with a one-hundred-dollar raise.[34]

Ethel Thomas's definition of patriotism also did not require her to further defy gender conventions. She had already broken with female tradition by declaring a history major in college so that she could work as a high school history teacher. But because of the war, she functioned as a surrogate patriotic mother in the classroom. As much as she had supported military preparedness and though she never questioned Elmer Herold's decision to join the army, she did not believe that she had to go into the military to lay claim to citizenship or to express her patriotism. She likely thought that supporting the war required different things from different people, and with some guidance from the government, she could decide how to make her contribution. Like other women, she heeded the warning from the *Ladies' Home Journal:* "Let every woman . . . be sure of her talent, and not hinder or complicate by offering herself for work for which she is not fitted."[35]

Ethel's support of America's involvement in the war and approval of the government's methods for securing home-front support made her particularly suited to teaching. She did not object that school boards expected teachers to follow a patriotic curriculum within the classroom, subjected them to loyalty oaths, encouraged the purchase of war bonds, and urged them to take on volunteer work.[36] Ethel eagerly cooperated, approaching her voluntarist duties as seriously as her paid job.

The federal government, through various boards and agencies, designed programs to support the war effort and to provide organization for voluntarist activities. Liberty Loans, launched in the spring of 1917, helped pay for the cost of the war. The Food Administration, Fuel Administration, and the War Industries Board all encouraged voluntary business cooperation and civilian conservation. Herbert Hoover, head of the Food Administration, eschewed rationing, convinced that Americans could be shown the wisdom of voluntary conservation. His agency inaugurated campaigns for "wheatless Wednesdays" and "meatless Tuesdays," reinforced by a half-million volunteers who visited housewives to secure their pledges to do without certain food items and stretch others. In August 1917, just before the start of the school year, the Bureau of Education and the Food Administration held a joint conference to plan an educational campaign on food conservation. Leaflets describing the program were ready for circulation at the beginning of October. Officials believed that schools were the most logical point of dissemination, since students could learn about food conservation through lessons on civic responsibility.[37]

Food conservation was not quite as coercive as the Selective Service, but since the government considered it important, Americans were expected to abide by Food Administration rules. Politicians like Wilson and Hoover viewed the Food Administration as "a model of voluntarism" designed to meet a particular wartime emergency. Cooperation was paramount, Hoover believed, because government-run rationing would require a "hundred thousand bureaucratic snoopers" to nose around in American homes, an intrusion he considered excessive. Male bureaucrats thought women ideally suited to monitor this domestic project. But as with knitting and sewing for the Red Cross, female volunteers for the Food Administration politicized their work for this agency, an approach supported by prominent women such as the progressive reformer Jane Addams. In 1918, Addams encouraged women "to connect their duty to feed their families with political obligations toward the nation and the world."[38]

The successful implementation of these voluntarist programs required state and county support to convince Americans to pitch in. As the seat of Grant County, Lancaster initiated many war projects and drives. The Community Chorus helped raise funds for the Red Cross; the superintendent of the schools, T. Emery Bray, headed up the Liberty Bond drives; and Ethel Thomas assisted with food-conservation efforts. Professor G. E. Wilson from the Platteville normal school had been appointed emergency food and farm labor agent for Grant County, and as Lancaster's agent, F. J. Glanville recruited volunteers to carry out government programs.[39]

Illustrating the link between women's domestic duties and their political involvement, the General Federation of Women's Clubs (GFWC) cooperated with the Food Administration to encourage women to embrace food conservation. The GFWC had been founded in 1890, and its members dedicated themselves to community improvement through voluntarism, endeavors that regularly brought them into contact with various levels of government. Throughout the 1910s, GFWC members worked for progressive programs and policies such as child labor legislation, workers' rights, the Pure Food and Drug Act, and prison reform. During World War I, the GFWC board determined that the most crucial issue facing the United States was the "conservation, development, and absorption of American ideals of National, Civic, and Social Life, particularly among the foreign born."[40]

Ethel Thomas directly supported a nationwide, voluntary food-conservation pledge drive named after the Food Administration's Herbert Hoover. Approximately five hundred thousand GFWC members visited the homes of nonmembers during three separate drives to convince housewives to sign a pledge card. About 14 million households complied, an example of one group of women "explicitly taking on the task of regulating the political obligations of other women." But the pledge drives, organized at the local level, also relied on cooperation from schools, churches, libraries, and places of employment. The local nature of the drives—neighbor woman visiting neighbor woman—made it difficult for any woman to refuse.[41]

The Housewife Food Pledge Campaign, initiated in Wisconsin at the end of October 1917 during the second of these three drives, enlisted the help of women in voluntary food conservation. Armed with myriad statistics about "what would happen if just one family wasted one slice of bread a day," Ethel Thomas lectured around Grant County about conservation and gave out recipes designed to assist housewives in creative cooking and baking. And everywhere she went, she sang: "Loyalty," "Keep the Home Fires Burning," "When the Boys Come Home," and especially "The Star Spangled Banner." The county campaign was considered a success, with 51 percent of its households signing pledge cards by the end of the year.[42]

For women, participating in food conservation was like knitting. It symbolized their voluntarism but masked any coercive methods that might have been used to prompt it. Because it was just "women's work," it was easy not to see it, easy not to think about what it meant. For Ethel Thomas, participation in the pledge drive meant that she had yet another opportunity to demonstrate that she was a good citizen, something she willingly did. But it also further confirmed that education, whether conducted formally in a classroom or informally in someone's kitchen, could be used to promote American values and goals. This lesson extended beyond the war years for Ethel as it likely influenced her decision to take up teaching in the Philippines.[43]

Boosting morale and encouraging support for the war seemed essential during the fall and winter of 1917 since Ethel thought it "looked worse for our side." The Germans and Austrians continued to serve up punishing blows to the Allies, and the Bolshevik Revolution in November, which prompted the Russians to sue for a separate peace, allowed the Central Powers to move more of their troops to the western front. It appeared that the Americans were in for a long fight. By the following summer, the initial excitement of the war had faded, and the reality set in. Ethel noticed more stars appearing in the windows of Potosi homes, signifying a soldier's death at places like Chateau-Thierry and Belleau Wood. This must have caused her deep sorrow since, in such a small town, she would have known these young men. Some of them, perhaps, had been the ones who escorted her home from Christian Endeavors during her high school years and tried to kiss her and elicit promises of marriage.

Yet in Ethel Thomas's memories of those years, almost everyone she encountered supported the war effort: most went "all out" to contribute what they could, and a steady stream of young men volunteered for military service. Grant County initially experienced little of the wartime divisiveness that plagued the rest of the state and the country. Rather homogeneous, the county had few people of German or Austrian extraction; by the 1910s the majority of its population was native born.[44]

At the state level, however, Wisconsin was not immune from the controversy that U.S. participation in the war provoked. Senator Robert LaFollette, a leading progressive, adhered to his pacifist beliefs, and eight members of the state's congressional delegation had voted against entry into the war. Congressman Victor Berger, a socialist from Milwaukee, was barred from his seat in the House of Representatives after being jailed under the Espionage Act. Nationwide, concern over this kind of divided opinion prompted President Wilson in the spring of 1917 to create the Committee on Public Information to promote the war aims and encourage "One Hundred Per Cent Americanism." Members of the American Protective League spied on friends and neighbors in an attempt to catch anyone impeding the war effort.

Maybe Ethel Thomas wanted to see only the unity, or maybe she only associated with people who supported the war. But after the first year of U.S. involvement, dissension cropped up in her own hometown. At the end of July 1918, a federal jury found Christian Yearous, a Potosi farmer, guilty of advocating the German cause in the war and declaring himself in favor of Germany. Two Potosi men were among those who gave evidence against Yearous, who received a one-thousand-dollar fine and spent a year in Fort Leavenworth. It is unlikely that Ethel Thomas had no knowledge of the Yearous case. Although she taught in Lancaster, she returned to Potosi on weekends and during the summer and was thus likely to have kept up with hometown news. It is also improbable, given her views on the war, that she would have had any sympathy for Yearous.[45]

Disloyalty was an especially serious problem for public school teachers, whose beliefs and behavior were subject to scrutiny from students, parents, coworkers, and school district officials. That she was a well-educated professional would not have given Ethel Thomas immunity from the Espionage and Sedition Acts, had she done or said anything to hinder the war effort. Women, perhaps because they were expected to act like patriotic mothers, found themselves facing federal or local charges when they violated these expectations. In the spring of 1918, the Brooklyn, New York, school board fired Gertrude Pignol, a 1905 immigrant from Germany who taught German at one of the high schools, because she had "personal reservations" about the war. The New York Board of Superintendents also charged Mary McDowell, a Quaker and a member of the Woman's Peace Party, with "conduct unbecoming a teacher" because she would not sign a loyalty oath or support the war in any way. Like Pignol, McDowell lost her job.[46] Ethel Thomas would not have dreamed of doing anything that could in any way be construed as opposing the war. Her sense of patriotism would not allow it, especially since the man she loved had put his life on the line to preserve democracy and freedom.

During that first summer of the war, Red Cross work and the war garden kept Ethel Thomas occupied physically, but her heart was with Elmer Herold. One day in mid-August 1917, she received a telegram from Elmer informing her that he would arrive on the early morning train. The two talked quickly for a few hours after he showed up that day; still, "so many things were left unsaid." But despite what they felt for each other, despite their worries that Elmer would be leaving soon for the front, they decided against running off for a hasty marriage. They were too responsible for that. When they parted that afternoon, they did not see each other again for two years.[47]

The Doughboy, the War, and the Influenza Pandemic

Elmer Herold wanted to get into something more specialized than the regular infantry, so he signed on with the new Tank Corps, the cutting edge of military strategy and technology in the war. By the fall of 1914, when the war was still new but already bogged down, a British officer had determined that some kind of armored caterpillar tractor was needed to help break the stalemate of trench warfare. At the Somme, two years later, the British sent forty-nine tanks into battle with encouraging results. In July 1917, American General John Pershing created a "tank board" to study the further development and usage of the vehicles. By the end of the year, the American Expeditionary Force had its own Tank Corps.[48]

Stateside training facilities were not ready in the fall of 1917, so Elmer Herold secured permission to teach science at New Richmond, Wisconsin. He remained in the states, but there is no evidence that he managed to visit Ethel during this period of time, though she must have been relieved that his departure overseas had been delayed. Elmer's job reflected not only the continuing shortage of qualified schoolteachers but also the rather casual nature of voluntary enlistment during the Great War. The army could not supply all of its recruits with uniforms, and many of the camps had not yet been fully constructed. It would take months before all of the citizen soldiers, eager or not, could be absorbed into military life.[49]

Dwight D. Eisenhower, a future president of the United States but then a young captain in the army, created the first tank training center in the country. In March 1918, Camp Colt in Gettysburg, Pennsylvania, was a skeleton of a place, with few men and no equipment. By the end of the year, however, ten thousand enlisted men and six hundred officers trained there. Elmer Herold received his call to duty at Camp Colt that spring, and he became a member of Company B, 337th Battalion Tank Corps. Upon completion of a course on surveying, he received a commission as a second lieutenant, under the command of now Lieutenant Colonel Eisenhower. Instead of receiving immediate orders for France—and to Elmer's consternation—he remained in Gettysburg, training men in land surveying.[50]

That Elmer Herold remained stateside for so long was not unusual. Although members of the American Expeditionary Force, led by General Pershing, arrived in France in June 1917, the War Department proved unable to quickly send large numbers of troops overseas. American doughboys continued to trickle into France until their numbers totaled about 175,000 by the end of the year. Overseas troop transfers did not pick up until the summer of 1918 when an estimated ten thousand men disembarked from eastern seaports.[51] For now at least, Ethel Thomas did not have to worry about Elmer enduring the trenches in France, but she did have to face another life-threatening concern.

Elmer Herold and millions of other American soldiers proved more at risk of contracting the Spanish influenza, which erupted in 1918, than of dying on the battlefield. Disease has always been a major killer in any war. In the United States, for example, two men died from disease for every one combat-related death during the Civil War. If a bullet or bomb did not hit a soldier during wartime, a germ probably did, and often with deadly consequences. The disease then usually spread into the civilian population. This 1918 strain of influenza thrived in wartime circumstances. Training camps, battlefields, and the dank close quarters of the trenches allowed the virus to rip into approximately one quarter of the people it encountered, killing even those in the prime of their lives.[52]

Most Americans were likely too caught up in war news that spring and summer to notice a mild, warning-shot epidemic of influenza that swept the country. The earliest outbreak has been traced to Haskell County, Kansas, and Camp Funston in early March 1918. Soldiers who traveled from Funston to other posts and then overseas carried the influenza with them. Although the spring outbreak was mild, causing few deaths, it had two unusual characteristics: the presence of bloody and fluid-filled lungs and the high number of otherwise healthy people in their twenties afflicted. The U.S. military, because of the large concentration of men in various camps, proved especially vulnerable to this flu.[53]

Elmer Herold contracted the flu as he trained tank operators at Camp Colt. Some soldiers from Camp Devens, just northwest of Boston, had arrived for machine gun training on September 14, 1918, bringing the virus along with them. One of Camp Colt's medical officers decided that the men were suffering from reactions to typhoid shots and saw no reason to keep them separated from the general population. It took a few days for the flu to be diagnosed, and by then it had already begun its astonishing spread through the camp. The afflicted complained first of headache, a general achiness, chills, fever—sometimes as high as 105 or 106 degrees—and nausea, and then extreme congestion in the entire upper respiratory tract. Most victims coughed constantly, eventually bringing up bloody sputum. Some battled for every breath and experienced searing pain in their limbs. Skin turned blue from a lack of oxygen in the lungs. Over the next two and a half weeks, the camp hospital treated 321 influenza cases and 106 of pneumonia. One hundred and fifty men died.[54]

Elmer Herold managed to scrawl a "scant note" to Ethel Thomas, reporting that he was getting over the flu, attributing his survival to "spirits of fermentis"—whiskey. Indeed, no medicines existed at the time that could effectively counter the virus's swift devastation. Elmer recovered by the end of September, even as another vicious wave hit. He joined the members of his tank battalion heading to Brest, France, on the troopship *Leviathan,* a tough, hulking, converted luxury liner capable of traveling at an impressive twenty-two knots per hour.

Over a three-day period, some ten thousand troops from a variety of different outfits plus supplies were loaded onto the *Leviathan,* which departed from Hoboken, New Jersey, on September 29, 1918. Elmer fainted as he boarded the ship and was carried into the infirmary, where he remained quarantined for the duration of the trip. Evidently his previous recovery had not been complete. Relapses did occur and often with fatal consequences, but Elmer managed to survive, this time in an enclosed environment that seemed to breed death. An officer from Vermont traveling on the *Leviathan* recalled, "Every available doctor and nurse was utilized to the limit of endurance. The conditions during the night cannot be visualized by anyone who had not actually seen them. Groans and cries of the terrified added to the confusion of the applicants clamoring for treatment and altogether a true inferno reigned supreme."[55]

Before the end of October, another of Elmer Herold's letters finally made its way to Ethel Thomas. Though it looked like "a bunch of ribbons" because of censorship, Ethel figured out that he was headed to the front to put his troops and tanks into action. In other letters, Elmer skipped over war talk and instead described the beautiful French countryside where he and his troops shared lodgings with an elderly couple on their farm. His bucolic missives skirted the martial reality: participation in the fall offensive at Meuse-Argonne from late September until November's armistice. During the last full month of the war, painstaking advances by the Allies cost about 550 American deaths per day. But Elmer Herold survived combat just as he had earlier survived the flu.[56]

The influenza epidemic that had afflicted Elmer and other soldiers was not, of course, confined to the military. When Ethel Thomas started teaching again in September 1918, she remembered that "the great war effort continued, history teaching was as vital as ever." But civilians had started dying in Philadelphia, New York City, and Washington, D.C. About midway through September, one of the first influenza-related deaths occurred in Lancaster; at approximately the same time, a Potosi military recruit was reportedly ill with pneumonia at Camp Grant. By October it was clear that influenza had infiltrated Wisconsin. When Dr. C. A. Harper, the state health officer, issued an advisory calling for the closing of all schools, churches, and theaters, the town of Lancaster obeyed. Ethel went home for a "short vacation" to wait out the influenza cycle. Toward the end of the month, so many people in Potosi were afflicted that doctors from nearby towns came in to help treat them.[57]

When the influenza seemed to burn itself out, the Lancaster schools reopened in early November, coinciding with the first reports of a firm armistice settlement to reach the town on November 7, 1918. On Monday, November 11, just after three o'clock in the morning, as soon as news arrived that the agreement had been officially signed, church bells pealed and the dome of the courthouse lit up. Soon a group of boys started a musical parade, automobile drivers honked their horns, and people shot off firearms. "Oh, happy day!" Ethel Thomas rejoiced. "A holiday at school. The day was cold, snow was trying to fall, but our spirits were gay." Students and teachers alike marched and sang all day. Main Street on the north side of the courthouse was roped off for evening entertainment: a dance, a jazz band, and a bonfire. But the euphoria of the armistice soon gave way to anxiety as Ethel wondered when Elmer would come home, wondered if by some cruel twist of fate he was killed on the last day of the war. Now that her war work had ended, she had even more time to dwell on such things.[58]

As some of the first American troops began their journey home, the influenza epidemic in southwestern Wisconsin again picked up steam. On December 3, 1918, the board of health, city officials, and the acting health officer decided to close all public places "until the epidemic now prevalent be, beyond a doubt, under control." School officials started Christmas vacation two weeks early, and Ethel Thomas, still healthy, went home to Potosi to ride out the flu and wait for word from Elmer. However, despite these best efforts and despite the closure of public places and orders that people wear face masks, the flu continued to spread.[59]

Ethel described this as a "weird time" because the quarantines cut down on the usual holiday socializing. The town doctors worked until they could not; nurses were nonexistent; and most people were too sick to help themselves, let alone their neighbors. The *Weekly Teller* reported that the "Reaper death has laid his heavy hand on Potosi": five deaths in just one week from flu and pneumonia. While Clem Thomas continued his mail route, his wife and daughter remained at home, observing quarantine rules and passing the time by sewing items for Ethel's hope chest.[60]

On a dark, snowy afternoon just before Christmas, Ethel Thomas walked to the post office and finally received a bundle of five letters that had been forwarded to her from her boardinghouse in Lancaster. Elmer Herold wrote about the armistice and how he and his men thought at first that it was a hoax. By early November, the Americans had pushed across the Meuse, and on the seventh, the Germans sent a delegation across the French lines to discuss peace, which prompted the premature assumption that the war had ended. Fighting continued for four more days until the Germans, French, and British signed the armistice. The guns finally stopped.[61]

When Elmer Herold and his men were convinced that the November 11 announcement was real, they expected to be put on the next ship back to the United States. But it took a while for the military to discharge its men and revert to a peacetime status. By mid-January 1919, about 818,000 men had been discharged; over 2.7 million left the service by June. Along with their separation from the service came a sixty-dollar bonus, and men who served overseas could take a souvenir gas mask and helmet. Instead of going home, though, Elmer Herold received orders to travel to the front lines for demolition work, after which he moved to Bordeaux to work at the headquarters garage. Before he returned home, he stopped in Paris for a couple of days and then went on to tour other European sites. If the delay in returning stateside disappointed Elmer Herold, he apparently kept it to himself, along with any opinions he might have formed about the French and German people he encountered and about implementation of the peace. He seemed satisfied that he had made an appropriate contribution to the war effort.[62]

The Lancaster schools reopened on January 6, 1919, ending Ethel Thomas's extended vacation, throwing her into a whirl of activity. During the late winter and early spring, she involved her history students in a mock organization of the House of Representatives and coached the junior history class in a rhetorical program on the war, which resulted in "splendid papers [that] showed the result of Miss Thomas' careful coaching in delivery of the papers and efficient teaching of the subject." At the end of March, she lectured the high school assembly on "the value of looking at things in the right light and working for the joy of working."[63] For Ethel Thomas, the "right light" was not subjective. Rather, it was a loyal, patriotic view that shone its brightest when citizens answered their country's call.

In April, as world leaders meeting in Versailles completed the terms of the peace treaty, Grant County geared up for its last Victory Loan drive. Ethel Thomas and two other teachers organized the production of a play called "Lest We Forget," performed for a standing-room-only crowd at the Lancaster Opera House. Eight English students took part in the "intensely patriotic and effective" one-act drama. The play capped a victory meeting that opened with a recital of the high school orchestra and included Ethel Thomas performing "two very beautiful selections," a community singing of patriotic songs, and a speech by Madame E. Guerin of Provence, France, about the patriotism and suffering of the French people. On the last day of April, hundreds of county residents braved cool and rainy weather to catch sight of an army tank that had been brought to Lancaster to boost enthusiasm for the loan drive. Ethel immediately "assumed authority" over it, rationalizing that she had the right because she was practically engaged to an officer in the Tank Corps. She rode down the main street on top of the tank, not inside of it as some of the other young women did, because she considered it too small.[64]

The school board decided to continue classes until June 20 to make up for some of the time lost to the influenza epidemic outbreak. Teachers received an extra month's salary. While Ethel Thomas appreciated the money, she felt exhausted at the end of that academic year. During those last couple of months, the makeup of the student body altered as the young Lancaster men who had gone off to war in 1917 returned to earn their high school diplomas. "Proudly wearing their uniforms . . . they all seemed much more matured than others in their class," Ethel observed. She found their opinions most interesting, admitting that, probably because of her ties to Elmer Herold, she "petted them a bit." By the time she headed home to Potosi for the summer, she knew she had been hired to return in the fall for her third year of teaching.[65]

Elmer Herold finally returned to Ethel in mid-July 1919. His arrival on the Friday morning train overlapped with a visit from the wife and son of Ethel's brother Roscoe, so the Thomas family home was too crowded to allow the young couple much privacy. Ethel had never seen Elmer in his officer's uniform and "at first sight of him a thrill of patriotism went through me." When she noticed that the hardy college boy who had gone off to war had returned a "filled out man with a stern face," she felt a bit afraid and shy. Liz Thomas broke the ice by hurrying everyone into the dining room for breakfast where Elmer Herold patiently answered all of Clem's questions about the war. As soon as it was polite, Elmer and Ethel went upstairs to the front parlor, where it took Ethel Thomas "only a few minutes . . . to realize that my college-boy sweetheart had become a powerful man-lover." Apparently she overcame her shyness and did not find Elmer's advances off-putting, but after some kissing and sweet talk, the two "had to come to reality." They agreed that it was not yet time to get married, and Elmer decided that he also did not have enough time to get a mechanical engineering degree. But as a college graduate he figured he could get a teaching job; then they could begin their life together.[66]

Elmer Herold returned for a long weekend the following week and again in the middle of August. While in Chicago negotiating with a teacher's agency, he must have seen some of the effects of the race riots and strikes that had been plaguing the city since the beginning of August. There is no evidence of Elmer Herold's racial views, but his life in rural Wisconsin had kept him separate from African Americans, and the U.S. military practiced segregation during both of the world wars. Still, the violence in Chicago that summer probably struck him as unpatriotic and disloyal. Indeed, many new veterans worried that an unstable postwar economy would lead to political radicalism, which they considered particularly intolerable after all of the sacrifices made during the war. Considering the choices that Elmer Herold and Ethel Thomas made over the next couple of years, it is apparent that Elmer believed that the Great War had done much to preserve democracy but that democracy needed to be continually nurtured and supported. As a loyal citizen, he would do whatever he could to make that happen.[67]

When Elmer Herold returned from Chicago to Potosi, he pulled Ethel into the Thomas's parlor to be alone with him, and presented her with a small box from Tiffany containing "the most beautiful diamond ring I ever hoped to see." Elmer told her that he had secured a job as the head of the science department at the high school in Kewanee, Illinois, where he would teach physics and chemistry, earning a salary of eighteen hundred dollars a year. He also signed up for correspondence courses through the University of Chicago to shore up his scientific expertise for teaching and to serve as the foundation for a graduate degree in engineering. They decided to get married the following June.[68]

These were not the actions of a disgruntled or discontented veteran. A college-educated man, Elmer Herold did not require any assistance from the U.S. Employment Service to find a job after the war, so he did not share the economic worries of his working-class counterparts. Despite any horrors he may have witnessed on the battlefield, Elmer seemed determined to put the war behind him and get on with the rest of his life.[69]

That fall of 1919, Ethel Thomas returned to Lancaster High School for her final year of teaching as a single woman. She continued to favor the returned veterans, and she taught with enthusiasm about the benefits of the proposed League of Nations, something she wholeheartedly supported, something that seemed positive in the months of postwar trauma. Ethel's support of the League put her at odds with the Republican majority in Congress and shows that she did not unquestioningly follow the party. Her exact reasons for that support are unclear but may have to do with beliefs that the League would contribute to the furtherance of democracy around the world and that the United States should play a leading role. In September, as Ethel Thomas helped organize an afternoon program honoring Theodore Roosevelt, the Boston police force went out on strike, and steel workers across the country walked off their jobs. President Wilson began his ill-fated campaign for ratification of the Versailles peace treaty and U. S. membership in the League of Nations. Although Ethel continued to pay attention to current events because she believed that aided her teaching, she was an engaged woman. She spent most of her spare time making things for her hope chest and trousseau.[70]

Ethel's school year wound down with her American history class debating the question of Philippine independence. Since April 1917, she had fixed her attention on Europe, but now that the war had ended with an Allied victory, the influenza cycles had died down, and Elmer Herold had safely returned, she started thinking about the Philippines again. She probably helped prepare the students for the debate by sharing what she knew about the islands from her brother Bart Thomas's years there. Not surprisingly, given Ethel's views on the situation, her students ultimately sided with retentionists, concluding that the Philippines should remain under the protection of the United States. The irony was, of course, that this "protection" denied Filipinos the right to construct and run their own government, a right that Americans claimed they had been fighting for in the Great War.

When the twenty-four seniors of Lancaster High School graduated at the end of May 1920, Ethel Thomas concluded her teaching career in Wisconsin. She had survived her first world war, which would prove to be the easier of the two by far, and took away the lesson that surviving a war depended on hard work, sacrifice, loyalty, and patriotism. The next time, though the work would be more difficult and the sacrifice more costly, Ethel would have Elmer Herold by her side.[71]

Chapter Three

An American Citizen in the Colonial Philippines

AFTER A COURTSHIP that survived four years of college, an influenza pandemic, and a world war, Ethel Thomas finally married Elmer Herold on June 24, 1920. Wearing a white satin dress trimmed with seed pearls and silver lace, she and Elmer exchanged vows in the daisy-festooned parlor of her parents' home in Potosi, where a local minister "tied a knot that will last through all eternity."[1] On this earth the marriage lasted fifty-one years, most of it spent thousands of miles from Ethel's southwestern Wisconsin home. Not long after the wedding, she and Elmer became active participants in America's colonial venture in the Philippines. The expatriate life Ethel Herold led over the next decades highlighted her American citizenship while deepening her beliefs about patriotism.

This chapter explores three aspects of those expatriate experiences. First, as an American teacher in the Philippines, Ethel participated in the United States government's promotion of democracy and other American values through a program of "practical" education. Then, via her volunteer work in Baguio and her various cultural activities, she carried out the colonial domesticity that was necessary for maintaining the colony and that clearly marked her as part of the elite. Finally, the establishment of the Commonwealth in 1935 and the events leading up to the Second World War gave her the first indications that the privileges associated with American citizenship were not immutable and could, in fact, lead to life-threatening danger. Throughout those years, Ethel Herold's actions expressed the sentimental, paternal (or, in her case, maternal) imperialism that Americans professed to practice in the Philippines to mask the unequal realities of colonialism.[2]

An American Teacher in the Philippines

A family reunion in Potosi during the summer of 1921 resulted in a decision that changed the course of Ethel Herold's life. The newlyweds had moved to Kewanee, Illinois, in the fall of 1920 so that Elmer could take up his position as a science teacher in the local high school. Ethel wanted to teach there as well, but Elmer, like many other white middle-class men of the time, considered it improper for his wife to work. So she threw herself into community activities: singing at the Congregational Church and participating in its Woman's Missionary Society, as well as volunteering at the Kewanee Public Hospital two mornings a week to do mending. By the beginning of the spring term of 1921, though, Ethel had convinced Elmer to let her teach part-time, which netted her a salary of forty dollars per month. As much as she enjoyed her time in Kewanee, she could hardly wait for summer vacation so that she and Elmer could spend some time in Potosi with her parents and her eldest brother, Bart.[3]

Bart Thomas and his family had driven over from Butte, Montana, in their new Model T to spend some time with Liz and Clem Thomas and to get acquainted with Elmer Herold. The adults spent hours playing cards as conversation flowed; much of the talk focused on Bart's adventures in the Philippines almost twenty years before. Bart probably discussed his meeting in Butte the previous June with Dr. Walter W. Marquardt, the Philippine educational agent responsible for recruiting teachers to work in the islands. As Bart showed Marquardt around during his visit to Butte, he may have mentioned that his youngest sister and her new husband were teachers. Marquardt remembered that Bart Thomas had been "still keenly interested" in the teaching program in the Philippines during that meeting.[4]

Ethel and Elmer Herold then decided that they would like to teach in the Philippines for a couple of years. After returning to Kewanee in the fall of 1921, they wrote to the Bureau of Insular Affairs, the division of the War Department that managed the Philippines, filled out all of the necessary forms, and passed the required Civil Service examination. Their timing was fortuitous. That spring the government of the Philippines, supported by U.S. Governor-General Leonard Wood, authorized the hiring of an additional sixty Americans to teach English to Filipino children. Ethel and Elmer Herold were conditionally accepted by the Bureau of Education in the Philippines,

Elmer at a salary of sixteen hundred dollars and Ethel at fifteen hundred, with all of their transportation costs reimbursed and half-salary paid during their trip. They predicted that at the end of their two-year contract, they could afford to come home following a European grand tour.[5]

In addition to seeing the world, Ethel Herold considered her new teaching job "a great opportunity to continue the patriotic duty of helping to educate the Filipinos." Much as her brother Bart had done his "patriotic thing" two decades earlier, she saw this as her chance to promote American interests in its Asian colony, to be an active citizen in the postwar world. Ethel's enthusiasm for colonization brought her into the "public sphere of empire" by channeling her patriotism into a government-sanctioned civilizing mission, often softened with the language of "social uplift."[6]

Ethel Herold's determination to do her "patriotic thing" was likely influenced by a set of intertwined factors that informed U.S. foreign policy around the turn of the twentieth century: economics, assumptions of cultural and racial superiority, and progressive notions of international reform. Many Americans viewed imperialism as an aspect of progressive reform—they equated expansion with progress, especially in connection with economic growth—or considered it an acceptable method of applying progressivism internationally. Either way, American control of the Philippines would bring order to society, economics, and government in the islands, thus contributing to the kind of stable world so prized by progressives. The Herolds' decision to live and work in the Philippines also reflected the leading role the United States played in world affairs during the interwar years. Ethel and Elmer would be devoted patriots and nationalists, but ones with a "world consciousness."[7]

However, the young couple still had to pass a personal interview, which Walter Marquardt, Bart Thomas's acquaintance from the Philippine Bureau of Education, conducted in Kewanee, Illinois, during the late winter. The recruiter regaled the Herolds with tales of the beautiful South Pacific and of the interested and committed Filipino students. Marquardt likely brought along an informational booklet he had put together for Americans interested in teaching in the Philippines. In a short foreword to one of the editions, Governor-General Leonard Wood described U.S. colonialism as an "experiment in altruism" and explained that Americans could handle the "problem" of preparing Filipinos for self-government with a "sound system of education." Wood wanted the "best teachers" for this project, and by this he meant American teachers. To Ethel Herold, these words would have been an enticing invitation to do one's patriotic duty.[8]

In his booklet, Walter Marquardt described the structure of the Philippine government, which, in this period of home rule, was similar to that of the United States with its three branches of government and elected officials. The centralized Bureau of Education was depicted as "a democratic organization" because its director relied on suggestions and advice from teachers and local administrators. Ethel Herold likely approved of these familiar structures because she believed that they were fit for all countries. She would have considered this information as proof that the United States was carrying out its promise to democratize the Philippines. Yet, like many other Americans at the time, she did not see the irony of using imperialism as a justification for promoting democracy.[9]

As educational agent, Walter Marquardt took special care to ensure that potential teachers were suited for this overseas assignment, particularly in matters of racial beliefs. At the end of the booklet, he included "A Few Personal Words" to hopeful hires, plainly stating, "If you possess racial prejudice or if you cannot sympathize with the endeavor of a small nation to prepare itself for independent national existence, you are lacking in at least two of the elements essential to your own peace of mind and to your future success in the Philippine teaching service." Marquardt found nothing unacceptable about the Herolds' racial views during their interview. In fact, he was so impressed with the young couple that he noted this in their employment file: "both experienced and of a good type . . . they should be watched for executive development." He also secured a higher-than-typical salary of eighteen hundred dollars for Elmer Herold.[10]

Walter Marquardt's stories, along with subtle appeals to patriotism, confirmed for Ethel that they would "be fools to miss all this while at the same time our salaries would pay for it." In early March of 1922, Elmer wrote to Marquardt that he and Ethel "definitely decided to accept our appointment to the Philippines." Yet patriotic motivations did not rule all of Ethel's decisions. She had almost backed out because her mother did not want her to go and because she worried she would miss her mother too much. But Elmer, perhaps anxious that his wife cut the apron strings, convinced her to stick to their original plan. They sailed from San Francisco on May 15, in first-class accommodations on the *Thomas,* the same ship Bart Thomas had taken twenty-one years before.[11]

Upon arriving in Manila, the capital of the island of Luzon, on June 9, 1922, Ethel concluded that the city "did not impress me. The streets were muddy and dirty. The buildings old with queer architecture." But she found that the fire trees, named for their resemblance to blazes, and the purple bougainvillea "lent spots of beauty" to this otherwise unimpressive city. This description stands in stark contrast to those written by other American women just twenty years earlier that focused on the "exotic" loveliness of the Philippine landscape. In such writings, these women presented themselves more as simple tourists reporting on their surroundings than as representatives of a colonial power. Considering Ethel Herold's interest in politics, her family's connection with the Philippines, and her self-conscious patriotism, it is unlikely that she felt a need for such subterfuge. She clearly understood her position as an American teacher in the Philippines.[12]

By the time the Herolds arrived in 1922, the United States had been the dominant force in the islands for more than twenty years. American expatriates numbered in the thousands by then, reaching about eighty-seven hundred by the end of the 1930s. Though these numbers paled in comparison to those of Chinese and Japanese immigrants (about one hundred thousand and sixteen thousand, respectively), the Americans and the Spanish wielded considerably more economic and social power. In 1916, the U.S. Congress established a general time frame for Philippine independence with the passage of the Jones Act, but President Warren Harding had no intention of allowing it to happen any time soon. The reciprocal trade relationship was too lucrative, and Harding worried that an independent Philippines would not be strong enough to withstand expansionist threats from nearby Japan. Harding's 1921 investigative commission to the islands concurred.[13]

President Harding's subsequent appointment of General Leonard Wood as the new governor-general of the islands exacerbated tensions between colonizer and colonized for most of the 1920s. Wood often behaved in an imperious manner, frequently clashing with Filipino politicians, doing little to give the Filipinos the impression that he believed they were capable of self-rule. Education was one such area of disagreement. Wood supported hiring American teachers as a means of improving the Philippine educational system, and in addition to English-language instruction, he promoted a vocational rather than academic curriculum. This emphasis, promoted by Americans as "practical," represented yet another method the U.S. government used for maintaining an imperial racialized hierarchy in the Philippines. This system, not coincidentally, mirrored the Tuskegee Institute model in the United States that promoted vocational training as a means for the economic advancement of African Americans. Many Filipinos resented and resisted this kind of educational system.[14]

Thus, the Herolds found themselves in the thick of this contentious situation, but they never wavered in their support of vocational education. Ethel, Elmer, and the other newly arrived American teachers received a general orientation from Dr. Luther Bewley, the head of the Bureau of Education, who steered clear of political issues during his welcome. Instead, Bewley gave tips about where to purchase supplies, warned against scrimping on food so as not to endanger their health, and encouraged a strong sense of humor. In fact, the "new teachers were a gay lot," Ethel Herold observed the next morning as they all departed Manila by train. "This is what we had asked for."[15] After a brief stop in the mountain city of Baguio, which would become the Herolds' home in 1927, Ethel and Elmer set off in a Model T for Abra, one of the most remote and poorest Luzon provinces. They had been assigned to Bangued, the provincial capital of about thirty thousand people.

In Bangued, the Herolds shared a tin-roofed brick house with another teacher, Frederick Roth, who had arrived just days earlier. The living arrangement worked out well, especially because Roth's duties included some travel, leaving Ethel and Elmer alone in the house for days on end—alone, except for the servants. The teachers hired a cook, a male household servant, an "aguasero" who kept the house supplied with water, and a "lavendera" for the laundry. This was a bit below the number of servants recommended by various European household manuals directed at colonial women in the early twentieth century but comparable to practices of the Dutch, who typically employed between four and six servants in their Javanese households.[16]

The presence of servants created a domesticity that had only an illusion of privacy. To establish a colonial home that reproduced the comforts of one stateside, Ethel Herold had to learn to ignore the other human beings in the household, the servants who represented the imperial relationship that she was there to sustain. But during her childhood in rural Wisconsin, Ethel had observed the comings and goings of paid domestics in her family home, so she was already familiar with residences that contained more than immediate family members. Therefore, even prior to her move to Luzon, she had learned how to not see servants, whether Caucasian or Asian: they were, in effect, invisible to her. Yet, however much she might have taken their presence for granted, it is clear that Ethel Herold refused to take undue advantage of them. When she told a Bangued city official how much she paid one of her household workers, his casual response—"You pay too much. You can buy a Kalinga boy for ten dollars"— horrified her. She did not want to participate in an arrangement akin to slavery.[17]

Employing household help was essential not only because of the colonial setting but also because Ethel had her own fulltime job. She taught six classes of English, from beginner to advanced, with up to sixty students in some of the classes. Elmer, although hired to teach physics and biology, was also assigned two first-year English courses. Though Ethel sympathized with Elmer's frustration that he had to teach subjects outside his area of expertise, she did not complain that she could not teach history. She made do, perhaps, with embedding lessons of democracy in her English classes. In addition to academic subjects, the school offered a vegetable garden designed to give students agricultural training and to introduce them to new foods. Though other American teachers complained about the low pay for such heavy teaching loads, the Herolds were pleased that they could bank all of Elmer's salary, and part of Ethel's as well, and still live very comfortably.[18]

Because servants took care of the rented house, the Herolds had time for an active social life that included evening sing-alongs, bridge games, and horseback riding. Yet the young couple endeavored to strike up relationships with Filipinos as well as with other Americans and Europeans in Bangued, a practice they continued throughout their years on Luzon. Ethel later explained, "We were in a foreign country and wanted to get the most out of it. Some Americans had the foolish idea of just clicking with other Americans. . . . Well, they were losers as the Filipinos, Chinese, and other nationalities were well worth knowing." Betty Halsema Foley, an American who grew up in Baguio, conceded that "individual Americans behaved in different ways" when interacting with Filipinos. "The Herolds and other teachers, sent to remote towns with few or no compatriots at hand, of necessity made close Filipino friends."[19]

Class and status mattered to Ethel Herold as she always distinguished between Filipinos who were servants and Filipinos and "other nationalities" who were social acquaintances and friends. Ethel's relationships with servants always maintained the employer/employee hierarchy, but she did not lump all Filipinos into the servant class. For example, she forged a lifelong friendship with Luisa Bersamin, a Filipina about fifteen years her senior, who had been educated by some of the first American teachers in the Philippines and had taught embroidery in the public schools. Ethel always called the older woman Mrs. Bersamin, the same form of address she would have used with her American and European friends, and for more than twenty years the Herolds and Bersamins visited each other regularly. It is unlikely that this was merely a "token" friendship. Among all the American women in northern Luzon, Ethel made only two close friends. Though she had many acquaintances, she was not the type who had many confidantes.

During those first years in the Philippines, Ethel collected much information about Filipinos and their heritage from her students and their families and from Luisa Bersamin, which satisfied her intellectual curiosity about the islands. But Bangued's cultural Americanization probably eased some of Ethel's homesickness and reaffirmed her sense of purpose in the islands. The American teachers organized a Fourth of July celebration that the Herolds and Frederick Roth kicked off with cold drinks—highballs for the men, lemonade for Ethel. And several months later, Ethel recalled that she had never seen such a fervent celebration of George Washington's birthday: "There was to be a parade of school kids from as far as they could walk to get there. The school special cadets had been practicing to perfection and polishing their wooden guns. There were also clever floats." Following hours of speeches extolling the first American president's virtues, the program concluded with Ethel singing "America the Beautiful." These kinds of programs not only provided entertainment but also served as civics lessons, backdoor reinforcements of America's democratic message.[20]

After the school year ended, the Herolds took an extended horseback-riding trip through the mountains to Baguio to reach Teachers Camp, the annual summer gathering of educators from all over the island. Elmer had planned this to divert Ethel's sorrow over the news of her mother's death in February, hoping that she would get caught up in planning the excursion and directing its daily progress. The Herolds' Filipino friends in Bangued tried to warn them off of such a journey, expressing concern over everything from headhunters to unsafe water. But Paulino, their household servant, was to join them to help with translations, look after the horses, and cook the meals, so Ethel felt confident that she and her husband, "with good manners and sweet smiles" plus assorted small gifts, could manage the trip.[21]

On the surface, this expedition appears to be an example of "domesticity on the move," in which the white colonial woman directed the work of her servants to create mobile, temporary domiciles. The comforts of the colonial home were supposed to be made effortlessly transportable whenever Americans wanted a tour of the natural beauty of the Philippines. But the fact that the Herolds chose to take a circuitous route on horseback to Baguio shows that they were after a different experience, especially since they engaged helpers outside of their regular household staff. Elmer Herold hired Igorot cargadores (supply carriers) for the going rate of twenty cents a day and dispatched them to find a hut for the evening and get a fire started. The presence of those cargadores introduced an element of danger not commonly found in "domesticity on the move" stories of the very early twentieth century.[22]

This mountain trip on horseback became one of Ethel Herold's favorite stories to tell about her colonial life in the Philippines. Her description of the cargadores cast them as "others": they wore G-strings, bore tattoos on their bare chests, and spoke with low voices in a local dialect. The men were not only different from the Herolds but also different from the Herolds' regular servants, and that led to considerable unease for the American couple. As they all settled down to sleep in a hut that had few comforts of home, especially with the cargadores inside, Ethel told her husband she wanted the door open so that they would not suffocate from the fireplace's smoke. Elmer knew that the men preferred to keep the door closed, and he warned his wife not to make a big deal about it or they might get their heads cut off. Stories about local "headhunting" tribes still circulated among Americans in the Philippines, who continued to believe that the alleged murderous ways of locals were only kept in check by a vigilant constabulary. The Herolds noted that the tattoos on the cargadores' chests supposedly meant that they had taken heads; thus, Ethel slept with one arm around Elmer's neck so that "in case they started chopping, I would be awakened quick."[23]

In recounting this story, which she did numerous times over the years, both in written and oral form, Ethel Herold did not rely on the "decidedly nonheroic, even half-mocking tone" adopted by American women from the previous generation who described their travels through the Philippines. Ethel's tale is heroic and romantic, and a bit tall. She claims the role of the hero for herself, as she refused to leave Elmer's side, even at the risk of losing her head—or at least her protective arm. But would Elmer Herold really have hired cargadores he believed to be headhunters or was he simply trying to inject some drama into the trip to keep his young wife distracted from her personal sorrow and clinging to his side? Elmer succeeded at least in diverting Ethel's attention, and everyone woke up alive the following morning, shared breakfast, and headed out for another day on the trail. There is no record of what the cargadores thought of their employers.[24]

On the eighteenth day of their journey, the Herolds reached the Trinidad Farm School. After boarding their horses, they proceeded to Teachers Camp, which, Ethel found, "came up to its reputation—it was a happy melting pot for the hundreds of Filipino teachers from all provinces." The mingling of the Filipino and American teachers reflected typical patterns of socializing in Baguio, including mixed dinners and parties, but racial segregation existed as well. Americans lived in cottages and tents, ate in a central dining room, and attended a variety of daily activities in a "fine big social hall." Filipino teachers stayed in dormitories, ate in a mess hall, and attended their own activities in a different social hall. Ethel stubbornly described this arrangement as "two parts—not segregation."[25]

That Ethel refused to recognize this as segregation is not surprising because she had grown up with U.S. Supreme Court–sanctioned Jim Crow laws. She probably could not conceive that the colonial system established in the Philippines by the United States government could have anything wrong with it. The reality of Americans' lives in the islands was that they did not interact with Filipinos on a totally equal basis, but the racism was obscured by subtlety, which was probably why Ethel Herold could deny it. There was some socializing, there was business and politics—but no recognition of true equality, which could not exist under imperialism. For most of the rest of her life, Ethel failed to understand the inherent unfairness of "separate but equal" racial policies.[26]

After a second year of teaching in Bangued, the Herolds felt satisfied with their Philippine adventure. They decided to return to the United States via an around-the-world tour, after which Elmer would finish his engineering degree and find a suitable job; then they would raise a family. The Bureau of Education invited them to stay on in the Philippines, but Ethel and Elmer had become disillusioned with the bureau's new emphasis on academic subjects over vocational training for Filipino students. Ethel still believed that aside from English-language instruction, classes should focus on agriculture and manual training. Other academic pursuits, she thought, were unnecessary and unsuitable as long as the Americans remained in charge.

The young couple traveled to Manila to disembark for their trip. Ethel and Elmer's tour, which would take them to Hong Kong, Shanghai, Yokohoma, Cairo, Jerusalem, and Marseilles, involved several different ships, on which they had booked second-class passages costing about four hundred dollars apiece. Their decision to undertake such a voyage may have been inspired by Elmer Herold's travels at the close of the Great War and may have also been influenced by the culture of international travel that had taken hold in the United States in the late nineteenth century. During the second half of the 1800s, American newspapers routinely ran advertisements for ocean liners, cruise ships, travel agents, and European hotels and shops, which attracted more and more members of the middle class. Even the General Federation of Women's Clubs promoted international travel. Traveling second class—what the middle-class traveler could realistically manage—was very respectable, and the cost of the Herolds' trip was on a par with what other schoolteachers could afford.[27]

Ethel Herold thoroughly enjoyed the travels, especially since their budget allowed for certain extras likely beyond the reach of stateside American teachers. For example, the Herolds indulged in a room at the Astor House in Hong Kong and purchased custom-made fur coats in Shanghai. Ethel loved to shop for souvenirs, and she bought generously, both for herself and for friends and family members at home. The fur coat would visibly mark Ethel Herold as an international traveler, and like the Chinese silk dress that Bart Thomas had given her years before, it would serve as a reminder of her family's contribution to American imperialism.

This trip introduced the Herolds to Japan, where Ethel admired everything from the lush countryside to the temples and shrines of Kobe. On the couple's second day in Tokyo, the welcoming climate they had been experiencing in Japan noticeably changed. They sat quietly together at a table in their hotel's dining room, wondering what had gone wrong, when an Englishman at the next table handed them a copy of the *Nippon Times* containing news about the passage of the National Origins Act in the United States. The Herolds understood immediately why their hosts were no longer gracious. Nativist sentiment had convinced Congress to drastically limit the number of "undesirable" immigrants; Asians topped the list. Embarrassed with their government's action and apparently uncomfortable with such blatant racism, Ethel and Elmer cut short their stay.[28]

They continued through China and India, then on to the Middle East. They sailed across the Mediterranean to Marseilles and boarded a train to Italy, stopping in Genoa and Milan before heading into Switzerland, where they celebrated their fourth wedding anniversary with a hike and a picnic. When they reached Paris, Elmer took Ethel to his war "haunts," showing her all of the places to which he had chauffeured high-ranking officials. Finally, at the end of the summer, after nearly five months of travel, the Herolds boarded their last vessel, this one bound for the United States.[29]

Home and Back Again

Although Ethel Herold remembered that she and her husband "were tired of foreign countries and wanted to live the American way again," they had a hard time readjusting to stateside life. The couple had not saved enough money to live on while Elmer Herold pursued a mechanical engineering degree full-time, so he accepted another teaching job, this time in Kankakee, Illinois. Ethel used her diaries to begin writing a book about their Philippine experiences, and her vivid stories made them realize how much they missed the islands. Part of that may have been associated with a sentimental longing for friends and favorite students, but it also likely had to do with missing the elevated status associated with being American teachers in the Philippines and the sense of larger patriotic purpose it provided. In the Philippines, the Herolds' American citizenship had taken on heightened importance; in the states, they were just average citizens.[30]

Fortuitously, in September 1924, Elmer Herold received an invitation from Walter Marquardt, now an agent for the American Book Company, to revise a textbook, *Civic Science in Home and Community.* For over twenty years, publishers like the American Book Company had taken advantage of the expanded market for educational books, producing textbooks that incorporated elements of Filipino culture into lessons for math, English, and other basic academic subjects. Marquardt hoped Elmer would do the same for science, but to do so, the Herolds needed to return to the Philippines so that Elmer could work on the revisions while teaching Filipino students.[31]

This meant yet another delay in Elmer's plans to obtain his engineering degree, and his wife would have to abandon her budding writing career. But according to Ethel, this was too great an opportunity for her husband to pass up; thus, within days of receiving Marquardt's proposal, Elmer wrote to the Bureau of Insular Affairs asking for reinstatement for himself and Ethel for the 1925 school year in the Philippines. They were accepted and assigned to Laoag, a city of about one hundred thousand in northern Luzon. Elmer Herold taught six science classes and Ethel Herold had six classes of fourth-year English, a teaching load she found terribly repetitive. And Ethel did not like the city of Laoag nearly as well as she had Bangued; therefore, she encouraged her husband to quickly finish the science textbook revisions so that they could once again leave the Philippines.[32]

Ethel Herold's willingness to leave the Philippines, which she actually did in 1924 but only contemplated in 1925, indicates that although she supported U.S. imperialism both in thought and in deed, she had her limits. She would not sacrifice comfort and professional accomplishment to further the aims of empire. As an American, she probably expected that they should all work together to her advantage, as well as to that of the Filipinos.

After about four weeks into their assignment at Laoag, however, the Herolds received a transfer to the Trinidad Farm School, where they had boarded their horses while attending Teachers Camp in Baguio in 1923. It "was like a release from prison," Ethel remembered, describing the Farm School as "the most coveted station in the whole Philippines. It was like being stationed next to heaven." Opened in 1916 as an agricultural extension school, Trinidad began offering classes in 1917, gradually adding new departments each year. Along with classroom instruction, each male student received a small plot of land on which he could grow whatever he chose and then sell the produce to the school exchange. About 225 Igorot young men attended the school, so all of the individual classes were small; female students were soon allowed to enroll as well.[33]

At Trinidad, Ethel taught English and composition to freshmen, sophomores, and juniors while her husband taught science, served as the school's principal, and worked on the science textbook for the American Book Company. After finishing the revisions, Elmer's busy schedule did not slow down; in addition to administrative duties and teaching, he kept the school's various pieces of equipment operating. Trinidad's emphasis on vocational training made the Herolds' assignment there a particularly good fit. "We loved it here at the farm school," Ethel later recalled, "and really felt we were accomplishing something with these Igorot people." Thus, they signed on for another two-year stint. Upon the recommendation of the local American businessman Herbert Heald and the American mayor of Baguio, E. J. Halsema, Elmer Herold set up a class in auto mechanics at Trinidad to prepare young Igorot men for the influx of cars that were certain to show up in the Philippines.[34]

At the beginning of 1927, Heald, impressed by what he had seen at the farm school, offered Elmer a job at his lumber mill in Baguio as a master mechanic. Ethel admitted that "it would be wonderful in many ways taking a job like that. But we had come out here in the first place as a patriotic thing. We went home because we did not agree with the system of education. But now we at the farm school were doing exactly what we thought should be done. And we were doing it for the Igorot people whom we like so much." Elmer declined Heald's offer. The Herolds were not quite ready to give up doing the patriotic teaching thing, even though a dramatic event at the school would soon cause them to reevaluate that decision.[35]

During the first week of February, about a month before her thirty-first birthday, Ethel Herold learned that she was pregnant. Among some white colonial settlers, especially French women in West Africa in the 1920s and 1930s, there was an assumption that colonial women's reproduction was vital to imperialism to maintain a racialized power structure. It is clear, though, that Ethel felt no such imperative. The timing of her pregnancy actually suggests that the Herolds felt well settled and financially secure enough to start a family, that the Philippine colony was stable, and that Elmer's salary at Trinidad was sufficient to maintain a comfortable lifestyle. There seemed to be no question that Ethel would soon quit her job to devote herself to domestic duties.[36]

On February 18, 1927, the Herolds, along with Jim Wright, superintendent of Trinidad, went to the Pines Hotel in Baguio for one of its famous seven-course meals. Ethel and Elmer had a wonderful time that night, telling friends their happy news and playing many hands of bridge after dinner, but when the trio returned home, they encountered unanticipated trouble. Wright got out of the car to unlock the front gate and Elmer drove on through to drop his wife at their cottage before putting the vehicle in the garage. At the front door of the cottage, one of the Igorot students who was on evening guard stepped out from the bushes and said, "Mrs. Herold, don't go in there, you will be hurt." Then Ethel saw a large group of students streaming out from behind the exchange, heading for the cottage. Elmer, startled at the sight, leaped out of the car. He and Ethel reached the front of the exchange at about the same time, shocked to see "our dear Mr. W lying on his back in the dirt with a rope around his neck."[37]

The Herolds managed to disperse the students and rescue Jim Wright, who was visibly shaken. Ethel locked the noose in a trunk in their cottage, but when she returned outside, she carried Elmer's walking stick with her for protection. The remaining students, now a bit calmer, informed Wright that they had grievances, but Elmer suggested they all get a good night's sleep and talk over the complaints in the morning. The students refused and started yelling, "Our fathers were head-hunters." While Elmer Herold and Jim Wright tried to reason with them, Ethel looked closely at every young man there because she knew that she would have to make up a list of the troublemakers' names. Suddenly Wright was knocked down again and Ethel lit into the attackers with Elmer's walking stick, hitting "as hard as I could and hit[ting] heads, backs, anywhere" until the students finally dispersed.[38]

The next morning, about two hundred students informed the Trinidad teachers that they were on strike. Elmer Herold then refused to release their weekly rations, telling them simply, "No work, no food." Jim Wright overrode Elmer's decision about the rations, and he later insisted to Mayor Halsema and a couple of other Baguio officials who had arrived at the school to investigate that there was nothing wrong. But by Sunday, Elmer Herold and Jim Wright were discussing the possibility that the student hostility might be an anti-American plot devised by Manuel Quezon, the Filipino senator known for his nationalistic views. If so, they believed that Governor-General Leonard Wood would want the trouble quashed. The two men knew Wood personally since he had traveled to Baguio many times on business and had visited the Farm School. Ethel remembered, "Elmer was all admiration for this great Governor-General."[39]

A subsequent investigation revealed the source of the riot. Two Trinidad sophomores had attempted to rape a young Igorot woman, and though Jim Wright expelled them, he allowed them to remain until they harvested and sold their potato crop. During this interval, the two students convinced others that they had a list of valid grievances against school officials. The students resented the paternalistic nature of the vocational educational system, especially since it was run by Americans who did not understand their culture. They informed Jim Wright and Elmer Herold that they did not want to wear G-strings while farming, wanted more beef at meals, and more sports equipment for physical fitness. They also demanded more money from the sale of their produce.[40]

A Baguio court found eight students guilty of disturbing the peace and ordered them to leave the Trinidad Farm School, but they continued to linger around town until a couple of days in jail encouraged them to go home. The riot was considered serious enough that Manila newspapers reported on it several times, and the governor-general, who viewed any uprising by Filipinos as a potential plot to overthrow or at least undermine American authority, had been apprised of the situation almost immediately. In his diary, Leonard Wood referred to the incident at Trinidad as "an unfortunate riot or strike" that was "a sort of bolshevik movement among the students."

His assumption that the students had to be "bolshevik" if they attacked Americans reflects the fears of radicalism that pervaded the United States in the years following the Great War. Americans could construe incipient freedom movements as threats to democracy, especially if those movements were aimed at Americans, even if the only real threat was to U.S. imperial power.[41]

The Bureau of Education held Jim Wright blameless for the student uprising; in fact, he and Elmer were complimented for their fine work at the school. Governor-General Wood accepted the findings of the report; yet he personally assessed the situation by making a trip to Trinidad. In his diary, he noted his belief that the rebellious students had intended to do lasting bodily harm to Jim Wright, and that, "fortunately," Ethel and Elmer Herold had been there to save him.[42]

The Trinidad riot did not compel Ethel Herold to revise her support of U.S. imperialism. She recalled, instead, that she and Elmer "were mighty sorry our Igorots had done this. It showed us clearly that they needed more help and guidance." She took the sentimental, maternal view that the Filipinos still had a long way to go before independence, that they still required instruction from Americans to improve their lives. She concluded, "It goes to show that force has to be used. All people recognize authority and justice." And Americans were the ones with that power. Even Ethel Herold, a pregnant American woman, felt justified in using violence against colonized people, no matter that they were her own students. Yet there was clearly a personal element to Ethel's use of violence: she saw her husband threatened and would not stand aside and do nothing.[43]

The riot did not sour the Herolds on teaching. In fact, it confirmed their belief in the importance of their positions—so much so that Elmer turned down the job of city engineer of Baguio because he wanted to continue working with the students at Trinidad. After all, as Ethel explained, "We really did like them and wanted to help them. We could not condemn all because a few were bad."[44]

For a short time, it seemed that Elmer Herold's role in quelling the riot would enhance his position with the Bureau of Education. Leonard Wood invited the Herolds to lunch at the governor's mansion in Baguio and asked Elmer if he would be willing to tour the farm and industrial schools in the United States for ideas to bring back to the Philippines. After that he would take charge of all of the farm and trade schools in the islands. Elmer immediately accepted the proposal, and he and Ethel returned to their work at Trinidad to await further instructions from the bureau. But at the end of May, instead of heading back to the states, Elmer received a transfer to the Munoz Farm School in Nueva Eceja, where he was to serve as superintendent at twice his current salary. This was an uncomfortably mixed message from the Bureau of Education. Despite having been absolved of any responsibility for the Trinidad riot, the bureau apparently believed that relocating Elmer would defuse any lingering hostilities; yet he received a promotion and salary increase.[45]

Munoz was the largest and richest farm school in the Philippines, something that normally would have impressed Ethel Herold, but she was bored there because school was not in session and she was anxious to move on to something even more prestigious. Elmer turned down another job offer from Herbert Heald while waiting to hear about his new duties with the Bureau of Education. But on the day the headlines of the *Manila Bulletin* blazed with the news that Governor General Wood had died in the United States from surgical complications, Elmer wrote to Heald, accepting his offer to work as the lumber mill's master mechanic at a salary of two hundred dollars per month. Without Wood's support, the Herolds probably worried that Elmer would never rise in the ranks of the bureau because of the Trinidad riot. Out of a desire for family security, they took a new tack in doing the patriotic thing, and a new phase of Ethel Herold's life began.[46]

Colonial Domesticity

Teaching had given Ethel Herold a clearly defined (and salaried) role in U.S. imperialism in the Philippines, but from the late 1920s until the Japanese attack on the islands in 1941, she would focus her attention on her husband and children, take part in Baguio's busy social life, and plunge into a variety of charity projects designed to demonstrate the beneficence of Americans. Years later, commenting on a New Year's Eve party in the 1930s, Ethel reflected on her Baguio activities: "All the men worked hard at difficult jobs. They deserved to tear loose and have fun. I thought I deserved to have fun too. In fact I believe I worked harder the last 5½ years than I had ever worked at teaching and I did my job then too. But except for the fifty dollars a month from Shevlin's [gold] mine for a year—I was getting no fat pay check. But that was all right."[47]

Men conducted the formal work of imperialism through politics and economics, but their success depended on women contributing their formidable domestic and organizational skills. Women like Ethel Herold expressed a "colonial mentality" of their own within the proper female domain of home and women's organizations. Furthermore, they had a patriotic duty to exhibit middle-class morality and respectability while living in proximity to colonized people.[48]

Ethel supported the American empire through her participation in several cultural organizations and her membership in the Monday Afternoon Club. Her concern with middle-class morality can be seen most clearly through the treatment of her servant, Tuding. Colonial domesticity afforded Ethel plenty of opportunities to be a useful member of the community as she continued to promote U.S. interests in the Philippines. But U.S.-Philippine relations were on the cusp of change as the islands inched closer to independence and the world moved closer to war.

Baguio in 1927 was a bustling city of eight thousand residents. In addition to the permanent population, about twenty-two thousand visitors came that year to soak up the city's cool climate and take advantage of its fine recreational opportunities. Teachers Camp made Baguio an educational hub on Luzon, and Camp Henry T. Allen, an officer training academy for the Philippine Constabulary, and Camp John Hay, a rest and recreational American army facility, generated constant military traffic. The city also attracted many successful business people. H. P. Whitmarsh, for example, founded gold and copper mines, launched a sawmill with Herbert Heald (who later employed Elmer Herold), and owned the Baguio Commercial Store. Although the Herolds did not attain similar wealth, Elmer's salary and investments, along with the couple's American citizenship, gave them an elevated social status, even higher than the one they had possessed as teachers.[49]

The Herolds' new home, built in the spring of 1928 near the Heald lumber office, was owned by the company; in addition to serving as a private residence, it also showcased Heald lumber products. As a company home, then, the Herold domicile became a site of American imperialism since it represented U.S. power and prestige, but the home's reflection of imperialism also signaled the impermanence of the colonial relationship. The house "belonged" to the Herolds only as long as Herbert Heald employed Elmer Herold, and even during that term of employment, neither Elmer nor Ethel had complete control over the house. At least twice, for example, while the Herolds were away on vacation, Herbert's wife, Florence (also one of Ethel's closest friends), made changes to the structure. Florence Heald always meant the home improvements as pleasant surprises, and Ethel publicly acknowledged them as such; but on some level she may have resented such impositions on the family's private living space.

Ethel Herold could and did exercise more control over her children and the household servants. Though she had two children (Billy, born in 1927, and Betsy, born in 1929), Ethel refused to hire an amah, or nursemaid. In colonial societies, there were often anxieties about children "going native." Dutch women in colonial Java, for example, had strict rules about how local servants could treat their charges; these restrictions were designed to school the colonial children in the correct social hierarchy and to prevent them from becoming Javanese. Ethel Herold, however, seems not to have shared such concerns. Rather, she worried more about servants spoiling her children than about her children turning into Filipinos. Ethel taught Billy and Betsy at home until it was time to send them to grade school; during their childhood, the young Herolds played with both Filipino and American children. But when it came time to enroll Billy and Betsy in school, Ethel Herold did not cross imperial lines: her children attended the elite Brent School in Baguio.[50]

In addition to taking care of her children, Ethel managed a household. The Herold home required the employment of four servants for its smooth operation—cook, "house girl," "garden boy," and lavendera—at the cost of about fifty dollars per month. Ethel functioned as the white mistress of local servants who not only supplied the necessary labor to keep the household running but who were also expected to adhere to Ethel's standards of white, middle-class morality. This is abundantly clear in her relationship with Tuding, a young Ilocano woman, a cousin of the Herolds' cook, who had been hired as a domestic servant shortly after Betsy Herold's birth in 1929.[51]

In early 1932, Ethel and Elmer Herold decided to take the family on an around-the-world tour, culminating in an extended visit with relatives in the United States. This would be the second such trip for the couple, the first with their children. Ethel thrived on these kinds of vacations. They satisfied her curiosity about people and places, gave her the opportunity to learn more about world history, and served as a very visible indication of her status. The Herolds had enough money to travel around the world and to purchase the right kind of souvenirs to give to family and friends and to decorate their home in Baguio.

Determined that she "was not going back to the states to wash dishes and wash clothes," Ethel announced that their servant Tuding would come along to perform these chores and to help watch the children. But in the midst of complicated travel preparations that involved producing Tuding's birth certificate so that she could get a passport, Ethel heard a rumor that the young woman and her boyfriend had been sleeping together every night in the Herolds' "puritanical household." Ethel worried about what might happen if, after they arrived in the United States, they "found our *saintly* Tuding pregnant." Here, morality (or "saintliness") clearly reflected a white, middle-class, Christian American perspective, which assumed that non-Caucasians possessed no natural sexual inhibitions. Ethel Herold probably knew something of Ilocano culture by this time, but that mattered little since Tuding was an employee in her household, a subordinate, single, young woman.[52]

Unwilling to directly confront Tuding, perhaps assuming that she would not tell them the truth, the Herolds contrived to get their proof by arranging to catch the young couple together in bed. When Elmer confirmed the unacceptable behavior, he and his wife decided they had the right to know if Tuding was pregnant. "We had Tuding examined," Ethel wrote very matter-of-factly. "No damage. After we had been more than half way ready to go, we skipped the morality and took her." That Ethel did not record Tuding's reaction to this forced medical examination demonstrates the silent, subservient status of women like Tuding. They were not expected or allowed to speak for themselves. It is probable that Tuding felt compelled to comply because she could not afford to lose her job, and a dismissal with no references would cut her off from employment by other Americans. Despite Ethel Herold's "puritanical" views, she genuinely liked Tuding and was too much in need of her services to let her go. Skipping the morality meant that Ethel could overlook premarital sex as long as it remained invisible to others and as long as it did not result in premarital pregnancy, an outward sign of immoral behavior.[53]

Ethel continued to monitor Tuding throughout the trip, and overall she seemed pleased with the young woman's behavior. While visiting Bart Thomas's family, some Filipino students attending the University of Montana offered to take Tuding out on dates, but Ethel refused permission even though Tuding seemed willing. The university's Spanish Club invited Ethel to give a talk and asked her to bring Tuding wearing a Filipina dress. Although Tuding was native to the Philippines, it was Ethel who lectured about the islands, but after she finished, someone from the club asked if Tuding would say a few words in her Ilocano dialect. To Ethel's amazement, "That sixth grade servant girl got up in front of those college kids with the poise of a queen. Talked in dialect and answered all their questions. I certainly was proud of her." Ethel's colonial-colored glasses did not allow her to imagine that a native of the Philippines, especially one with only six years of schooling, could have more knowledge of those islands than she did.[54]

Tuding had promised that in return for the opportunity to travel with the Herolds she would continue working for the family for two years after their return, and she kept her word. Then she quit to marry the young man who had come to sleep with her in the servants' quarters, a tailor working in Bangued. Thereafter Tuding traveled to Baguio twice a year to purchase cloth for her husband's shop, often bringing along her newest baby. She stayed in the Herolds' servants' quarters, and Ethel invited her up to eat one meal with the family. Ethel's relationship with Tuding can be read as imperialism personified. She treated the young woman as a subordinate, assuming authority not only over the work Tuding was expected to perform but over her private life as well. Ethel believed it necessary to shape Tuding's morals according to her own, which meant no premarital sex, and believed that her rules and instructions would only serve to improve Tuding. Even after the Ilocano woman stopped working for the Herolds, Ethel never considered Tuding an equal. She maintained the imperial hierarchy with the visiting arrangements; moreover, she always referred to Tuding by her first name and never even revealed the young woman's last name in any of her writings.

In addition to monitoring the morals of her servants, Ethel Herold participated in the cultural uplift of Filipinos. Her work on the Baguio Spring Festival especially illustrates her understanding of the link between such programs and the American colonial mission in the islands. At the end of the 1930s, she helped organize and served as secretary of the Spring Festival Society, which was dedicated to showcasing the musical talent of Filipino students throughout Luzon. Ethel advertised the program and then helped coordinate housing and transportation for the student musicians to attend the festival. Herbert Zipper, an Austrian refugee from Nazi Germany and the new conductor of the Manila Symphony Orchestra, presided over the five concerts performed during Easter weekend of 1939.[55]

The Spring Festival was considered a success, but Herbert Zipper complained that the stage of the Baguio City Auditorium was too small for such a gala event. Society members asked the City Council to build a bigger stage, but the request was denied. After the second festival in 1940 turned out to be an even "bigger success," bringing more visitors than ever to Baguio over the Easter weekend, Ethel, Zipper, and a few others approached the City Council, but its members again refused to build a bigger stage. Livid at being turned down, Ethel "could not hold in any longer. I told how we had worked, spent our own money—all for the Filipino people, giving them enjoyment and encouraging their musical ability, bringing business to Baguio." Then she dissolved in tears as she told them, "I as an American [am] doing all this for your Filipinos and you [are] not caring a bit."[56]

Ethel got her way by playing the citizenship card, which in this case had the force of imperial relations behind it. Although the men of the City Council may have been more persuaded by economic arguments that the festival boosted tourism, Ethel saw its importance in terms of cultural uplift. In any event, the City Council footed the bill for the construction of a new stage, and the 1941 Spring Festival was even more successful than the first two. Society members planned to enlarge the event over the next few years, but war intervened.

Cultural events and social acquaintances provided Ethel with interesting pastimes but afforded only limited opportunities to promote the American values she held so dear. She still needed to find a way to combine her cultural pursuits with practical, useful programs. Coincidentally, in the summer of 1933, Flora Colbath Crosby, an American woman from Manila and the wife of a mining executive, announced that the Baguio women spent too much time playing bridge and that they needed to organize a club that would do some good for the town. Ethel Thomas Herold already had considerable experience with women's organizations, dating back to her childhood in Potosi, when she assisted in Woman's Relief Corps and Ladies' Aid Society activities. From her mother's example, Ethel had accepted the belief that a good woman contributed to the betterment of her community. She incorporated notions of citizenship and patriotism into this belief during the Great War when she heeded the call of the U.S. government to donate her efforts to support American servicemen, mostly through Red Cross and Food Administration work organized by local women.

In the early 1920s, while living and teaching in Bangued, where there were few other white people, Ethel had contemplated joining its women's club, which had been influenced by American clubwomen in the United States and in the Philippines. The National Federation of Women's Clubs (NFWC) dominated Filipina groups from its inception in 1920, providing guidance and suggestions for women's civic and charity work. It is not clear whether the Bangued group was part of the NFWC or whether it represented one of the earlier provincial women's clubs. Nevertheless, Ethel Herold's friend Luisa Bersamin advised her against joining. As she diplomatically explained to Ethel, the club had a rule "to begin its meeting promptly at 3:00 p.m. but the women don't ever get there until 5:00. Now Mrs. Herold, I know you would not stand for that and would criticize them. Then you would argue and not be friends any more. So you stay out of it." Luisa Bersamin did not come right out and say that an American woman's presence in the club would be socially uncomfortable; instead, she focused on cultural differences, pointing out that because Ethel Herold was American, she could never fully grasp local ways and that everyone would suffer for it. "Bless Mrs. Bersamin's heart, she was so right," Ethel later acknowledged.[57]

However, after the Herolds moved to Baguio in 1927, Ethel joined the Baguio Club, an organization run by local Filipinas. Her level of involvement in the group is unclear, though the fact that she wrote little about it in her memoir indicates that hers was perhaps a courtesy membership rather than an active one. With the Baguio Club, there was apparently no concern about a culture clash, perhaps because Baguio's population was more racially mixed or because of an implicit understanding that Ethel Herold would not actually attend the meetings.

On July 31, 1933, despite her previous involvement with women's organizations, Ethel only reluctantly attended the planning meeting of what became the Monday Afternoon Club, more commonly referred to as the Monday Club. Her reticence stemmed not from an aversion to the work associated with such a club membership but because she feared being drawn into some kind of religious missionary society. Although Ethel was raised by a staunchly Methodist mother and had graduated from a Methodist-affiliated college, religion never played a major role in her life. As an adult, she routinely attended Sunday services at an Episcopal church, and for a short time she even belonged to the Woman's Missionary Society in Kewanee, Illinois. But she had little in common, for instance, with nineteenth-century American women of the Presbyterian Board of Foreign Missions, who considered religion and patriotism the same thing.[58]

It does not appear that Protestantism was the foundation of or at the forefront of Ethel Herold's support of American colonialism. She and her husband chose to relocate to the Philippines and work as public school teachers to inculcate Filipino children with the benefits of democracy and capitalism, which they accomplished through lessons in government rather than religion. Even when Ethel labeled the household servant Tuding's sexual behavior "immoral," God did not enter into her justification for correcting the young woman's behavior. Christianity may have been an implicit factor in Ethel's beliefs and actions, but it was not the overriding one. She never tried to proselytize Filipinos; for her, imperialism was secular. It was explicitly about government, politics, and economics.

Once assured that this proposed women's organization was not affiliated with any one particular church, Ethel helped found the Monday Afternoon Club and for over twenty years served either as its secretary/treasurer or president. The new club recruited American and European women, describing itself as a nondenominational organization whose purpose was "to mete out aid where required." Filipino women were not invited to join. Just as she had observed of the racial separation at Teachers Camp, Ethel Herold insisted that this did not represent segregation since Filipinas had their Baguio Club. Everyone felt comfortable with this mostly separate-but-equal arrangement, she believed, so there was no need to challenge it. Moreover, she lauded the Monday Club because it put American women "in touch with the Filipinos and Igorot people."[59]

The creation of the Monday Club can be read as a reflection of the imperial relationship. Ethel acknowledged that the Baguio Club officers met once a year with their counterparts in the Monday Club "to coordinate our efforts." That Ethel referred to this as a coordination of efforts indicates that the Monday Club did not dictate to the Baguio Club, that the American women willingly sought and acted on the recommendations of the Filipinas. This once again points to the importance of class in Ethel Herold's perception of the imperial relationship, but it also suggests that she and the other Monday Club women knew that this was a temporary relationship because the Philippines would not be an American colony indefinitely. It mirrors the delicate and sometimes contentious relationship between the United States government and the colonial Philippine government, which also had to coordinate their efforts in pursuit of democracy and capitalism.[60]

The Monday Club sponsored a variety of social and cultural events to raise money for its many charitable projects that ranged from providing kimonos for Igorot babies to paying tuition and expenses for some qualified students to attend the Trinidad Farm School. The annual tea dance at the Pines Hotel brought in about five hundred dollars through an admission fee, corsage sale, and raffle. According to Ethel Herold, this "grew to be one of the big social events of Baguio," attended by Americans, Europeans, and "upper class Filipinos [who] came in flocks." For two years she also organized and directed a Christmas Concert with the Baguio Glee Club, featuring carols from all over the world, which attracted hundreds of people and brought in hundreds of dollars.[61]

Ethel Herold's involvement in the Monday Club provides a glimpse into colonial women's benevolent activity during the interwar period. Though few documented comparisons exist, it appears that American women living overseas modeled their organizations on stateside counterparts, infusing the clubs with their own racial, religious, and class beliefs. In the Philippines and in other territorial locations, U.S. imperialism provided these women with the additional authority to set and carry out their agendas, which varied from place to place. For Ethel Herold and the other American women in Baguio, this meant providing material assistance to the Igorots, while in Hawaii, for instance, one of the most powerful women's clubs, Honolulu's Outdoor Circle, focused its considerable efforts on beautification projects.[62]

"The work I did for the Monday Club was necessary and interesting and greatly appreciated," Ethel Herold concluded. "The interest I took and the time I spent was much appreciated by the Filipino people. I thought it also helped my husband's business." Her observation illustrates the workings of colonial domesticity. American men could not have been successful in building this overseas empire if American women had not been willing to support it. Ethel Herold's charity work extended to the YWCA, American Red Cross, Philippine Anti-Tuberculosis Board, Girl Scout Board, and the Baguio Hospital Advisory Board. She later explained, "Elmer and I had learned that to live in a foreign country and to earn one's livelihood there, one must give something of himself to that country."[63]

All of this can be read as an expression of her position in the imperial relationship, for the fact of her U.S. citizenship provided an extra level of power to her public activities in Baguio. However, given Ethel Herold's background, it is likely that she would have engaged in similar activities wherever she lived, always setting herself up as the woman with intelligence and means who could help those less fortunate. Class, even more than race, categorized "the other" for Ethel. She carried out similar benevolent work whether she lived in Potosi or Kewanee or Baguio. Her sense of patriotism and civic duty transcended the physical borders of the United States and led her to America's furthest colonial outpost in 1922. Now that outpost was on the brink of extinction.

The Commonwealth

In 1935, the United States established a commonwealth government in the Philippines, the final step to independence. Initially, the 1932 Hare-Hawes-Cutting bill, which outlined the process, passed the U.S. Congress but stalled in the Philippine legislature. The two most powerful Filipino political leaders of the time, Sergio Osmeña and Manuel Quezon, opposed the bill, and the American governor-general, Frank Murphy, remained neutral. Finally, the new Tydings-McDuffie Act won over both American and Filipino legislators. It provided for a commonwealth government largely concerned with domestic issues, independence in ten years, and Philippine imports subjected to American tariffs, but it came with no promises that the United States could have army posts in the islands. In early 1935, a constitutional convention created the structure of the new Philippine government.[64]

The act also raised the issue of citizenship status. As a territory or insular area, indigenous inhabitants of the Philippines were considered U.S. nationals rather than U.S. citizens, which was made clear shortly after the U.S. Senate ratified the Treaty of Paris that ended the Spanish-American War. Filipinos were entitled to the protection of the United States and were expected to be loyal to its government but did not enjoy equal political rights with American citizens. This legal definition of "national" supported imperialism by emphasizing the difference between the colonizers and the colonized. Because the Philippine Islands were an administrative colony and an unincorporated territory, they were not destined for U.S. statehood, and their inhabitants were not entitled to equal citizenship with Americans. Tydings-McDuffie stripped Filipinos of their status as nationals, reclassifying them as aliens for purposes of immigration.[65]

The passage of Tydings-McDuffie was mired in economic fears, xenophobia, racism, and isolationism. President Franklin Roosevelt, like many of his predecessors, had no clear idea on Philippine independence. In 1934, during the debates over the bill, FDR remarked in private, "Let's get rid of the Philippines—that's the most important thing. Let's be frank about it." Severing the colonial relationship would benefit the United States by eliminating free trade and by removing the costly obligation to protect the islands. In altering the trade relationship with the United States, Tydings-McDuffie had the potential to harm the Herolds' economic prosperity and weaken their social status. With independence, Americans would lose their privileged position. From that standpoint, Ethel Herold may have viewed the Commonwealth with suspicion and may have hoped that something would interfere with the independence timetable.[66]

The launch of the Commonwealth got underway with the usual governmental pomp. Forty-three American senators and representatives, accompanied by their wives, along with Vice President John Nance Garner and Secretary of War George Dern came to Manila in November 1935 to participate in various ceremonies and celebrations inaugurating the Commonwealth and its first president, Manuel

Quezon. Many of the American visitors traveled up to Baguio on November 9 for a celebration in the popular resort city and to show off American business ventures there. Elmer Herold had charge of some of the visitors, including Senator F. Ryan Duffy of Wisconsin, a member of the Foreign Relations and Military Affairs committees.[67]

Afternoon entertainment for the visiting dignitaries included golf at the Baguio Country Club and a dance performance by local Igorots and Ifugaos at the Camp John Hay amphitheatre. The Gold Mining Association of the Philippines hosted an informal dance at the Pines Hotel Annex that evening. The Herolds attended. After dinner, while most of the guests danced, Ethel Herold and a California congressman got up on a table and belted out the song "San Francisco." Afterwards, the Herolds and others went over to the country club, Ethel drinking champagne in the car along the way. Apparently almost everyone else continued to imbibe as well, making "fools of themselves," but, as Ethel Herold conceded, "who was I to criticize?" The drinking picked up again the following afternoon during farewell luncheons. Several senators ended up at the Herold home, first sleeping off their alcohol on Ethel's Chinese rugs, then fortifying themselves with a lot of very strong coffee for the trip back to Manila. With rest and caffeine, "the dignitaries became dignified again."[68]

As Ethel Herold observed the behavior of many of the visiting Americans, especially their consumption of alcohol, she recalled that she "did not blame the Filipinos for wanting their independence." This rather vague comment about impending Philippine independence may have been tempered through time. Writing about the Commonwealth celebration more than thirty years after it had taken place, Ethel already knew the outcome. In retrospect, she wrote that she did not blame the Filipinos for wanting independence, but at the time she may have distinguished between wanting independence and being prepared for it. As committed as she was to the American colonial venture, it is doubtful that she believed the Philippines would be capable of self-rule by 1945.[69]

Senator Duffy concluded that the Filipinos "were truly grateful that the American Congress had passed the law that would give them ultimate independence." And what would independence mean? Duffy saw a bit of Luzon, traveling to some of the small villages, and speculated about the future of the Philippines: "It is hard to forecast the future of the islands. Japan is close at hand; the Japanese people need more land. The Philippines soil is rich. In addition to gold, valuable deposits of manganese chromite have been discovered. These are extremely valuable in war." Just six years later, this would become a near prophetic statement.[70]

Signs of War

During the 1930s, the Herolds became one of the most well-known and influential American families in Baguio. "We were really living on top of the world," Ethel later recalled. "Elmer with a difficult job that he liked. Two healthful intelligent children. A beautiful home with everything a heart could desire. I believe Elmer and I both realized we were living in a heaven on earth."[71] But political and military developments in Asia would soon bring an end to their comfortable expatriate life. Stung by the economic reverses of the Great Depression and a rapidly growing population, Japan embarked on a plan to dominate Asia in order to seize its raw materials and the laborers needed to revive its own prosperity. In 1931, Japanese troops occupied Manchuria and staged an unsuccessful attack on the port city of Shanghai the following year. When the League of Nations criticized these actions, the Japanese simply withdrew from the organization and continued to attack China. In 1937 came the Rape of Nanking—the brutal six-week Japanese assault on that Chinese city and its population.

Like many people in the Philippines, Ethel Herold expressed concern for the Chinese but worried less about her own immediate situation. With General Douglas MacArthur advising the Philippines army, she felt safe. "We had seen our vast military forces," she wrote later. "We had no worries." MacArthur's father, Arthur MacArthur, had been a military governor of the Philippines in the early twentieth century, and Douglas served with distinction during the First World War. In 1922, the same year the Herolds went to the Philippines, Douglas MacArthur took command of a U.S. infantry brigade there. Over the next dozen years, a series of promotions bounced him back and forth between the states and the islands.[72]

MacArthur returned to the Philippines in late 1935, after the establishment of the Commonwealth, to serve as President Manuel Quezon's military adviser, taking the unusual rank of field marshal.

When MacArthur reportedly told Quezon, "I *know* that the islands can be protected, provided of course you have the money which will be required," the president was convinced that MacArthur was his man. The American general intended to prepare eleven thousand Filipino soldiers to train four hundred thousand reservists, in the event of an attack, to harass the Japanese and hold the islands until American reinforcements arrived. By the end of 1939, however, his aide, Colonel Dwight Eisenhower, had only managed to raise a Filipino reserve of about one hundred thousand soldiers. Despite MacArthur's optimistic insistence, chances for defending the Philippines did not look good.[73]

When war broke out in Europe in 1939, Ethel Herold was "shocked at the weakness of England and France." Still the war had not come as a total surprise. The Herold family had taken another around-the-world tour in 1938 and saw firsthand the results of land grabs by Germany and Japan. While the Japanese continued to threaten more territory in Asia at the end of the 1930s, she did not initially believe the Philippines were at risk: "For years they [the Japanese] had been taking over parts of China and China was fighting them back. Why not let them fight it out and the Yellow Peril exhaust itself by fighting each other." While Ethel clearly supported the right of the Chinese to live peaceably in their own country, her comment shows that her main concern would always be for the security of the United States and its people. If the Chinese and Japanese wore each other out, they would not be able to threaten the United States.[74]

In a strange about-face, President Quezon—now convinced that the islands could not be defended and reluctant to antagonize the Japanese—undercut MacArthur's authority over the military, stopped the draft, and requested and received from the national assembly special emergency powers. This strained his relationship with Francis Sayre, the American high commissioner, who worried that such actions would interfere with America's ability to defend the Philippines. These qualms were compounded by concerns over how Filipinos would respond to a Japanese attack. Would they turn against their American colonizers and greet the Japanese as liberators? Or would they continue their loyalty to the United States and fight against the Japanese?[75]

Then, in 1940, President Roosevelt cut off fuel and scrap-metal sales to Japan; the country responded by entering into a political and military pact with Germany and Italy. This action heightened concerns about the probability of a Japanese attack on English colonial possessions in Asia, so dependents of British military personnel serving in Shanghai and Hong Kong were relocated to Manila during the summer. Over twelve hundred made their way to Baguio, where they remained for six weeks until the British government sent the majority of them on to Australia. Missionaries from China also arrived in the Philippines in greater numbers as a variety of missionary boards decided that their people simply were not safe.

The Special Division of the U.S. State Department, organized in 1939 just as war broke out in Europe, bore the responsibility for protecting Americans in war zones by arranging for repatriation. In October 1940, it requested that the dependents of American military personnel living throughout Asia return to the United States. It then made a similar request to all American civilians living in China and Japan. Though the Special Division had a $500,000 budget to assist in these matters, transportation costs were left to the evacuees. Part of this had to do with the financial tightness of the division's director, Breckenridge Long; part had to do with delicate foreign relations matters. The State Department "requested" and "suggested" that Americans leave these areas but did not demand it because the government did not want to give Japan the impression that it was preparing for war.[76]

Ethel Herold helped outfit thirty-nine cottages on Baguio's Military Cut-Off Road to handle the overflow population of British civilians. Near the end of 1940, hundreds of American women and children heeded the State Department's suggestion and left the Philippines. Just after Christmas of 1940, the Herolds took a short vacation to Abra and also visited the Trinidad Farm School. One of Ethel's Filipino friends suggested that if war came to the Philippines, she and the children should move back to Trinidad, where the people would supply them with food and shelter and Ethel could teach English again at the school. Elmer Herold, who presumably would be tied up with business matters, could visit on weekends. "We all agreed that that would be a good arrangement," Ethel said, adding, "Such a lovely pipe dream." Though this entire scenario did not come true, the Herolds' former students proved instrumental in providing them with much-needed food and other supplies during the war years.[77]

Ethel Herold refused to believe that the Japanese would attack the Philippines. She trusted General MacArthur's pronouncement that the islands could be defended, that it was impossible for the Japanese to take them over. Her husband apparently shared this belief because he did not uproot the entire family or even send Ethel and the children back to the states. As a veteran of the Great War, Elmer well understood the realities of war, and it is difficult to believe that he would have willingly put his family in danger. The Herolds had the economic means to pack up and go home, and with Europe at war again, Elmer probably could have found a good job commensurate with his experience and education. They stayed because they saw little reason not to do so.

Yet, the Herolds realized that the Japanese were capable of organizing a successful blockade and thus prepared for this contingency. Elmer stockpiled spare parts, cables, and fire bricks so that Heald Lumber could continue to operate, and he also ordered the construction of two huge crude-oil tanks so he could lay in a supply of fuel. On the domestic front, Ethel realized "there would always be rice, camotes, sugar, fish, pigs, fowl," but she collected canned goods nevertheless. If their formal schooling was disrupted, Ethel would teach Billy and Betsy at home.[78]

The year 1941 began with the usual social and cultural events in Baguio. Ethel Herold attended picnic luncheons and farewell parties called despedidas, helped plan a concert by the Manila Symphony Orchestra, and participated in the annual Roosevelt Birthday Ball. Amid these activities, Baguio residents continued to prepare for hostilities. A City Council candidate proposed building air-raid shelters; Mayor Nicasio Valderrosa called together a city emergency committee to draw up plans for a home guard; and Baguio Rotarians were asked to help prepare for refugees in the event of war as Baguio had been chosen as an evacuation center for people from lowland cities. Elmer Herold, a longtime Rotary member, served on a committee responsible for protecting utilities and industries.[79]

As Ethel continued her charitable activities, made all the more urgent because of the preparedness activity, she must have been remembering the first time she supported preparedness: back in 1914, when war already raged in Europe but had not yet drawn in the United States. Then she worked with the Red Cross in Potosi and Appleton, knitting and rolling bandages. Now, she used her position in the Monday Club to recruit women for Red Cross work in Baguio, most of which was still dedicated to making bandage kits destined for China and Europe.[80]

During the summer, Douglas MacArthur, who had officially retired from the U.S. military at the end of 1937, was called back into active service, an action prompted by escalating Japanese aggression. Japanese troops occupied Saigon and on July 25 announced a protectorate over Indochina. The next day, President Roosevelt froze Japanese assets in the United States and the Philippines and forbade the export of iron, rubber, and oil to Japan. The American high commissioner, Francis Sayre, then received word that the president had ordered the Philippine military to merge into the American, putting the sixty-one-year-old MacArthur in charge as the commanding general of the United States Army Forces Far East (USAFFE). In September, Baguio residents began practicing for blackouts and soldiers trained from dawn until midnight. The following month, a command and staff school opened at Camp Allen to train American and Filipino division commanders. Tourist traffic to Baguio slackened as the city busied itself with preparations for an attack.[81]

On December 1, 1941, Ethel Herold and other members of the Monday Club enjoyed a visit to the high commissioner's summer residence in Baguio, courtesy of club member Elizabeth Sayre. "It was an unusually large meeting, as all the gals wanted a look at the mansion," Ethel recalled. "I was glad so many were present as we had a lot of business to do." Elizabeth Sayre surprised the women by announcing that "it was expected that large numbers of U.S. troops would be in hospitals by Christmas time and would need Red Cross comfort bags." She asked if the Monday Club would purchase the material and make the bags—women in Manila had volunteered to fill them—and the club committed to two or three hundred bags. Ethel Herold wondered, uneasily, why the High Commissioner's wife expected this to happen, but uncharacteristically did not speak up.[82]

The Monday Club held a basket social on Saturday, December 6, at the Baguio Country Club. Each woman who attended had to bring a decorated basket filled with enough food for two people. Each basket would then be auctioned off, and the highest bidder would win the basket and the right to eat with the woman who prepared it. Ethel asked that each woman prepare enough food for three people because she expected a large number of military guests. Dinner, followed by square dancing, was, according to Ethel, "a yowling success. Elmer almost swung the life out of me." The money the club collected, to be used to help fund China Relief and the Red Cross, was locked up in the Brent School safe until it could be taken to the bank on Monday morning. On Sunday, the Herolds "just rested and enjoyed our lovely house"; in the evening they attended a performance of the Philippine Military Academy band at Camp Allen. It was the last pleasant, carefree night they were to spend together for over three years.[83]

Chapter Four

Enemy Alien: Citizenship and Patriotism in the Occupied Philippines

ON MONDAY MORNING, December 8, 1941, Elmer Herold rose at 5:00 a.m. as usual, waking Billy and Betsy so that they could practice their music lessons before school. At 6:00, he switched on the radio for the day's first news broadcast from Manila. Within minutes, the children rushed to their mother's bedroom door shouting, "Pearl Harbor has been bombed!" Ethel Herold replied, "How dare they attack us? I can't believe it." She got out of bed to talk to her husband about the Japanese strike. Although Betsy Herold remembered that while her mother looked alarmed, her father radiated calm. Elmer Herold quickly reassured them all that Pearl Harbor was many thousands of miles away. He believed distance was a safety feature. Also, a whole squadron of B-17 bombers had recently arrived from the United States, and General Douglas MacArthur had been rigorously training Filipino soldiers. They had nothing to fear from the Japanese.[1]

The Herolds' overconfidence stemmed from nationalistic pride tinged with racism. Ethel Herold avidly followed world events—she regularly listened to radio news broadcasts and read newspapers and magazines—so she knew that the Japanese had been having considerable success in conquering portions of Asia. The 1937 Rape of Nanking loomed especially large in her mind, but she refused to believe that the Japanese, whom she viewed as racially inferior to Caucasians, could do the same to American-held territory. Civilians in the Philippines received no formal evacuation notices, so leaving would look cowardly and un-American. Besides, Elmer Herold's work was in Baguio, and he would not leave it. Thus, Ethel and the children also stayed.

That decision cost Ethel Herold over three years of freedom. Because of Japan's swift military victories in December 1941, her American citizenship took her from a position of power and privilege to one of dependence and fear as the Herold family, along with other Allied nationals, spent the war years as interned enemy aliens in Japanese-occupied territory. Nevertheless, Ethel once again drew on her pride in that citizenship and her notions of patriotism to get through a world war. Surviving internment required not only the psychological boost patriotism provided but also the considerable organization and hard work to which she was accustomed.

Though her status as a prisoner in the Philippines isolated her from the propaganda that the U.S. government created stateside to sustain support for the war, she would have embraced those campaigns. Government propagandists tapped into what Americans chose to believe about themselves, crafting campaigns that portrayed the Allied war against the Axis powers as an "all out fight between democracy and dictatorship." Ethel Herold believed it was her patriotic duty, an answer to a higher political calling, to help bring democracy to the Philippines, and with Americans in place as colonial masters she could easily convince herself that the goal was altruistic. But a Japanese victory in this new war would mean an end to American supremacy, an end to the spreading of democracy.[2]

This struggle between the free and democratic United States and the authoritarian Japan probably led Ethel to consider the political differences between the two countries. To Americans, the Japanese represented an "alien political culture" that provided a clear contrast to democracy. Furthermore, U.S. government propagandists insisted that perceptions of morality differed as well, that good and evil simply did not mean the same things in both countries. Such issues were not theoretical to Ethel Herold, not simple rhetorical flourishes for propaganda purposes. She believed them and she lived them. As an internee, she daily confronted what she viewed as the evil and alien nature of Japan's undemocratic regime, first-hand experiences that convinced her that the Americans had to win the war.[3]

This chapter explores how perceptions of Japan's "alien political culture" shaped Ethel Herold's internment experiences. From her perspective, the fact that the Japanese interned civilians and disregarded the Geneva Convention in their treatment of prisoners proved their evilness. The Japanese directives to their captives about the ways in which they should organize their camp life represented an unfamiliar political culture to the Americans, for whom communal living and authoritarian rule were not the norm. Yet the very organization and running of the internment camps required the internees to create a government, which in turn sparked debates on voting rights. The chapter also looks at the relationship between gender and patriotism in connection with Ethel Herold's reactions to military events and with the internees' involvement with guerrilla forces on the island of Luzon. Even—or especially—within the confines of a civilian internment camp during an enemy occupation, Ethel Herold strove to be a loyal American citizen.

"Who Has Guts?"

On that Monday morning in December, in addition to their attack on Pearl Harbor, the Japanese struck the Philippines as well. After hearing the news about Hawaii, anxious to maintain a semblance of normality, Ethel Herold got dressed and dropped her children off at the Brent School at 7:30 as usual. From there she headed to the post office, where she stopped to chat with friends. Several planes flew overhead, and Ethel cheered them on, thinking they were American planes on their way to bomb Tokyo. When several loud booms followed, she assumed that soldiers at Camp John Hay, the U.S. military recreation post, had fired salutes to the planes. In fact, those were Japanese planes, and they would drop a total of seventy-two bombs on John Hay that day.[4]

The Herolds' property ran adjacent to Camp John Hay, and when Ethel returned home from her errands, she saw that the pavement on the asphalt road that led to the house was peppered with large cracks that had not been there earlier that morning. Elmer Herold, working amid the noise of the lumberyard's machine shop about seven kilometers away, knew nothing about the bombing until someone from the main office telephoned to report it; then he came home immediately. Planes screeched overhead, sirens blared periodically, the radio broadcast war news every hour, and the telephone rang incessantly with friends desperate for information. Listening to radio reports of local bombings, Ethel agonized, "Oh, God is this the year of our Lord 1941? Is this Baguio?"[5]

Under the extraordinary circumstances of a Japanese attack, and considering her upbringing and her experiences during the Great War, it is hardly surprising that Ethel Herold looked to men to handle the situation. To her, the political and military aspects of war were primarily men's business, with loyal women offering their support. She believed that the American men in the islands would quickly repel the enemy attack and reestablish the colonial order, but in fact from the very beginning the United States Army Forces Far East (USAFFE) did not stand a chance against the Japanese. Thus, with her ordered world collapsing around her, Ethel Herold railed against what she perceived as the stupidity of men, and she even took some matters into her own hands. In the confusion during the first days of the Japanese invasion, she accused some men of cowardice—or lacking guts as she put it—a condemnation that called into question their masculinity and their loyalty.

Though she could not believe that the Japanese would actually be able to conquer the Philippines—a blockade was more likely, she thought—she took their attacks seriously. As a safety precaution, Ethel and Elmer Herold sent their children to spend a few days with family friends Herman and Anna Kluge up the Mountain Trail at Kilometer (KM) 67, just until the USAFFE mopped up the Japanese. With her children as safe as they could be and her husband occupied with protecting the lumber business, Ethel did what she did best. She helped organize and prepare the Baguio community for whatever might come next and started calling Monday Club women about first-aid classes at the Baguio Country Club Pavilion.[6]

The Japanese landing at Vigan, north of Baguio, on December 10 proved that the enemy was capable of more than air attacks and that occupation would follow. Baguio lay right in the Japanese path to Manila. Because of the repeated bombings and fear of an imminent invasion, few Baguio residents willingly ventured out of their homes by mid-December. Ethel Herold, not content unless she had something to do, continued her first-aid activities up at KM 67 where Billy and Betsy had been staying with the Kluges. "No air alarms up here," she reported, but she could "see the Jap planes coming and going—presumably as they please." She and the doctor from the lumber mill held three first-aid classes per day, and just as with an earlier generation of students, she found the classes "wonderful, how eager those Igorotes are."[7]

But within a few days, Ethel returned to Baguio. The Japanese had not yet made it that far, and besides, she missed her husband. "How glad I am to be with Elmer during these awful times," she confided in her diary; a couple of days later she reunited the entire family when she retrieved the children from KM 67. On December 21, Ethel hung both Christmas decorations and blackout curtains in her home, noting that "Elmer *shows* he is worried—for the first time." She also expressed her first frustrations with what she perceived as men's inability to effectively organize: "Elmer trying like the devil to get in more rice for the men. Such fool red tape and such delay. Heald Lumber trucks hauling dynamite from Balatoc, Benguet, etc. to Balate Pass and Lingayen Coast Defense—then bringing back truck loads of rice—but that fool City Hall has to have records. DUMB." Results, not procedure, mattered the most to her.[8]

In the early morning of December 22, in advance of an enemy attack, some women and children were evacuated from Baguio and the nearby mines; then the main road between Baguio and Manila was closed to civilian traffic. But Ethel Herold would not leave because her husband would not, and she rationalized that the family was "much safer in the mountains among the Igorots [where] we would always have camotes, sugar and coconuts."[9] Some forty-three thousand Japanese troops landed just north of the Lingayen Gulf that morning and began their unchallenged ascent up five thousand feet in the mountains to Baguio. Ethel did what she could to prepare, taking cash out of the bank for family supplies and making sure that the patients in the tuberculosis hospital had a sufficient stock of food.

By noon, the USAFFE retreated, and Baguio quickly descended into chaos. American officers and soldiers stationed at Camp John Hay had no time to control the civilian population. The next morning, Lieutenant Colonel John P. Horan, commander of the camp, came roaring up to the Herold home in a military vehicle, excitedly explaining to Ethel that he had just returned to John Hay from a reconnaissance mission only to find no one there, the radio station destroyed, and all of the code books burned. "Mrs. Herold, what shall I do?" he asked.[10]

To Ethel, Horan's request was a bizarre and unwelcome gender-role reversal. At once furious and frightened, she thought to herself, "MY GOD! That I should live to hear the commander of John Hay say anything like that." She did not offer any advice to Horan but took him over to the Heald Lumber office, where Elmer, E. J. Halsema, and a few other Baguio men had been meeting daily to figure out how to maintain law and order. She had confidence that those men would provide the lieutenant colonel with the assistance he required.[11]

Though she considered it improper to counsel a military officer, Ethel Herold did not hesitate to provide assistance to troops in need, the kind of aid she considered appropriate for a woman. Later on during that afternoon of the twenty-third, after Elmer and the other men had left the Heald Lumber office, "two young unshaven, red-eyed young soldiers" arrived looking for food. Their mess had been destroyed, and they had hoped that someone in Baguio would donate enough food to keep the troops going. Unable to locate a key to the company store, Ethel and one of the lumber mill employees broke the door down so that they could help load the soldiers' truck with cans of sardines, salmon, sausages, and fruit. With a heavy heart, she watched as "those precious sons of someone drove back down into the valley of death." By the time Ethel sank into her bed that night, she admitted, "Never did I think I'd live to see such a day. Balatoc, Benguet, Cal Hor deserted. City officials all gone. Who has guts?"[12]

The day after a low-key Christmas celebration, she once again assisted in supplying the USAFFE. Lieutenant Colonel Horan notified Elmer that his men, now congregated at Heald's sawmill at Lusod, needed more food. Ethel quickly helped organize the loading of five lumber trucks with all of the foodstuffs left over from the Camp John Hay commissary. When J. J. Keith, Baguio's chief of police, tried to take over the operation, Ethel Herold "learned then and there that I could swear like a drunken sailor—I ordered him out."[13]

It is likely that she viewed this as a woman's project—directing the distribution of food, which she had done during the Great War. It is also likely that she considered the American police chief tainted by cowardice. On December 22, 1941, Keith, along with Baguio's mayor Nicasio Valderrosa, had left the city in a premature attempt to negotiate a surrender with the Japanese. Many people in Baguio believed other factors—including self-protection—motivated this action and speculated about the loyalty of the two men. Ethel Herold concluded that loyalty and bravery were not race-specific: "After seeing and knowing how my own country men have turned tail and run like scared people, what can one think? It takes guts and fortitude and discipline to live in the world. Certain men of ALL races have it.

And many do not."[14] Though she bemoaned the fact that some men lacked guts, she herself did not directly accuse Keith and Valderrosa of disloyalty, but the aspersions she cast on their masculinity implied it.

December 26 was, Ethel admitted, "my first time to blow up." In addition to her confrontation with Chief Keith, she railed against what she considered useless conversation among the men at the lumber office. "Meeting in Heald Office for about 3 hours to send word to Manila about what should be done here," she wrote in her diary. "Then instead of immediately sending the couriers—no, they must wait for a report on Benguet, etc. Why in hell weren't those reports made last night or early this morning? Some men are too DAMNED *slow.*" Even as Japanese troops approached Baguio on the following morning, Ethel criticized the city leaders for not declaring Baguio an open city: "My God why such procrastination? Can't anyone think straight and ACT? Why do men talk so much and do so little? I would like to take the chance and send word myself and suffer the consequences."[15]

It is tempting to dismiss Ethel Herold as a termagant, but behind her scolding lay a deep and very real fear for the safety of her family and community. She had already lived through one world war but had experienced and supported it from the safety of the United States. Now she faced one of the realities of imperialism. Though the U.S. government still held the Philippines as a territory, it did not place the security of those islands on an equal basis with its own mainland; the Philippines and the people living there were expendable. This became increasingly clear to Ethel as events unfolded in December, so she became frightened and lashed out at the men on whom she had counted for protection.

The Japanese reached the Baguio city limits on the morning of December 27, 1941, and worked out peaceful occupation terms with city officials. Ethel remembered that Baguio "fell silently, there was no crash, not a shot fired. A section of the Jap army just marched up the Naguilian Road. The City Hall was occupied. The telephone office was occupied. All plugs pulled." Elmer, at work as usual in the Heald Lumber office, sent a message to Ethel apprising her of the latest developments, instructing her and the children to remain in the house. When Ethel looked out the window and saw one of the Heald lumber trucks speed by with a Japanese flag waving on the front end, she observed that "the world was fast coming to an end." Her world of privilege rooted in American imperialism was about to be replaced by Japan's Greater East Asia Co-Prosperity Sphere. Americans were no longer colonial masters; Asia, the Japanese pronounced, was now for Asians.[16]

Citizenship, Internment, and International Law

The Herolds ate "a quiet apprehensive supper," after the Japanese Ninth Infantry occupied the city, and exhausted from the day's events, they retired early. "Well, so far so good," Ethel thought. "Elmer had not been shot, I and the servant girls had not been raped. I could go to sleep once more in the arms of my husband." Later that night, though, some Japanese soldiers turned up at the Herold home, searched it, and informed the American family that they were not to leave their house. The soldiers remained through the night and then took them to the Brent School in the morning for registration. The use of the word "registration" was a bright spot. The Herolds believed that the Japanese intended to record their names, addresses, and nationalities before allowing them to return home to await repatriation to the United States. Instead, the Japanese interned these civilians first at the U.S. Army's R&R facility in Baguio, Camp John Hay. Then, in the spring of 1942, they moved their captives farther up the Mountain Trail to Camp Holmes, the former Philippine Constabulary base. A final, harrowing transfer to Old Bilibid Prison in Manila occurred in late 1944.[17]

At the Brent School, Ethel Herold described "bedlam: cars coming and going. Americans and Japs all around. Everybody scared." Soldiers led the Herolds into the empty infirmary and left them there. Japanese guards came in that afternoon and took Elmer Herold away to talk with them, a process they repeated the following morning. When he returned, he told his wife that the Japanese had designated him liaison for all the prisoners—they intended to hold the Allied civilians as such—with the manager of the Baguio Bank, Wally Moore, to serve as his assistant. American missionary Fern Harrington later described Elmer as a "natural choice" for liaison since he had had considerable experience working with Japanese employees in his capacity as manager of Heald Lumber, the largest employer of Japanese laborers in the Baguio area. Elmer Herold had won their "confidence and respect," according to Harrington, and they regarded him as a "man of integrity."[18]

The Japanese decision to hold the Allied nationals captive rather than repatriate them signaled to Ethel Herold that the enemy rejected western traditions of wartime conduct. Typically, civilians trapped in enemy territory at the onset of hostilities are returned to their home country. But in this case, the Japanese resisted repatriating the more than twelve thousand Americans in the Pacific, partly because of the logistics involved and partly because they anticipated that these civilians might be valuable bargaining chips. Both Japan and the United States bore some blame for the limited repatriation during the war, with each side unwilling to release people who might turn out to be of particular value to their native country. Nevertheless, neither her American citizenship nor her civilian status nor her gender was enough to qualify Ethel Herold for repatriation. The Japanese agreed to exchange official diplomatic personnel, municipal officials, employees of "public organizations" who had been sent to Asia, students, and missionaries, but not other American citizens who had chosen to live in the Philippines.[19]

Two repatriation swaps took place, one in the summer of 1942 and a second in September 1943, but Ethel only made brief mention of them in her diary. She never recorded the repatriation rumor that circulated in December 1943 and the Baguio internees' vote on whether or not to participate. Perhaps she saw no point in dwelling on something unlikely to happen. If so, she was right to not waste her time; a third exchange did not materialize. With the second repatriation, the U.S. government had apparently done all it could for Americans held captive by the Japanese. Now Ethel Herold and the others could only wait and hope for liberation, praying that they would survive the ordeal.[20]

That wait proved long and difficult. From the beginning, the Japanese showed that they cared little about the needs of their captives; they only wanted an orderly occupation. But any occupation is a brutal intrusion on a society. It does not recognize tradition or cultivate consent; yet it enforces authority and demands obedience, and somehow the occupiers and the occupied have to learn to coexist. The Japanese expected Elmer Herold, as their designated liaison, to make sure that their rules were passed along to the internees, who would unquestioningly adhere to them. But the Allied nationals struggled not only to adjust to their new circumstances but also to comprehend and negotiate with an enemy they perceived as possessing alien and inferior social and political structures.[21]

On December 29, 1941, the Japanese moved the internees to a larger location, forcing the captives to walk the three miles from the Brent School to Camp John Hay, their first internment site of the war. For Ethel Herold, "it was awful marching along—Americans as prisoners. How degrading in front of the Filipinos who lined the way." Yet, according to Americans who recorded this event, the Filipinos witnessed this in near silence, with no wild exuberance at the sight of five hundred hot, exhausted, and thirsty prisoners prodded down a road. Ethel Herold took this as a sign that America's imperialism had in fact been so benevolent that the Filipinos would support the United States in its fight against Japan.[22]

Still, for the first time in her life, Ethel's patriotism would have to see her through a personally dangerous situation, and her citizenship would bring hardship rather than privilege. The United States military, which she believed invincible, had not been able to save her from an enemy occupation. Now, she and the other captives could only pin their hopes on the Geneva Convention and international law to guarantee them good treatment until they could be repatriated or rescued. But the ways in which the Japanese did or did not adhere to international law confirmed for Ethel Herold Japan's evil and alien nature.

In the early twentieth century, many countries sought to mitigate the carnage of modern warfare with international agreements that set up standards of decent treatment for wounded or captured military personnel. Forty-two nations signed an agreement at The Hague in 1907, which guaranteed "humane treatment, protection from violence, freedom from reprisals, and the provision of sufficient food, medical, and sanitary supplies and facilities to sustain life in a reasonable manner" for military prisoners. The horrors of protracted trench warfare during the Great War prompted additional guidelines. The 1929 Geneva Convention decreed that "it will be the duty of every Power to diminish, as far as possible the unavoidable rigors thereof and to mitigate the fate of prisoners of war." Article I defined prisoners as "all persons belonging to the armed forces of belligerent parties, captured by the enemy," but the agreement stipulated that captured civilians should be "treated as military prisoners of war." By 1939, most countries, including Japan and the United States, had signed the agreement, though Japan's Diet failed to ratify it.[23]

"Elmer and Wally [Moore] constantly argue with [Lieutenant] Mukibo about our rights as prisoners of war, the Geneva Conference, the Red Cross," Ethel Herold wrote in her diary in early February 1942, "but nothing doing." The Japanese announced their intentions to treat the internees according to the Geneva Convention, but in reality they rarely did. The Japanese disregard for legal documents and agreements led to their officials making up the guidelines of internment as they went along, giving them considerable leeway in how they treated prisoners. And the prisoners invariably suffered.[24]

Though the Japanese also insisted they would treat U.S. internees in the Philippines on a par with the American government's treatment of Japanese-American internees in the United States, there was no such reciprocity. In early 1942, citing fears of possible sabotage and espionage, the U.S. government established "relocation centers" for people of Japanese descent in the United States. That such internment camps were established is today regarded as a gross injustice, a reflection of long-standing racism directed against Asians in the United States. Yet, despite the fact that Japanese-American internees were deprived of their liberty and property without due process of law, the camps generally offered them sufficient food, shelter, and medical care as well as opportunities for education and work. Spain, Japan's designated protecting power, along with both the International and American Red Cross and the American Friends, regularly visited these locations; U.S. courts heard challenges to internment; and the government even offered ways out of internment.[25]

Japan did not allow such opportunities and oversight in the Philippines. Because American internees in the Philippines were not citizens of that country, to the Japanese they were conquered enemy nationals who merited scant attention and who could certainly not claim any civil-liberties violations. As the Japanese contributed minimally to their internees' upkeep and refused Red Cross intervention, the captives struggled to find enough food and medicine to keep themselves alive. They quickly learned that they did not enjoy the protection of international law.

Japanese authorities also violated other aspects of the Geneva Convention. For instance, during the third week of January 1942,

Elmer Herold engaged in a running argument with Lieutenant (later Major) Musa Mukibo over submitting a list of internees' names to the International Red Cross, so that relatives could know where they were, that they were alive, and that they might exchange correspondence with them. Elmer cited international law as the basis for his request, and indeed Article 8 of the Geneva Convention states, "Belligerents are bound mutually to notify each other of their capture of prisoners within the shortest period possible." Mukibo replied, "There is no International Law, we are the laws."[26]

To Ethel Herold, Mukibo represented everything that was evil in the Japanese, especially when, in early 1942, he threatened the safety of the interned women. He approached Ethel at Camp John Hay "with that damned smirk on this little old straight mouth" and informed her that the Japanese officers billeted at the Pines Hotel in Baguio needed waitresses to serve them. This marked one of the "all time low moments of the Camp" for Ethel because Mukibo's request was a thinly veiled demand that American women work as prostitutes for the Japanese.[27] She protested to Mukibo that the internees had too much work to do and could not be sent away to work elsewhere. Mukibo was insistent, however, emphasizing that the officers wanted young women. "So scared inside that I could hardly think," Ethel continued babbling objections, trying to convince him to relent. But when Mukibo cut off the conversation with "you will cooperate," she dashed off to find her husband.[28]

Elmer Herold called an emergency meeting of the internees' governing body, the Men's Committee, and news of Mukibo's demand "spread like wildfire through the women's barracks." Ethel Herold advised the young women to stick close to the children in camp and to "make yourselves look like ugly married women." Though her description of a potentially disastrous event for the young women clearly shows how she perceived the Japanese as evil, she never completely revealed the outcome: when the Men's Committee vigorously protested this moral outrage to higher-ranking Japanese officials, those officials quashed Mukibo's plans. Clearly, not all Japanese believed it appropriate to force conquered women into prostitution; yet the very threat frightened Ethel Herold so much that she never admitted that the Japanese themselves called it off. And she worried for the rest of the war that they might change their minds and round up the young women.[29]

Treatment of the interned children provided another sharp contrast between the cultures of captives and captors. Though in general the Japanese guards dealt benignly with them, often playing games and sometimes sharing food, Ethel Herold and the other parents constantly worried about how the children would fare under these circumstances. In addition to living in the fear and uncertainty of enemy-occupied territory, the interned children had to cope with having their families separated—women and children in one set of barracks, men and older boys in another. Parents struggled to maintain some semblance of normal life for their children, and they considered the continuation of education a key part of that. Near the end of January 1942, while still in Camp John Hay, Ethel said to her husband, "Elmer, we must have a school for these noisy kids. They are driving me crazy. It's a waste of time for these kids to be running around like this." Elmer agreed. Other parents had made the same request, and since thirteen teachers, most from the Brent School, were among the internees, opening a school seemed the logical thing to do.[30]

Elmer Herold and a couple of other camp men took the request to Japanese authorities, who gave their conditional permission. Japanese censors evaluated textbooks brought in from the Brent School and either blacked out or ripped out sections that contained "dangerous ideas"—mostly concerning the subjects of history and geography. Despite the censorship, Ethel proclaimed that the camp school was a "great success with few books." To get around Japanese control of the curriculum, Jim Halsema, a journalist, taught the children his own version of history and geography with news items he picked up from outside the camp while he was on garbage duty and from the radio the men had smuggled into camp. Thus, Billy and Betsy Herold, along with the other schoolchildren, received an American education during internment, one infused with patriotic lessons in defiance of Japanese rules.[31]

That the Japanese prevented the delivery and distribution of food and medical supplies from relief organizations to the internees also confirmed to Ethel Herold that the enemy was evil and uncivilized. But in this case, unlike with Mukibo's demand for "waitresses," she realized that not all Japanese were the same. In December 1943, the internment camp commandant, Rokuro Tomibe, secured 576 cases of Red Cross materials for Camp Holmes, bringing in much-needed food, clothing, and medical supplies. The Baguio internees, including the Herolds, considered Tomibe a humanitarian and a gentleman, even crediting him with safeguarding their survival because he made sure that those parcels got to them.[32]

The Red Cross packages provided a psychological boost as well: the internees no longer felt forgotten. Wrappers on the Old Gold cigarettes in the parcels contained an inspiring patriotic message that the Japanese tried but failed to confiscate: "FREEDOM. Our heritage has always been freedom—We cannot afford to relinquish it—Our armed forces will safeguard that heritage, if we, too, do our share to preserve it." The cigarette wrapper also reassured Ethel Herold of what she was due as a citizen. If she did her part to support the government, the government would ultimately save her. She expected reciprocity from her various organizational activities as well. "A memorable day," she wrote of receiving her family's share of the relief packages. "I am glad of all I have done for the Red Cross, will surely do more."[33]

Those Red Cross parcels literally saved the lives of the Baguio internees. In early 1944, piqued by Japanese military losses, camp authorities announced that internees could no longer accept food parcels from the outside, go to the Baguio market, read the *Manila Tribune,* or listen to the radio at the guardhouse. The prisoners suffered without those outside food parcels, especially as the Red Cross supplies dwindled. Commandant Tomibe found his hands tied by his superiors, who soon transferred him out of the camp, correctly suspecting his sympathy for the captives. On June 10, 1944, Ethel Herold wrote in her diary, "Elmer and I exhausted with hunger. Little money and terrific prices; we afraid to touch Red Cross things for fear times will get worse. All four of us lost much weight again. I feel so sorry for Elmer and Billy, they never get enough to eat. Imagine Elmer and I not interested in a dance."[34]

In August 1944, the Japanese claimed that since food had become so scarce, the Baguio internees must work in a camp garden. It was not the forced, uncompensated labor outlawed by the Geneva Convention, but it certainly violated Articles 29 and 30, which said that "no prisoner of war may be employed at labors for which he is physically unfit" and that the length of the labor "shall not be excessive." According to Ethel, "Japs threaten to take away our private cooking unless we work in the 12.5 acre garden. Forty-four women and forty-three men volunteered at the point of the bayonet. Camotes and onions chief things to be planted. I hope to God we are not here for the harvest." By that time, she feared, they would all be dead from hunger.[35]

Work, Politics, and the Preservation of Democracy

When the internees had first arrived at Camp John Hay on December 29, 1941, they found the place barely fit for human habitation. "There were 3 barracks," Ethel Herold wrote in her diary, "but we could use only the ONE—it had been built for 60 Igorotes, we were 500 people. It had not been cleaned since the war started; all 3 barracks had been bombed and were full of holes and windows smashed." The Japanese directed the Herolds to a seven-by-twelve barbershop room where they made their beds on the floor. "Japs told us to organize ourselves and live as a community," Ethel explained. "We aimed to follow the skeleton organization of Brent." She was referring to the school where some had voluntarily concentrated themselves just before the occupation. There, a small group of men had established a ruling committee, with several subcommittees responsible for carrying out various tasks.[36]

At the Brent School and then at Camp John Hay, the internees largely bore responsibility for food, shelter, and sanitation, and the Herolds pitched in from the start. Elmer spent the first full day of internment at John Hay trying to fix some electric pumps. A group of internees cooked breakfast for everyone in the camp, and missionary Fern Harrington noted this of Ethel Herold: "a woman with graying hair swept up in a bun on top of her head, wearing a light blue housedress, white anklets and oxfords, stood near the kitchen door supervising waitresses like a maitre d' at a fancy restaurant." While Ethel lauded the kitchen workers that morning, saying that everyone was "doing their bit," by the end of the day she noticed that "a lot of people just sat in a DAZE—too stunned with events to do anything."[37] With Japanese administrative inconsistencies and without access to international relief organizations, the Baguio internees had to organize themselves. If too many people sat around in a daze for too long, they would all die.

Surviving internment required effective organization, skills Ethel Herold possessed. Her dedicated work over the next three and a half years can be viewed in terms of patriotism—that every action she took to survive enemy captivity was an expression of loyalty to the United States. Ethel's position on the Women's Committee in the Baguio internment camps and her revival of the Monday Club illustrate the politicization of civilian women's work in wartime, of how even the most mundane domestic tasks could be infused with patriotism.

The U.S. government created two main lines of propaganda during World War II. One involved the necessity of preserving the "presumably universal human rights and liberties of liberal democracy" threatened by the Axis powers. The other was the preservation of "essentially private moral obligations to individuals and interests similarly threatened," such as families, friends, and neighbors. Fighting for both would preserve the "American way of life." The Baguio internees attempted to preserve this way of life by establishing a democratic-style government within the confines of their camps and by preserving their family and community structures, none of which was easy under the Japanese. Ethel Herold worked hard not only to protect her family and community but also to prove to her nemesis, Lieutenant Musa Mukibo, the superiority of the American way of life.[38]

To facilitate internee organization, the Japanese appointed several of the male prisoners, including Elmer Herold, to an executive committee (commonly known as the Men's Committee), which created various subcommittees to handle all of the necessary work, including kitchen, hospital, sanitation, garbage, and mechanics. Ethel described this as "similar to setting up a new United States or something—only we have those damned Japs over us—but it surely is an experience in government." The Men's Committee in turn appointed a Women's Committee to divvy up their own camp responsibilities, delegating to the women childcare and other tasks considered "women's work." On January 5, 1942, Ethel noted in her diary, "Women's Committee named by the men. Committees for everything appointed."[39]

The Men's Committee tapped Ethel to head the women's work committee, but she tried to resist, not because she was afraid of the work but because she knew the position would make her unpopular with many people. Arthur Richardson, a minister from the Brent School, knew just how to convince her: "Now Ethel, you're a good

American. You're not going to let this Japanese business put you down. You're just going to show what you can do." Ethel maintained that the appointment came as a surprise, and she surmised, probably correctly, that the men drafted her for the job because of her position as president of the Monday Club and her service on various boards in Baguio. She finally could not resist the appeal to her patriotism, concluding, "Well, this was war, and I'd do my duty."[40]

Positions on the Men's Committee and Women's Committee then became elected rather that appointed, one of the few ways that the internees had of exercising some autonomy from their captors and of demonstrating their continued allegiance to the democratic system. The elections also probably cut down on graft and charges of favoritism in connection with work assignments. Still, the policies for the committee elections were neither clear nor consistent, and the gender differences were obvious. "Men having a new election," Ethel reported on February 1, 1942, just over a month into internment. "Wish the women would have one as I'm fed up with this chairman of Women's Committee—nothing but work all the time and listen to troubles day and night."[41]

It is a testament to the tenacity of gender roles that the two main committees were divided by gender, with the Men's Committee taking responsibility for things like overall camp organization and camp money while the Women's Committee focused on issues concerning the women's barracks. And even more important to the preservation of gender hierarchy, the men's group had veto power over the women's. For instance, during March 1942, members of the two committees discussed where the "big boys" should live—with the women and children or with the men. Though the Women's Committee voted to send them to the men's barracks, the Men's Committee voted for the boys to remain with the women, and so they stayed.[42]

Even more telling about these gender divisions, though, was the controversy over voting, which first surfaced in August 1942, a few months after the Japanese moved the 500 internees to Camp Holmes, the former Philippine constabulary base that had originally housed about 120 men. Adjusting to the new location, which like Camp John Hay offered only damaged and cramped accommodations, put additional stress on the Men's and Women's Committees. On April 22, 1942, the day of the move, Ethel Herold had noted, "We had a Women's Committee meeting about every hour, to try to decide things the best way." The repeated meetings had gone on through the next day as well, until Ethel had to often "stop and cry—I am so utterly tired."[43]

As part of her duties as head of the Women's Committee, Ethel sat in on Men's Committee meetings, trying—not always successfully—to forge consensus on organizational matters. "Our policy" on the Women's Committee, she explained, "has always been to put all cards on the table and then thrash things out. This is surely an experience in government." She seemed most comfortable with this arrangement: using her powers of persuasion to influence men but ultimately leaving the final decisions to them. In the internment camps, she did not deviate from the organizational approaches that had served her well throughout her life. Thus, in a way it is not surprising that when some of the women in Camp Holmes raised objections about committee voting procedures, Ethel Herold did not weigh in.[44]

Women's voting never ranked high on Ethel's priority list. While she had worked on the suffrage campaign as a college student, her support had been prompted more out of a sense of duty to her political science professor than out of a sense of gender equality. Her expatriate life in the Philippines physically removed her from the practice of U.S. elections, though her extensive work with women's and other charitable organizations in Baguio, especially her leadership in the Monday Club, provided her with small-scale political experience. Yet, for Ethel Herold, women's participation in the political process did not matter as much as the actual fruits of the organizations, and this viewpoint continued throughout the war. In June 1942, for instance, the Monday Club met for what had become in wartime only an annual meeting and "voted to retain the same officers until the emergency is over—or after the war."[45]

This suspension of the democratic process did not bother Ethel: she considered it an acceptable wartime measure. (She had, after all, admired Emmeline Pankhurst's 1916 lecture that encouraged women to set aside their work on behalf of woman suffrage and focus instead on securing an Allied victory in the Great War and alleviating the plight of civilians.) But one of Ethel's acquaintances, Natalie Crouter, apparently had gotten wind of what was going to happen at the Monday Club meeting, and she emphatically disapproved, refusing to attend and resigning from the club. Two months later, Crouter would raise the issue of women's suffrage in Camp Holmes. "It is election day for our men," she wrote in her diary on August 13, 1942. "It still surprises me that the chairman [of the Men's Committee] doesn't want the women to vote or have any kind of election."[46]

Though Ethel Herold noted the Men's Committee election in her diary as well, she did not take note of the issue of women's suffrage, probably because the Japanese Military Police had taken Elmer away for questioning on August 14. Camp politics ran a very poor second to Ethel's concerns for her husband's safety. But Natalie Crouter had apparently been vocal enough in her criticism of voting procedures that the Men's Committee quickly organized elections for the Women's Committee. After a lengthy description of the work she accomplished on August 20, Ethel jotted in her diary, "Primary election of Women's Committee." For Natalie Crouter, "It was a sensation to cast a ballot, to be considered people again. The chairman's excuse that the Japanese kept us from voting was rather thin."[47]

Members of the Men's Committee had in fact used the Japanese as the reason to block women's suffrage in Camp Holmes. The Japanese did not regard women as political actors, the Baguio men pointed out, so to allow women to vote in the camp would only further antagonize the captors. But Natalie Crouter and other female internees recognized this as an aspect of the enemy's "alien political culture" and reacted against it. Japanese men had achieved suffrage only in 1926, and even those voting rights had been subjected to enough restrictions to weaken their political power. Japanese women could not vote or participate in political organizations because authorities feared that would have a negative impact on the family and upset the social hierarchy.[48]

Though Ethel Herold also viewed Japan's political system as undemocratic and therefore inferior to that of the United States, there were at least two interrelated reasons why she did not push the matter of women's voting rights in the internment camps. First, she probably accepted the Baguio men's argument about not antagonizing their captors: after all, Elmer Herold had spent a lot of time dealing with Japanese authorities, and she would have taken his word about the enemy's views on women. Second, if the primary purpose of the committees was to organize the internees so as to facilitate their survival, then any other purpose, including democratic expression, was less important and had the potential to put survival at risk. Apparently, Ethel did not consider women's suffrage more important than survival. Yet, when the men changed their minds and allowed Women's Committee elections, she accepted that, too.

In the new election in August 1942, Ethel maintained a place on the Women's Committee but not as its chair. She expressed surprise over the outcome of the election because she thought "everybody was ready to shoot me" and described it as "an awful load off my shoulders" not to be chairing the committee. Elections were then held every eight months, but the controversy over women's suffrage in Camp Holmes did not end. In March 1943, again with Natalie Crouter's prodding, the Women's Committee asked the Men's Committee to consider the question of universal suffrage so that men and women together could vote for members of a governing committee comprising both sexes. The Men's Committee put the question to the adult internees of voting age, but the men and women voted separately. Although the total "yes" votes in support of universal suffrage outnumbered the "no" votes, the Men's Committee decided that elections should continue in the original manner.[49]

Ethel did not comment on this issue in her diary but described the committee elections that followed in April 1943 as consumed "with the usual mud-throwing." She refused a nomination to serve again as chair of the Women's Committee but still secured a seat on it. "I confess it did my heart good to get the plurality of votes in the finals," she wrote, "after all the bossing and swearing I have done around here." The interned women continued to elect Ethel Herold to a seat on the committee, often putting her in the top three vote-getters. She saw nothing unusual in only women continuing to vote for members of the Women's Committee, nor did she find it odd when in May the Men's Committee established a Welfare Committee, with men and women serving together on it. "The Women's Committee still has its meetings," Ethel reported at the end of November 1943, "but our power has been usurped by the Men's Committee which I guess is just as well; things are organized now and we are not kept separated like the first year." Three months later, after the Japanese Army took over control of the camp, the Men's and Women's Committees merged into one that had little power.[50]

Survival had important political implications. If the United States ultimately triumphed in the war against Japan, then Americans could once again assert their right to spread democracy, even if that meant resuming colonialism. Survival meant demonstrating superiority; work increased the likelihood of survival. Therefore it is not surprising that the results of the Women's Committee's work mattered much more to Ethel Herold than the manner in which women were chosen to serve on its various subcommittees. She used that work to prove to her Japanese captors the mettle of American women and to prove to herself and others that she was a loyal American.

As she had done before, Ethel Herold not only supervised the work of others but did a lot of the work herself, toiling for up to sixteen hours per day doing everything from helping to clean out gutters to overseeing the kitchen work to investigating cases of theft. When she was not busy with her Women's Committee duties, she turned to Monday Club activities, which she revived in Camp John Hay and continued in Camp Holmes. Since survival was at stake, Ethel often had to boss and bully the other women to ensure that everything got done. She would never become one of the beloved "angels" of internment like the famed military nurses who had been at Bataan and Corregidor and then were separated from the soldiers after the surrender and held with civilians. The toughness of those women, which had enabled them to live through such horrors, was softened by their medical caring, whereas nothing seemed to soften Ethel Herold. In all matters, though, she strove to be fair, leading her to beg one day in her diary, "Oh, God, help me to do right and to be JUST in this mess I'm involved in. Above all help me to be a good American."[51]

Ethel viewed her camp work as an expression of her American pride and patriotism, both influenced by race and gender. During the first week of January 1942, she reported on a Japanese inspection of Camp John Hay: "The mighty general and much staff looked us over as so many chattels. One of their favorite sports was to inspect us and let us know how *INFERIOR* the white man is. It is worth it, to have had this loss of ours, and to know we have the guts to take it on the chin." When Japanese officials came through for a follow-up the next month, Ethel noted sarcastically that they "tromped through without even looking at us insignificant women." The Japanese, she hinted, were not intelligent enough to recognize that the women's work was hardly insignificant—indeed, it was critical for the internees' survival.[52]

For nearly a year and a half, Ethel found herself responding to criticisms from Lieutenant Mukibo about American women, which rankled her to no end. In early January 1942, Mukibo allowed one of the male internees to haul wood for the women's kitchen stoves but turned down other requests that Elmer Herold brought to him on behalf of the women. "After long arguments," Ethel Herold wrote, "Mukibo always says NO and ends with a dissertation on the inferiority of American women—'NO GOOD.'"[53]

"Everybody has 2 or 3 jobs," Ethel recorded in her diary on January 20, 1942, "how I hate this business of slave driving. We must all try to be clean and sanitary for our own good, not just jap inspection—how that devil Mukibo takes it out on Elmer because American women are so dirty 'No gooooood.'" Two months later, preparing for yet another inspection, Ethel admitted there was an "awful mess to clean under our dirty barracks and I find I'm always the goat for that—as one cannot make white women do a job like that—if it is dirty, Mukibo gives me hell."[54]

There were very few ways in which the internees could resist their captors. The Japanese held all of the power and capriciously punished their captives—or not. But Ethel Herold had determined from the start of internment that she would never bow to a Japanese. Internment was humiliation enough. Since Japanese authorities had decreed that all prisoners must bow when they came into contact with a Japanese, Ethel avoided meeting them. Still, one day as she walked from the camp hospital back to her barracks, she realized she was about to cross paths with a Japanese general. "I wouldn't be a coward and turn back and run and I was not going to bow," Ethel remembered. "I stepped aside and gave the general the best American salute Elmer had ever taught me and the white haired old man saluted me in kind and actually smiled at me. That made me feel good for about two days." She had been lucky. Had the general not been amused, the four officers accompanying him would have done more than give her dirty looks.[55]

Singing helped improve Ethel Herold's morale, and it provided a welcome patriotic boost. About thirty internees sang in the camp choir, directed by a man who had once worked with the famous singer/actor Nelson Eddy. "The singing in that choir kept me from going insane," she remembered. "It lifted me from drudgery and the status of a scrub woman. The singing released the hatred of the Japs in me." The choir performed once a month on a Saturday night, mostly singing religious songs since the Japanese had forbidden anything patriotic. "That was quite a blow" to Ethel Herold, who nevertheless found ways to infuse ordinary lyrics with patriotic meaning. The overtly patriotic songs she reserved for private settings, such as when she sang her World War I favorites "Loyalty" and "The Americans Come" at a 1943 dinner for the Camp Holmes teachers.[56]

The most tangible expression of Ethel Herold's patriotism came in the form of sewing an American flag to celebrate the Fourth of July in 1942. Members of the Women's Committee first began working on the flag on July 3 and continued into the holiday. The women had to rely on their memories of what the flag looked like, piecing together stars, stripes, and the blue field background from carefully hoarded lengths of fabric. Each committee member invited a friend to sew some stitches, with that friend inviting another and so on, until all of the women had an opportunity to participate. The women celebrated subsequent Fourths of July and Armistice Days in internment by stitching on the flag "until every seam was beautifully done over and over, each star securely done. Even the men came to put in just one stitch and wipe away tears."[57]

During a Monday Club meeting, the women discussed what they should do with the flag after the war. One suggested it should be exhibited at the Baguio Country Club, but others worried that after a few years no one would remember the flag's particular significance. Another thought that the flag belonged in the Baguio City Hall. But someone, perhaps Ethel Herold, pointed out that the Philippines would soon become independent and "would care nothing about our flag." The women never reached a decision, but the comment about independence indicates that many already realized that even with an Allied victory, things would be different after the war.[58]

When the Japanese shut down Camp Holmes as an internment site and transferred their captives to Old Bilibid Prison in Manila in late 1944, Ethel tucked that American flag into her brassiere. She remembered that "the carrying of it in my bosom was a great comfort and a good talisman" on the trip, as the internees feared that American planes might inadvertently strafe them as they moved from Baguio to Manila. On February 4, 1945, the day American forces liberated Old Bilibid, Ethel "publicly unfurled" the flag, and the internees "all cried for joy and through tears tried to sing 'The Star Spangled Banner.'"[59]

Loyalty, Resistance, and the Guerrillas

In early August 1942, Ethel Herold recorded a couple of rumors in her diary: "Hear the guerrillas raided Capiz and shot all the guards and stole all Jap commissaries. Atok—far off in the valley here—also raided last night and the supplies taken by guerrillas; could see flares from our hospital." These kinds of actions proved two things to Ethel: first, that the imperial relationship between the United States and the Philippine Islands had been so special and beneficial to the Filipinos that they rejected Japanese promises of a Greater East Asia Co-Prosperity Sphere and cast their lot with the Americans; and second, that some American men, both civilian and military, had refused to accept defeat and engaged in guerrilla activities, sometimes alongside their Filipino counterparts.[60]

From the beginning, Filipino authorities made clear that their allegiance was to the United States. After the Japanese first bombed the islands, Philippine President Quezon asked for and received from his congress emergency legislation to deal with the war, along with an official statement of loyalty and assistance to the United States promising "the full support and cooperation of the Filipino people to the government of the United States." The Philippines, because of its colonial status, could not issue a separate declaration of war against Japan, but even when a puppet government replaced the exiled Quezon, most Filipinos continued to demonstrate allegiance to the Commonwealth and to the United States.[61]

Ethel Herold began experiencing this loyalty even in the days prior to the Japanese occupation of Baguio. When Filipinos at a school near the city offered her gifts of food and coffee, she wrote in her diary, "I don't think I was ever so touched before. Those poor kids giving us food at a time when we need it most. The bread I cast upon the waters is surely coming home." She also reported that once the invasion had begun, the Igorots and the Kalingas declared against the Japanese. Throughout her captivity, Ethel frequently acknowledged "an eternal debt of gratitude to these Filipinos who are so good to us now."[62]

Filipinos also expressed their allegiance by participating in guerrilla activities. Men and women even joined various guerrilla groups for reasons besides patriotism, including economics, greed, political rivalry, family feuds, and grudges. Many American soldiers who escaped from or evaded capture at places such as Bataan and Corregidor also engaged in guerrilla tactics against the enemy. The Japanese, determined to break these underground fighters, ruthlessly hunted them down, putting those who supported them in as much danger as the guerrillas themselves. Despite their own precarious position but eager for the opportunity to show their loyalty and patriotism, the Baguio internees did what they could to assist the guerrillas. And Ethel Herold found herself and her family directly involved.

At noon on Ethel Herold's first birthday in internment, March 25, 1942, Japanese guards took Elmer away to question him about Herman Kluge, a family friend and an employee of Heald Lumber. Kluge had abandoned his work for the company and disappeared into the mountains to help the guerrillas. Elmer had already been questioned several times at the headquarters of the Japanese High Command in Baguio, but apparently those sessions had mainly focused on conditions in the camp. This time, however, the Japanese wanted information about one of the Herolds' closest friends, information that could not only threaten Kluge's safety but also disrupt guerrilla activities in northern Luzon. Though Elmer admitted that Kluge had worked for him, he convincingly denied knowledge of Kluge's whereabouts.[63]

It is likely that the Japanese did not press Elmer Herold on this issue because things were going well for them in the Philippines and they did not yet anticipate much resistance. "We hear Corregidor has fallen," Ethel Herold wrote on May 7, 1942, and "that put us in the depths. Where are those reinforcements? The guerrillas here in the mountains are doing their stuff against great odds." The next day, the Japanese proudly confirmed the news about Corregidor, and the day after that, Ethel reported a rumor that Herman Kluge had been made a captain of the guerrillas. Because of their prewar friendship, Ethel kept close track of stories about Kluge, urging him on from the privacy of her diary, taking pride in his activities.[64]

On August 14, 1942, Billy Herold came looking for his mother, asking whether she knew where Elmer was. Ethel told him that she did not, initially unconcerned because she typically did not see her husband during the day. But her heart sank as Billy informed her,

"The Jap Military Police took him to the Military Prison for questioning at 2:30." That had been three hours earlier. Billy, almost in tears, reminded Ethel, "And you know what they do with them there."[65]

They were right to be terrified. The Kempeitai, originally established in Japan in 1881, worked closely with the Army Intelligence Service and served as military police. Kempeitai officers and enlisted men were trained in, among other things, criminal detection, indoctrination and thought control, and unarmed combat. They used these skills despite the provisions in the 1929 Geneva Convention which stipulated that prisoners "must at all times be humanely treated and protected, particularly against acts of violence" and that they "have the right to have their person and their honor respected." Despite her fears for her husband's safety, Ethel never worried that Elmer would betray the guerrillas.[66]

At 8:30 that evening, two of the camp doctors delivered to Ethel Herold her husband's empty wallet and his watch, its crystal ominously broken. The men explained that the items had been sent over from the prison and that they had managed to send him some blankets. All they knew at that point was that the Kempeitai had taken Elmer Herold along with Richie Greene, head of the garbage crew, because they believed the two men had contacts with the guerrillas. A half-hour later, Ethel tried to question a couple of the camp guards about Elmer, but they pretended not to understand her. After a sleepless night of worry, she did as much work as she could stand and then took a walk out to the pig pen for some time alone to cry. Soon she heard a police car arrive and, in "the happiest moment of my life," she watched as her husband got out of the car. After greeting his relieved family, Elmer went to the hospital to attend a hastily called meeting of the Men's Committee, finally returning to the barracks at 9:30 to find his wife quietly knitting.[67]

Elmer Herold told Ethel his story while drinking a cup of hot cocoa. The military police had picked him up for questioning about his contact with the guerrillas because they suspected, correctly, that Elmer's trips to the Taboras tienda, a local store, on camp business had given him the opportunity to pass along information to Herman Kluge. The Japanese locked Elmer Herold in an eight-by-twelve prison cell "just high enough to stand up; wooden bars about six inches thick and 1½ inches between; dismal electric light from somewhere; toilet—a square can in the middle of [the] floor—smelling to high heaven; high window four inches square." He received a cup of water and a ball of rice at each meal. His interrogators did not mistreat him, he claimed, just shined a bright light in his eyes as they asked about the guerrillas. After he finished his story, he violated camp rules and took a late-night bath, then sat in the dark and ate some food. Ethel observed that Elmer's return was "electric," that everyone was "overjoyed" he had safely returned to the camp.[68]

Because of Elmer's position as liaison, his role on the Men's Committee, and his prewar knowledge of Luzon's terrain, the Japanese strongly suspected that he was a supporter of the guerrillas. But comments by Natalie Crouter indicate that almost everyone in Camp Holmes passed information to the guerrillas when they could. When she recorded Elmer's return to camp, she explained that "the Japanese figure we are giving information to the guerrillas as well as getting it from them." Camp guards carefully examined all items entering the camp, and on September 12, Elmer was once again taken to the Kempeitai for questioning because some notes had been found in a bag sent into Camp Holmes. "Thank God, they kept him only a few hours. A low day," Ethel recalled.[69]

These interrogations continued into the next year. In March 1943, Natalie Crouter wrote in her diary that Elmer Herold was "called to the guardhouse by the Intelligence man from town, and a smooth, casual proposition was put [to him]." Elmer and a few other men were to go to Kapangan and Balacbac to bring in Herman Kluge and his wife, Anna. If the men refused to cooperate and the Kluges refused to surrender, the Japanese would hunt them down and kill them. According to Crouter, Kluge had maps and other information about northern Luzon the Japanese believed valuable. "Of course they want him alive and healthy," Crouter observed, "and there is nothing like a good friend as bait in the trap." Still, she did not believe that Elmer would cooperate to the extent of actually locating Herman Kluge, as "he cannot believe they [the Kluges] will be well-protected and cared for if they surrender."[70]

On March 17, Elmer and the other men, along with a dozen or so Filipino cadets serving as their armed guards, went off to, as Ethel Herold put it, "pretend to look for Mr. Kluge and not find him, if he does not want to be found." She noted that her husband had been ordered to take on this job: it was not something he could decline.

Natalie Crouter's comments confirmed this: "None had any choice but to go on this miserable manhunt, this quest which is typical of occupied countries and total war where all are helpless, no one free to be decent, straight, loyal or honorable. . . . We all feel lead in the stomach, hate in the heart, bitter dismay at our helplessness." But even as Crouter lamented that under these circumstances no one could act decently or honorably, Ethel understood the theatrical aspects of the hunt. Kluge would not be found unless he wanted to be. Elmer Herold could certainly take his cue from Kluge, thereby honoring their friendship and maintaining his own allegiance to the United States.[71]

Ethel's diary entries for March 17–20, 1943, are compressed together into one. She admitted with her characteristic understatement, "We extremely worried the four days, as one never knows what fool accident might touch things off." Her intense fear may have prevented her from writing much during those days when her husband was out leading the search for Herman Kluge. But the fact that Philippine Constabulary soldiers, rather than Japanese, accompanied the internees, worked in Elmer's favor—and Kluge's as well. As the American guerrilla leader Robert Lapham explained it, the "guerrillas managed the Philippine Constabulary—and the PC allowed themselves to be so 'managed.'" Intelligence reports showed "a large majority of PC men stayed at their posts merely to make a living and would turn against the Japanese if the Americans ever returned." The Constabulary even provided guns to the guerrillas.[72]

By the time the men from the internment camp reached Kapangan on March 17, the locals knew why they had come, and since Filipinos escorted them rather than the Japanese, they were cordially received and well fed. But whenever they attempted to learn anything about Herman Kluge, "it was a blank wall of non-cooperation in full view." Given the likely sympathies of the constabulary members, it is not surprising that they did not punish Elmer Herold and the others for their failure to locate Kluge.[73]

Though Ethel did not dwell on her fears during her husband's four-day absence, she carefully documented his return. In the late afternoon of March 20, 1943, while at choir practice singing "Peace," she saw two of the cadets and an internee come back into camp, and she broke off in mid-song to see if Elmer had come with them. He had, returning with "loads of good chow" from the Igorots plus an invitation from one family for the Herolds to come and live with them for the duration of the war. Ethel Herold took these as signs that the Filipinos were "all 100% for us, just waiting for THE DAY" when the Japanese were defeated.[74]

Because they believed the constabulary had made an honest effort to compel Elmer Herold to find Herman Kluge, the Japanese did not punish Elmer when he failed to do so, nor is there any evidence that he divulged the whereabouts of his friend. If there had been a whiff of scandal in the camp that Elmer had betrayed the guerrillas, Natalie Crouter, consistently critical of the Herolds, would have reported it. The fact that Elmer successfully negotiated this difficult mission represents the unique and often lucky position of the Baguio internees. Though dedicated to wiping out resistance and seemingly suspicious of everyone, Japanese authorities chose to believe that Elmer had been most diligent in the search for Kluge and that the Filipino Constabulary was loyal to them.

On the afternoon of April 1, 1943, the Kempeitai came for Elmer Herold once again, purportedly to inspect some equipment at the sawmills on the Mountain Trail. This time Ethel was not as concerned: "I do not visibly worry as I think Elmer has a chance to visit his beloved machinery." When her husband "came back o.k." on April 8, he told Ethel that he had "hiked all around the mills at 52 and 72, presumably looking for Mr. Kluge." When the Japanese approached Elmer about another manhunt the following month, he successfully declined. As the search for Kluge continued with no results, the Japanese tried a different tactic. When they threatened to kill civilians in the area where Kluge was operating, he finally surrendered and was executed. His wife, Anna, survived the war by hiding out in the mountains with friends and being smuggled through enemy lines in northern Luzon in 1945 to safety.[75]

The internees' insistence on helping the guerrillas in spite of any punishment they might receive is evident in the escapades of Herb Swick, an American gold miner who joined the army when the Japanese attacked the Philippines. Swick evaded capture after the fall of Bataan and Corregidor and by late summer of 1942 had met up with Lieutenant Don Blackburn and Colonel Russell Volckmann, a senior U.S. instructor with the Philippine Army's 11th Infantry. The three men cast their lot with the guerrillas in northern Luzon, some of whom were led by Bado Dangwa, a former student of the

Herolds. Dangwa had learned auto mechanics from Elmer Herold at the Trinidad Farm School in the 1920s and later opened a bus and transportation company. When the Japanese invaded Luzon in December 1941, he donated his buses to the USAFFE to help move troops down to Bataan and then began organizing guerrilla resistance in the area.[76]

In 1943, the Japanese intensified their efforts to break that resistance and managed to capture Herb Swick, whom they suspected was a former USAFFE member and a guerrilla. Despite a month of interrogation and torture, Swick stuck to his story that he was an innocent civilian, and with no confession and no proof to the contrary, the Japanese sent him to Camp Holmes in February. Information about his guerrilla activities quietly spread among the internees—Ethel Herold identified him in her diary as a lieutenant—but no one ever gave him up. The following February, Colonel Volckmann set out to establish a new guerrilla headquarters in western Benguet, not far from the Lingayen Gulf, in anticipation of a U.S. invasion. Word went out that he needed all the help he could get, so in early April 1944, Herb Swick and Richie Greene, another bachelor in camp, simply walked away from their garbage-crew duty and joined up with Volckmann. Upon learning of their escape, Ethel commented, "Power to them, I hope they are safe on an American submarine by this time."[77]

Not all of the internees may have agreed with her, but none betrayed the two men. The Japanese had always threatened to deal harshly with escapees, and since most of the men had wives and children in camp, they stayed put to spare their loved ones possible punishment. Herb Swick and Richie Green had no such ties; still, the entire camp would likely bear the brunt of Japanese anger over their escape. Commandant Rokuro Tomibe called the men into a two-hour meeting the morning after the escape, questioning them about what happened and explaining the new restrictions that would be imposed as punishment. Tomibe felt hurt by the two men's actions, taking it as a personal affront after all he had done to help the internees; yet he successfully mediated with his superiors against any harsh punishments.

Nevertheless, ninety new Japanese guards were posted to Camp Holmes, the entire area was fenced in, and no one was allowed outside for any reason. The Kempeitai came in and interrogated some of the internees and then took away three men, including Jim Halsema, son of the Herolds' close friends. The Men's Committee, fearing that the men would be tortured, asked Tomibe to intercede with the Kempeitai, and by April 14 all three returned to camp. Ethel Herold reported that Halsema and Bill Moule had been "badly beaten up, both hung by the thumbs," while Gene Kneebone went to the hospital for a broken rib. The Kempeitai had taken these men to confirm information they had already obtained by torturing some Filipinos. Jim Halsema and the others successfully convinced the Kempeitai that information they had about the war had come from the *Manila Tribune* and radio news overheard at the guardhouse, not from contact with guerrillas.[78]

Guerrilla activity increased in the area during the fall of 1944 in response to the changing military situation as the Americans geared up to invade the Philippines. That October, about a month after the Baguio internees spotted their first American planes, General Douglas MacArthur made good on his "I shall return" promise, landing troops on the island of Leyte, about four hundred miles south of Luzon. Finally, on January 9, 1945, his forces arrived at the Lingayen Gulf. By then, the Herolds and the other internees had already been evacuated from Camp Holmes to Old Bilibid Prison in Manila, where they would spend the remainder of their internment. For the trip, Ethel had stuffed her brassiere with family papers, American money and traveler's checks, and the precious American flag she and the other women had sewn and hidden away in camp.[79]

It took six weeks for American forces to make their sweep down from the north, through the central plains, and into Manila; meanwhile, the internees in Old Bilibid teetered on the brink of starvation. Ethel Herold described the prison as "the filthiest hole I have ever seen." Already a crumbling wreck before the Japanese invasion, it had sustained structural damage during the war and now swarmed with bed bugs, lice, and green flies. "Our aim now," Ethel wrote, "was to keep body and soul together." She estimated that they existed on about 650 calories per day; food once doled out by the tablespoon was now scraped out by the teaspoon. Their survival was down to a matter of days when at dusk on February 3, they caught a glimpse of tanks making their way down Quezon Boulevard. Eight tanks in all rolled past the prison before the Herolds realized what was happening, and then Billy blurted out, "My God, they are AMERICANS."[80]

Filled with American soldiers, trucks and jeeps—these latter vehicles were unfamiliar to the internees—followed the tanks. The Herolds were "almost petrified with joy." A battle broke out at the Japanese general headquarters at the Far Eastern University, located just across from Old Bilibid; the Americans had been able to take the Japanese by surprise because Filipino guerrillas had cut Japanese communication lines. Huddled inside the old prison, the Baguio internees could hear the fighting and knew that liberation was imminent. It turned out to be a bit accidental as well. Ethel Herold believed the troops stopped just because they were curious about what was inside the old prison. But MacArthur knew where American prisoners, both civilian and military, were being held, and these American soldiers simply happened upon Bilibid before they reached Santo Tomas.[81]

For two weeks, the Herolds lived in the middle of a pitched battle, somewhat safe but never assured that a stray bomb would not find its way to Old Bilibid. Only the abundance of food from army K rations and reliable war news courtesy of the Red Cross made the sleepless nights bearable. Life outside the walls was horrific as American troops fought the enemy, street by street, building by building, and even floor by floor. About one hundred thousand civilians died during the month-long fighting.

On February 15, 1945, Ethel and Elmer Herold secured passes to Santo Tomas University, the largest site of civilian internment, so that Elmer could talk to Rose McKee, the treasurer of Heald Lumber. Elmer Herold wanted to establish an official chain of command for the resumption of the business before he and his family went home to the United States. Ethel Herold found the streets of Manila strange, "full of military traffic going and coming to beat hell. Streets and sidewalks full of the holes of war, dusty. All the GIs yelling greetings at white folks. Manila seems just a rubbish heap." Bolstered by food and medical attention, Elmer Herold began to rethink his decision to leave the Philippines and within days sent a letter to Judge Haussermann telling him he wanted to remain on Luzon and restart the business.[82]

Walking back to Bilibid after a late February afternoon stroll near the Pasig River, Ethel and Elmer Herold felt almost lighthearted and "like a couple of kids loose from school, we could not resist the temptation to go take a look at the destroyed Escolata." As they viewed the rubble in the street, a reporter from the *Denver Times* approached and asked what was so special about this place, so the Herolds explained that it was Manila's grand main street. The reporter then took their picture in front of the ruins, recording for posterity their liberation appearance. The couple were gray-haired and, although they had both gained more than ten pounds, still thin. Ethel wore a dress refashioned from an old holiday costume of Betsy's; Elmer was clad only in shorts and shoes.[83]

As Elmer Herold was preparing to resume his business career and trying to salvage the family's finances, his wife had begun to contemplate their wartime experiences. One night in February, as she listened to the sounds of the battle still going on around Manila, she thought about God: "I wondered is there a God? Prayer was always in my soul. This awful war. Why was it? All this death before my eyes. I looked at those great stars [of the Southern Cross] again and felt, Yes, there is a God." Ethel Herold tended to keep her religion private, as evidenced in this diary entry, but it is not surprising that she would have turned to God in such a trying time. Still, the god she acknowledged and prayed to was likely one of retribution. Later that same month, when she reported "much fighting again last night," she admitted, "How I would like to get out there and kill some Japs too."[84]

On March 10, 1945, Billy Herold flew to Leyte, where he immediately boarded a troop ship bound for the United States. Five days later, the three remaining Herolds followed to Leyte and then waited in a military camp for weeks for available transport home, reveling in the abundant army rations and the movies and shows at the Red Cross recreation hall. But politics and war were never out of Ethel Herold's thoughts as she struggled to make sense of her wartime experiences. For instance, on her birthday, she saw the movie *Woodrow Wilson*. "Of course it was propaganda," she wrote, "but all right. The GI reaction was as a good American reaction should be. This is not [a] war of politics." She was probably referring to stateside American partisan politics and the function of the U.S. government because on March 27, she wrote admiringly of the army's vast offerings to military personnel and civilians alike: "Uncle Sam has not forgotten anything—it surely takes our capitalistic government to get things done." On April 13, Ethel recorded reactions to President Roosevelt's death: "How terrifying to hear at 7:30 A.M. that our President is dead.

Whether we are Republicans or Democrats, he was our President and we are fighting a fierce war which must be won, and so must the peace be won."[85]

The stakes of that war became immediately evident three days later when the Herolds were told to prepare for departure. After a visit to the G-2 (intelligence) office, Ethel Herold reclaimed her diary and other personal papers, "officially sealed in a big envelope and I am not to open it until after I get to the States." She had been reluctant to turn over the items in the first place, especially because she had carefully recorded all of the money that individual internees owed to Filipino benefactors. Without that, Ethel wondered, "How could I ever see to it that these amounts were paid back?" She also bristled at the sight of "Censored" stickers all over her papers. In late March an intelligence officer had told her, "The American people will never believe the cruelty of the Japs, that we internees should talk and talk when we got home." But now she had been instructed not to look at her diary before she got home and not to talk to anyone about her experiences once she got there. Ethel testily informed the officers that when she got home she would "tell the TRUTH about anything" she was asked.[86] As she saw it, Americans had fought and died for freedom of speech, and she and her family had suffered terribly during that fight. Now, no one—even a member of the mighty American military—could take that right away from her.

During the early morning hours of May 9, 1945, the military convoy approached San Francisco, and Ethel Herold noted that it was "exactly 3 years 5 months ago, all hell broke loose—and today we go under the Golden Gate Bridge, at 7:15 A.M., what a thrill." That night, finally alone in a hotel room that provided luxuries they had almost forgotten about, Ethel Herold and her husband and daughter "ate a dozen oranges. All three of us took a hot soak in a real bath tub. Falling into bed and stretching out was like in soft sea foam—bottomless comfort. We prayed and thanked God for our liberation."[87]

Chapter Five

Postcolonialism: An American Citizen in the Independent Philippines

HOME. After more than three years of imprisonment by the Japanese, the Herolds returned to the United States. "It was so wonderful to be on U.S. *free* soil," Ethel Herold remembered, "we felt like bending down and kissing it. Every time we saw our flag, a thrill of joy went through us." Though she basked in the benefits her American citizenship accorded her stateside, a true feeling of home eluded her. Friends and family members fussed over the Herolds—"everybody wanted us to visit them indefinitely"—as they traveled eastward from California toward Wisconsin. In Potosi, Ethel returned to the large stone house her parents had purchased near the beginning of the century, the place where as a child she had explored the advantages and responsibilities of middle-class town life, and declared that "it still seemed home." It "seemed" like home but not quite, for she had not lived there in twenty-six years, and with her parents both dead, the house was now occupied by one of her nieces. Ethel began to realize that her real home was thousands of miles away, buried in the ruins of a Japanese occupation.[1]

All of the abundance the Herolds encountered stateside only highlighted the family's precarious economic situation as they mostly lived off the kindness of friends and family. Elmer, now in his early fifties, needed to restart his career, and he believed his best chance lay with Heald Lumber. Ethel not only supported her husband in this but she also wanted to return to the Philippines to help rebuild Baguio as repayment to the Filipinos who had assisted the Americans interned during the war. As they had done more than twenty years before, the Herolds hitched their future prospects to American interests in the Philippines, and Ethel spent the next thirteen years trying to rebuild the home and community that war had destroyed.

This chapter examines Ethel Herold's perceptions of citizenship and patriotism in the postwar period. The United States had been on the winning side in World War II, which shored up her pride in her country and confirmed her commitment to democracy; yet that victory set in motion major international changes, including decolonization and the fear of the spread of communism. Ethel strove to be a "good American" of the Cold War era, a time in which the definition of patriotism expanded to include social conventions and cultural ideals. She demonstrated this patriotism by reestablishing her expatriate home and engaging again in various charitable activities in Baguio, activities designed once again to highlight American superiority. But try as she might, she could not replicate her prewar life because of the changes the war had brought to the Philippines.[2]

Ethel's difficulties in reestablishing what she had had prior to the war stemmed in large part from Philippine independence and from Cold War challenges to American democracy, both of which affected how she viewed her position in the islands and America's position in the world. Though home and heart were still in Baguio, that city was now a changed place. With independence on the horizon, Americans living in the Philippines no longer enjoyed the power and status they had in the prewar years. If nations are "imagined communities" because their disparate members cannot realistically know each other, then independence and its attendant social and political unrest upended Ethel Herold's imagined community of the Philippines. It was a vision steeped in the sentimental imperialism of the colonial period, one in which wise Americans guided grateful Filipinos. As an expatriate American citizen in the Philippines, she now proved her patriotism by becoming a committed cold warrior, convinced that fighting the spread of communism would both protect the United States and demonstrate the continuing ability of the country to be a leading world power.[3]

A Stateside Interlude: The Illusion of Home

While the Herolds convalesced in California, Elmer worried over family finances and his stalled career. A meeting with his boss, Herbert Heald, proved only mildly reassuring. Heald explained that his assets in the Philippines were still frozen as long as the war continued in the Pacific theater, so he encouraged Elmer to relax and get his health back before he started thinking about work. But that was all Elmer Herold could think about. He did not have a job, and the Japanese had burned the Herold home and looted their property in Baguio; yet he and Ethel started to think that they had the best chance of starting over in the Philippines. Fortunately for their short-term monetary concerns, cash gifts from Elmer's fraternity brothers and Ethel's sorority sisters from Lawrence College tided the family over until Elmer resumed his career with Heald Lumber. "Never did a thousand dollars seem so much or come at a better time," Ethel Herold recalled of that generous windfall.[4]

Throughout the spring and summer of 1945, as the family traveled east across the United States heading for Wisconsin, Ethel received invitations to lecture about her family's experiences in the Philippines. She put the spirit of the Monday Afternoon Club to work during these talks as she drummed up donations for the war-ravaged islands. Once again, she could present herself as the wise maternal American helping the needy Filipinos, an indication that she assumed the colonial relationship would resume after the war. Moreover, she set the stage for transforming the Monday Club from a local charity to a transpacific one. The speaking engagements also gave Ethel an opportunity to assert her rights as an American citizen. As she had assured the intelligence officer on Leyte who had tried preemptively to muzzle her, she intended to say what she wanted about her years as a Japanese prisoner, the truth as she saw it. What had all the sacrifices and hardships of the war been for if not to protect such liberties?

While back home in Potosi in early August 1945, Ethel and Elmer learned about the atomic bombings of Hiroshima and Nagasaki. Ethel did not remember expressing any animosity or vengeful thoughts when she heard about the bombs, only that she was "surprised" at the news. She did not ruminate on what the postwar world should look like. What seemed to matter most was that, with the war finally over in the Pacific, the Herolds could soon return to Baguio. Potosi, the place Ethel had long called home did not quite match up to the home of her memory. Her mother had been gone for more than twenty years; her father, Clem Thomas, had died at the beginning of the war; and her only sister, Edna, died near the end. The "important ones" of her Potosi family were gone from there, Ethel noted. Though Ethel's niece graciously opened the former Thomas house to the Herolds, it clearly was not the same place of her youth.[5]

Home and family were shifting for Ethel Herold. By the fall of 1945, she noticed that "Elmer's health and strength were coming back, he was getting to be his same good-looking self again. . . . his thoughts of going back and doing real work again put new life in him." The necessary permits to start up the lumber business were secured by November 1, but only Elmer and several other men headed for the Benguet region received permission to travel to the Philippines. Still, Ethel took all of the required shots for overseas travel so that she could be ready to join her husband at a moment's notice.[6]

During the winter of 1945, Ethel and her children, Bill and Betsy, lived in Missoula, Montana, so that she could be near the surviving "important ones" of her family—her brothers, Bart and Fred Thomas. As they had done in childhood, the brothers spoiled their little sister, this time, perhaps, with more reason. For over three years, they did not know for certain whether or not she was alive, and if she were alive, they did not know what she was enduring in Japanese captivity. In violation of rationing rules, Fred butchered one of his prize cattle and stored the meat in Bart's freezer locker as the families worked their way through it. "No government official is going to stop me from feeding my sister," Fred proclaimed. Ethel reciprocated by sharing her ration coupons with her brothers, but she could not understand why people complained about those consumer controls. "I could feast on the hundreds of things they were allowed to buy," she observed, even as she admitted, "I just about went wild in the food stores—so many things to buy." Yet many of the items she purchased were headed to the needy in the Philippines, and every two weeks she posted a box of food to Elmer to insure that he had enough to eat.[7]

Ethel Herold loathed to be separated from her husband. She described his departure for the Philippines as "sad," comparing it to when he had enlisted in the First World War. Though somewhat comforted that he would not be dodging enemy bullets this time, she still had a lot to worry about. "I knew that things were an awful mess," she wrote, "hidden mines, Japs still in the hills. Accidents on the worn out roads." Inconsistent mail delivery and Elmer's irregular correspondence exacerbated her concerns. Though Ethel wrote long, detailed letters, her husband's tended toward brief sketches in which he outlined the realities of postwar Baguio. Life was still so difficult in the area that the Herolds' former servants had returned, eager for work and food, and Elmer quickly rehired them because he had little time and inclination to attend to domestic affairs.[8]

Ethel could have used these hardships as an excuse not to return to Baguio, but the desire to reunite with her husband was stronger than anything else, even the opportunity to move with her children back to Potosi. The former Thomas house was no longer her home, but the death of her old friend, Bertha Bonn, provided the Herolds with a place of their own. Bertha's mother, Anna Bonn, had known Ethel Thomas Herold since childhood, had cultivated her interest in benevolent associations, and had encouraged her musical talents. Bertha, an only child and without a family of her own, remained close to Ethel, often visiting the Herolds after they returned to Potosi in the summer of 1945. One day Bertha Bonn had insisted that Ethel and Elmer come to her farm—she even picked them up in her car—to pick blackberries, which were already out of season. Nevertheless, Bonn spent considerable time showing off the farm to her friends.

When Bertha Bonn died later that year, she willed her family farm to Ethel Herold. "She had left her entire 260 acre farm to me," Ethel wrote of her friend's generosity. "I just could not believe it." Although Ethel admitted that her inheritance was "really something to think about" in terms of where her family should settle, she concluded that the Bonn farm would be a perfect location for stateside vacations and as a future spot for retirement. Even if she wanted to live with Bill and Betsy on a comfortable farm with well-producing acreage in the place where she had grown up, that would not have been a real home to her yet. Elmer was in Baguio and wherever he was, that was home. Ethel may have believed that life on the farm would not provide her with enough useful work to do. With her two children now safe in the United States and old enough not to require constant mothering, she clearly expected to make a significant contribution to her community, even if it was overseas.[9]

So, once again Ethel Herold traded the security and abundance of the United States for the challenges of the Philippines. Despite the postwar hardships outlined by her husband, she likely viewed the current situation in the islands as very similar to the way it had been for Americans there since the Spanish-American War. There had always been challenges. When her brother Bart took up his first teaching post in the islands in 1901, disease, rough terrain, and Filipino "insurrectionists" posed dangers. Two decades later, when Ethel and Elmer arrived, those threats had considerably lessened, but Americans living outside of Manila still faced privations of food and other supplies. Yet even after World War II, as before, the Americans were in charge, at least for a while. Ethel Herold inferred from her husband's letters that many Filipinos still looked to Americans for protection and guidance; in her mind that was the natural order of things.

By the spring of 1946, however, when Ethel Herold finally received permission to return to Baguio, Philippine independence was scheduled for the coming July; thus, the imperialist privilege she had enjoyed in the 1920s and '30s now had a firm expiration date. In addition to defeating fascism, World War II had dealt a death blow to imperialism, and the United States showed its acceptance by honoring the provisions of the prewar Tydings-McDuffie Act. The Philippines would have their freedom.

As Ethel's days of demonstrating her citizenship and patriotism through participating in colonialism drew to a close, the deepening Cold War provided a new outlet for transnational expression. The U.S. government worried about the strength of a newly independent Philippines and hated to lose its lucrative trade relationship with the islands. Economic prosperity, most American politicians agreed, would serve as a bulwark against communism. Citing concerns about collective security in the Pacific region, Congress passed the Philippine Trade Act in April 1946. Among other things, this piece of legislation contained a parity provision that gave Americans equal rights with Filipinos to own mines, forests, and other resources in the Philippines, which bode well for the revival of Heald Lumber and the Herolds' finances. To sweeten the deal for the Filipinos, Congress then approved some $620 million in aid to help rebuild the islands.[10]

Now, as a good American, Ethel Herold would be helping prevent the spread of communism in the Philippines as she helped rebuild the country. She could hardly wait to return to Baguio, and she was basically the kind of person that the United States government would soon recruit to work in postwar Asia. A 1951 National Security Council report on American foreign-policy goals in that part of the world specifically addressed the qualifications of American personnel there. If the United States hoped to achieve its objectives in Asia, it had to have a sufficient contingent of people who were not only knowledgeable about Asia and who exhibited a "temperament suitable for life in Asia and creditable to the United States Government" but who also could also make it clear that the United States did not intend to "colonize" or "Americanize" Asian countries. Though Ethel Herold never held an official government position, she was one of the first Americans to return to Asia who possessed the requisite knowledge of the Philippines, demonstrated an appropriate temperament for living in that part of the world, and accepted the end of colonization. However, despite her acknowledgment of Philippine independence, she still saw Americanization—whether a lot of it or a little—as a good thing, and indeed American consumer goods would spread rapidly around the world during the postwar period.

After arranging for her son, Bill, to attend her alma mater, Lawrence College in Appleton, Wisconsin, while enrolling Betsy at a private boarding school in Kenosha, Ethel said "tearful goodbyes to my two precious children." But she was excited to be "at last . . . on my way back to Elmer. Elmer and I would be together, and we would be free." With her ship delayed for two weeks in San Francisco, she "shopped madly for the thousand things I wanted to take with me." Some items were still scarce because of rationing, but she managed to track down mattresses, mirrors, electrical appliances, pots, pans, and even a bridge table and matching chairs. Now fortified with basic, practical domestic items, Ethel Herold felt prepared to deal with whatever lay ahead.[12]

A New American Home in Postwar Baguio

Elmer was waiting for his wife in Manila, coming out at dawn on the pilot boat. "I can see him yet in a blue shirt down there smiling at me," Ethel later recalled. "This was a real honeymoon." She noticed that little had been cleaned up in the capital city since the year before, and during the drive up to Baguio, she got her first look at the devastation wrought by the final stand the Japanese had taken in the mountains: partially destroyed military vehicles, artillery caves, shrapnel-ridden pine trees. Yet Filipinos had already resumed farming—growing sugar cane and corn and tending the surviving livestock. As he drove, Elmer provided a rundown of postwar Baguio. All of the nine Heald lumber mills were gone, looted by either the Japanese or the Filipinos. The United States Army had set up a makeshift mill at KM 72 and then had given the operation over to the Philippine army earlier in 1946. Elmer Herold told the captain in charge that if he turned over the mill to Heald Lumber, Elmer would not lodge any charges against the army for the trees that had been illegally cut. The captain agreed, so that was the one mill Elmer had to manage.[13]

As they passed through Baguio, Ethel observed, “Whoever said nine tenths of the town is destroyed said it right. One wanted to pass through it quickly and not see it again.” Then she braced herself for the most heart-wrenching sight: “Our house and the guest house were burned flat. Other Benguet [company] houses on our hill had been badly shelled and most of the lumber carried off by Filipinos to build shelters of their own.” Despite extensive damage, the Heald home still stood, and with no other housing available, Elmer established his lumber office in the rooms in the front part of the house with living quarters in the back. Even with the help of two servants, housekeeping proved difficult for Ethel. “One cannot buy a thing here,” she wrote in a letter home that June. “I am using some tea cloths I had in my trunk for necessary curtains.” Commissary privileges at Camp John Hay provided “wonderful help” to the Herolds, as the same food purchased at the market, if it could be had, would cost eight times as much.[14]

Establishing a postwar expatriate home as a private haven proved especially difficult for Ethel Herold because of the political and cultural anxieties caused by the unraveling of U.S. colonialism in the Philippines. The Herold house and the Heald house, both elegantly appointed abodes in the 1930s, carefully outfitted with the latest conveniences and home furnishings, symbolized U.S. imperialist power before World War II. With the Herolds’ original company home destroyed during the war, Ethel had to turn someone else’s company house into her own. The Heald house had sustained heavy damage and was only barely habitable, much like Baguio itself. The house’s state of disrepair also reflected the rocky road of American decolonization. Ethel had to figure out how to repair the damage, how to project American strength in the face of dwindling U.S. authority in the Philippines.[15]

During those early months of reconstruction, the Herolds occasionally drove around Baguio, "just to see what we could recognize," leading Ethel to mourn that "we were lost in our own home-town." Almost all of the beautiful prewar homes had been destroyed during the final months of the Japanese occupation, replaced by hastily constructed shacks of old boards and tin roofing. The majestic trees, so essential to the lumber business, had been damaged by bombs and shrapnel. Surrounded by all this devastation, Ethel threw herself into reconstructing Baguio. The work left her little time to think about how much she missed her children, though she rationalized that Bill and Betsy were too old to need constant mothering. During a time when Americans placed great emphasis on family, Ethel Herold concentrated her domestic, maternal skills on the needy city of Baguio, treating it as a surrogate child.[16]

In late July 1946, Ethel's barrels and duffel bags of supplies from the states finally arrived. On the heels of those came additional boxes of clothes donated by people who had heard her lectures in Wisconsin, California, and Montana about her wartime experiences. Using one of the back bedrooms in the Heald house as her base of operations, Ethel and a few friends began sorting through the donations, determining where the items should go. With the work of the Monday Afternoon Club resumed, Ethel, still officially the club's president, decided to formally relaunch it on November 18, 1946, her daughter's seventeenth birthday. She prepared an elaborate party for club members at her house, but of course it was not entirely a social occasion. The People's Bank and Trust Company, working with affidavits and reconstructed club records, finally released Monday Club funds totaling over seven hundred pesos. With money and goods, the organization could officially operate once again.

A mythology of voluntarism developed after World War II, one that hailed voluntary associations as essential to the preservation of democracy because they helped safeguard individual rights from the long reach of the government. It is likely that Ethel Herold, with her decades of involvement in women's and other charitable organizations, would have bought into this mythology, especially with the war years still so fresh in her mind. Since totalitarian regimes forbade these kinds of associations, they must have contained seeds of liberty that dictators felt compelled to eliminate. This may have been how Ethel Herold perceived the activities of the Monday Club during internment, especially since the women had feared asking the Japanese for approval to run the club and had kept their projects hidden from their captors.[17]

By linking voluntarist groups with the promotion of democracy and freedom—even by the slenderest threads—American women carved out an important place for themselves in the postwar fight against communism. Ethel Herold's reestablishment of the Monday Afternoon Club represented her understanding that an economically strong and prosperous Philippines was not only a testament to the enduring benefits of imperialism but also served to undercut the appeal of communism. For her, this linkage of club activities with U.S. foreign policy goals was another variation on a theme. Ethel's early involvement in women's benevolence in Potosi helped her develop a nationalistic pride mostly domestic in scope. Her work for the Red Cross and the Food Administration during the Great War expanded her perceptions of citizenship and patriotism to include American interests overseas, which turned into direct support of imperialism when she and Elmer moved to the Philippines in 1922. Now her charitable endeavors would serve yet another purpose for the American government.

Shortly after World War II, eleven Monday Club members, including Ethel Herold, had returned to Baguio; she invited all of them, plus the military wives from Camp John Hay. Of those thirty American women, twenty attended the club's first official postwar meeting. The others declined, citing lack of transportation. The new members proved especially helpful when, using their position as military wives, they convinced the U.S. Army and Navy to donate "jeep loads" of surplus clothing, blankets, and other necessities. The Monday Club then had a tremendous amount of useful items for distribution among those in need in Baguio, things that would ease the distress caused by wartime destruction, poor health, high prices, and unemployment. The Puericulture Center, a hospital for sick babies that Ethel Herold had helped establish before the war, received blankets and sheets, as did the Baguio Hospital, which was still in the process of rebuilding. These local efforts were bolstered by the assistance of former club members now living in the states, women like Marie Halsema, Anna Kluge, and Betty Foley, who had suffered during the war in the Philippines and who now donated boxes and boxes of goods for Filipinos still struggling to resume their normal lives.[18]

Recognizing that the club's success rested on transpacific cooperation, the Monday Club women voted in 1948 to join the General Federation of Women's Clubs, a U.S.-based organization with an international scope. First established in 1890, the GFWC had had connections with the Philippines since at least 1912. That year a visit by the American suffragist Carrie Chapman Catt, president of the International Woman Suffrage Alliance and a frequent GFWC speaker, prompted the formation of the Manila Woman's Club, the first of hundreds of such clubs that would spring up in the islands. During World War II, the GFWC used its vast network to support the Allied war effort through spearheading the "Buy a Bomber" campaign (a war bond drive), providing scholarships for nursing students, and organizing salvage and conservation programs. In 1945, three GFWC members attended the planning meeting for the United Nations, a very public recognition of the group's international efforts. When GFWC president Dorothea Buck toured Asia in the late 1940s, she made such a positive impression on the Monday Club women that allying with the organization proved an easy decision for them.[19]

As during the interwar years, Ethel Herold worked for a variety of community and charitable endeavors in addition to the Monday Club. In 1947, she chaired the first postwar Philippine Red Cross fund drive and continued to serve on its local Baguio board. She rejoined the Baguio Women's Club, went on to chair the Baguio Public Hospital Advisory Board, and sat on the Girl Scout council. Still, the Monday Club remained at the heart of her club work.

One of the major projects she launched in 1946 that eventually came under the purview of the Monday Club especially illustrates the link between women's charity work and international relations. Shortly after returning to Baguio, Ethel ordered a large quantity of seeds from a Burpee catalog she had brought with her so that she could help the Igorots, both the adults and the school children, resume farming and gardening. She continued this process for several years; and in 1952, a program called Seeds for Democracy, sponsored by the Committee for Free Asia, began sending the Monday Club enough seeds to supply the Trinidad Farm School, where the Herolds had taught during the latter half of the 1920s. Seeds for Democracy distributed its goods in thirty locations throughout the islands in an attempt to improve the standard of living and to "develop unified resistance to Communism." After receiving the fifth large carton of seeds from the program, Ethel Herold wrote to the Committee for Free Asia, "With such wide distribution, seeds for democracy is accomplishing great good. To grow more food on one's own land is the hope of all Asia." In 1952, the program aimed to collect and send one million packages of vegetable seeds to the Philippines, especially Chinese cabbage, green string beans, green pepper, mustard, eggplant, cucumber, tomato, and lettuce.[20]

The Committee for Free Asia, founded in California in 1951 as a private, nonprofit corporation, operated on the belief that Americans should assist Asians in resisting communism. In addition to Seeds for Democracy, the organization introduced Radio Free Asia in September 1951. By 1953, though, committee members realized that the most successful projects were those created and implemented by Asians, an acknowledgement, perhaps, of the unpopularity of blatant Americanization programs. The Committee for Free Asia then abolished Radio Free Asia and reconstituted itself as the Asia Foundation in 1954, which by the end of the decade had field representatives in thirteen Asian countries. Many of the Foundation's projects had strong educational components and supported youth programs and farming organizations.[21]

Directing the Seeds for Democracy program for the Monday Club allowed Ethel Herold to draw on her own considerable educational expertise and experience with farm school students. For more than a decade, her assistance in reviving agriculture in and around Baguio clearly helped resuscitate the economy. She shared no official affiliation with the Asia Foundation and earned no formal recognition as a forerunner of Seeds for Democracy, but she certainly believed in the link between a strong, stable economy and democracy. Ethel's endeavors to promote democracy in the Philippines connected her political past with the present. This kind of benevolent work expressed her continued admiration and support for what the United States had tried to accomplish with its colonial rule of the islands and her willingness to participate in the Cold War by undercutting communist aggression.

By the end of the 1950s, Baguio and other locations in the Philippines were showing clear signs of growth and affluence, yet Ethel Herold did not let up on her volunteer work. Though her level of commitment to community causes remained consistent, her attitude toward racial mixing within women's organizations showed indications of change. Before the war, she had insisted that it was entirely proper and just as effective for the American women of the Monday Club to work separately from the mostly Filipina Baguio Women's Club. Aside from some token combined meetings, the two clubs kept apart. However, that segregation began to break down at the beginning of the 1950s for reasons likely connected to both the growing influence of the civil rights movement in the United States and the end of American colonialism in the Philippines with the attendant declining influence of Americans there.

In 1951, the Monday Club moved beyond the annual combined meeting with the Baguio Women's Club to identify and work on cooperative projects, the first of which was to design educational programs to promote protein as a necessary part of a balanced diet. Ethel paid the Women's Club dues for a dozen of the lumberyard workers' wives, describing them as bashful among "all this P.I. so-called brass" who were "so snotty with each other." Still, she considered it a successful meeting and expressed confidence that the two clubs could work together to achieve these goals. The joint project apparently exceeded its goals, because in January 1952 the Baguio Women's Club presented Ethel with a gold medal and named her the outstanding social worker of Baguio. Delighted with the recognition, she realized that "all the dirty work I keep busy at is more or less appreciated."[22]

On May 5, 1958, the Monday Club elected Ethel Herold president for the eighteenth time—"which is too many times," she declared. Still, she was proud of the club's accomplishments: "Our Revolving Loan Fund has really gone over the top now. We have loaned to more than 70 now. About 35,000 pesos. It is slowly being paid back—very slowly, as these first few years are really hard." Ethel also managed to talk Bob Manley, a representative of Cooperative American Remittance Everywhere (better known as CARE), into recommending that his organization purchase a couple of tractors for farming settlements that the Monday Club supported and admitted that the club "feels quite puffed up and we hope all this really materializes." In December, the Provincial Board of Mountain Province issued a special resolution thanking the Monday Club for its support of students, farmers, and those in need, for "their valuable contribution to the economic, educational, cultural and social development and upliftment of Mountain province and its people." Ethel Herold's work there was just about done.[23]

Philippine Independence and the Beginning of the Cold War

When Ethel Herold had returned to Baguio in June 1946, the Philippine Islands were in their final days as an American colony. She had come back knowing that independence was a foregone conclusion. Even as the U.S. military fought to drive the Japanese from the Philippines in early 1945, General Douglas MacArthur cautioned the War Department that the "utmost care should be taken that an imperialist policy not be introduced into the situation under the guise of military operations and necessities." Before his troops secured Manila, MacArthur moved to reestablish the Commonwealth government at the traditional seat of its power, a clear sign that the United States intended to honor the prewar path to independence. During a ceremony on February 27, 1945, at Malacañan Palace, miraculously undamaged despite the battle for Manila, the general described a "soul-wrenching moment" as he prepared for the official transfer of military rule to civilian. In the same room where he had received his command as field marshal of the army, MacArthur told Philippine president Sergio Osmeña that the country was "again at liberty to pursue its destiny."[24]

Because the Commonwealth government had functioned smoothly before the war and because most Filipinos had resisted the wartime Japanese occupation, the United States had no excuse to further delay independence. General MacArthur, who remained in the islands during 1945 to help prepare for the transition, supported Manuel Roxas as the first president of the postwar independent Philippines, as did Paul McNutt, the last U.S. high commissioner for the islands. Roxas was duly elected, defeating Osmeña by a 10 percent margin, and on July 4, 1946, just after nine o'clock in the morning, he raised the flag of the Philippines as McNutt lowered the American flag. About a million people showed up for the ceremony at the Luneta Park in Manila on that rain-drenched morning. There was a twenty-one-gun salute, bands played both "The Star-Spangled Banner" and the "Marcha Nacional," and church bells rang. MacArthur, not surprisingly given his lifetime association with the

Philippines, flew in from his occupation duties in Tokyo for the ceremony. He described the event as "the end of empire as the political chain that binds the unwilling weak to the unyielding strong" and told a friend, "America buried imperialism here today."[25]

Ethel Herold, participating in celebrations held in Baguio, viewed independence cautiously, referring to it as an "experiment" that would have to be closely watched. A few months later, she commented to her friend Marie Halsema, "Yes, this is the worst time in the world for independence," but again failed to specify her concerns. Postwar nationalist rhetoric in the United States constructed a Cold War ideology that divided the world into sections of good and evil. Ethel Herold, of course, cast her lot with the "good" faction—the democracy faction—by reestablishing an American home and resuming charity work in Baguio. Also during the Cold War, almost any criticism of the U.S. government was considered communist-inspired and therefore unpatriotic, but it is difficult to believe that Ethel Herold felt so muzzled by Cold War fears that she would not denounce a government policy with which she disagreed. Besides, widespread hostility to communism was just beginning to spread in that first year after the war, and her residence in the Philippines kept her removed from the worst of the American anticommunism hysteria. So why did she not let loose with her opinions about independence?[26]

Her rather measured comments concerning Philippines independence may have reflected her belief that it was a consequence of the war, that since military and political leaders had come to this conclusion, it must be right. A national heroic figure like Douglas MacArthur, whom she credited with her family's liberation from Old Bilibid Prison, supported independence. Certain elements of postwar patriotism seemed to depend on traditional ideals of white, male heroism, and Ethel Herold likely viewed MacArthur as the personification of U.S. postwar authority in Asia, a patriotic symbol of the American victory over Japan. Thus, she willingly embraced his acceptance of the end of imperialism as an inevitable consequence of the war.[27]

Additionally, her labeling of independence as an experiment may indicate a wait-and-see attitude about how much the United States—and especially its expatriate citizens living in the Philippines—would actually lose. Though Ethel Herold worked her whole life to promote democracy, she also worked hard for the material benefit of her family, so she probably supported independence as long as it did not create economic hardship for her. The governing structure of the Philippines was democratic in form, with a president, bicameral legislature, regular elections, and political parties; but in reality, a handful of political and business elites controlled the country. Ethel Herold often criticized Filipinos for their imperfect democracy, but the United States continued to direct much of the islands' economy through the Bell Act, which kept the Herolds and other Americans economically prosperous. She would have taken that as a positive sign that all of her efforts in the Philippines would not go unrewarded.[28]

The Herolds attended a program on July 4, 1946, held at the Baguio city flag pole, listening to the speeches given by local dignitaries and watching a parade. The 150 former guerrillas who marched received the most applause, Ethel Herold recalled, while the float proclaiming independence "got barely a sign of applause." The commander of Camp John Hay lowered the American flag, and the acting mayor of Baguio raised the flag of the Philippines, bringing Ethel to tears. After the program, she and Elmer went for champagne at the makeshift city hall in the old Japanese school, where they met up with many old friends who greeted them with the familiar refrain "Well, we are alive" before launching into their own versions of what had happened in Baguio during the war. That evening, the Herolds attended a reception and dance at John Hay, complete with champagne, sandwiches, and a band. Decked out in a new brightly colored blouse over a long black jersey skirt and black evening sandals, Ethel danced with Elmer, who sported a suit and tie for the first time since returning to Baguio. It was a bittersweet evening that served as the official reminder that the days of American privilege had ended.[29]

As the United States relinquished its colonial hold over the Philippines, American politicians carefully considered national-security issues and concluded that the Philippines had a part to play in protecting Asia from the spread of communism. U.S. Senator Millard Tydings, chair of the Insular Affairs Committee, identified the connection between Philippine independence and Asian security as "Siamese twins." Building and staffing American military bases in the Philippines would strengthen the newly independent islands and provide an impressive show of American power. In the spring of 1945, before the end of the war, the American military identified fourteen locations in the Philippines that would be ideal for bases. President Osmeña, eager for American economic assistance, quickly gave his approval. His cooperation sent the correct signal to the U.S. government about Philippine pro-American attitudes, and in return the United States soon bestowed aid upon the war-ravaged country. It also seemed to prove to Americans that they had been "good" colonial masters since Filipinos remained willing to follow their guidance.[30]

Even with the war over, the devastation it had wrought sometimes made life in the Philippines dangerous. Still desperate for food and shelter, still smarting over conflicting wartime allegiances, people turned against each other, exacting revenge or taking what they wanted. A few months after independence, a close friend of the Herolds was shot and killed during a payroll robbery on the Mountain Trail. In a scene that could have come straight from an American western, a man with a kerchief masking his face stood in front of some large rocks blocking the road and flagged down the car carrying Emil Jorgensen and his two Filipino assistants. As the car swerved to avoid the man and the rocks, gunfire erupted from both sides of the road, instantly killing Jorgensen. Ethel Herold blamed an ex-convict from Bilibid Prison, claiming the man had been inciting others in the area to thievery. "God, it makes me so mad that this had to happen to an American and to good old hard-working Emil," she wrote in a letter to Florence and Herbert Heald. "We have always had such faith in the Igorotes and our beloved Mt. Trail."[31]

This kind of violence prompted Ethel to ponder the wisdom of choosing to live in a potentially dangerous place. At the end of her graphic letter to the Healds, she told them, "Don't worry about the rest of us. When our time comes, it comes." Yet she did not express such fatalism in a subsequent letter to her son when she encouraged him to spend the summer of 1947 in Wisconsin. "But of course anything can happen out here," Ethel wrote to Bill. "This is not rosy by any means. Your Dad gets fearfully disgusted many times with many things. And if just the wrong thing turned up, he would not stand for [it], then home we would come to the Bonn farm." Ethel did not specify what had been irritating her husband, but it likely had to do with adjusting to new business regulations that had been imposed after independence. And if Elmer Herold should decide that continued employment with Heald Lumber was not worth the effort of dealing with the difficulties of a decolonized Philippines, then Ethel, still ambivalent about the situation, would gladly return to the United States to set up housekeeping in Potosi.[32]

Murderers and thieves posed worrisome threats in the years after the war, but Ethel Herold also fretted about Philippine politics and the governing of the islands, especially because of the increasing agitation of the Huks. The *Hukbong Bayan Laban sa Hapon* (also known as *Hukbalahap* or Huks), a Tagalog phrase for the People's Anti-Japanese Army, originated as a large, successful guerrilla group during the war. The Huks admired Mao Zedong's style of guerrilla warfare and embraced communism and socialism as methods for improving the position of agricultural workers after the war. Many people viewed the Huks as a communist menace, as a threat to the newly independent and democratic Philippines, even though they participated in the political process through their coalition party, the Democratic Alliance. Seeking reform of a corrupt system rather than revolution, the Huks were concerned with obtaining from their landlords easy credit terms, a fair share of the agricultural yield, and a safeguard of their liberties.[33]

Just how closely the Huks toed the communist line is debatable. Though the United States had committed itself to the battle against the spread of communism, President Harry Truman did not see the Huks as a big enough threat to warrant U.S. assistance in getting rid of them. Ethel Herold worried that every country was vulnerable to communist infiltration. She closely followed the case of Alger Hiss, the former New Deal official accused by Whittaker Chambers of being a communist. She lauded the arguments in John Thomas Flynn's 1949 book about socialism called *The Road Ahead: America's Creeping Revolution,* which she believed every U.S. congressman should not only read but also be tested on. Ethel thought that communism threatened the security of both the United States and the Philippines. Yet, she did not see communism behind all unrest. In 1959, after the height of the red scare had passed, she demonstrated savvy about Philippine politics when she wrote to her children about some uprisings in southern Luzon and noted, "but of course the govt. says they are communists." Ethel dismissed the notion, arguing that the protesters "are just opposed to this awful [government] extravagance."[34]

In late 1949, discontented laborers at the Balatoc mine in northern Luzon divided into factions, one of which supported the Huks. Members of the outlaw group held up two buses on the morning of December 10. "What a mess," Ethel Herold observed. The disturbances continued into the spring of 1950 when mine workers, probably encouraged by the Huks, called strikes at Balatoc and Benguet, resulting in over $300,000 worth of gold losses and damages to mine property. Ethel speculated that the American owner, Judge Haussermann, would not give in to the striking workers and might let work stop at the mines even if that meant putting some six thousand Filipino workers, plus the American employees, out of jobs. While she believed that the strikers were "entirely without reason," she agreed they deserved better living accommodations at the mines.[35]

Despite the level of agitation, the strikes lasted only a week. "Judge took it calmly," Ethel reported. She anticipated that criminal charges would be brought against those striking workers who had damaged the mines. As usual, however, she insisted that all of the trouble had to have been caused by outside agitators. "The Igorotes never did want to strike," she asserted in a letter to her friend Marie Halsema. Her lingering sentimental affection for the Mountain Province people, who she believed had always been so grateful for American assistance, would not allow her to think otherwise.[36]

Ethel Herold assumed that the mine strikes would not have an adverse affect on Heald Lumber, telling her son, Bill, "Your Dad is always so proud that he has not ever had any labor trouble; and that when these devilish lawyers went to our mills to organize labor unions—that our men were not interested—but satisfied with the treatment of Heald Lumber. Your Dad really has a way with these people that is right. And you as kids were taught to be polite to these people—whether laborers or not." Ethel's repeated reference to "these people" reveals the persistence of an "us-them" mindset that was nevertheless tinged with sentimentality. While she wanted fair treatment for the workers, she viewed them as very different from herself and the other Americans, and she expected that the workers would understand that Americans still knew what was best for them.[37]

The Philippines suffered from a variety of troubles in the years immediately following the war. Between 1946 and 1950, the government went through more than one billion dollars of U.S. aid, but the economy showed no improvement. In 1950, the United States dispatched the Bell mission (not to be confused with the earlier Bell Trade Act) to the islands. After a five-month study, it concluded, "The profits of businessmen and the incomes of large landowners have risen very considerably [but] the standard of living of most people is lower than before the war." Offering an incentive of $250 million in American aid, the mission recommended that the Philippine government increase taxes, establish controls on foreign-currency transactions, introduce a minimum wage, and implement land reform.[38]

But what was good for the Filipinos, Ethel Herold realized, was not necessarily good for the Americans: "One never knows what is going to happen next in this cock-eyed country—now the legislature has passed an import-control law which has sky-rocketed prices that we foreigners get caught on. . . . And also a law that no money can be sent out, except with a license through the Central Bank. Gold must also have a license to go out. So all that is going to cramp business." It was the American businesses, of course, that felt the pinch of these new regulations, rules that left Elmer Herold, still struggling to revive Heald Lumber, disgusted and frustrated but never actually broke. The Herolds found themselves increasingly in the minority, viewed with suspicion as outsiders in a place they considered their home.[39]

These economic troubles translated into personal ones for Ethel Herold. She hoped that after his graduation from Lawrence College, her son, Bill, would return to the Philippines and take an engineering job at one of the mines. As much as she looked forward to this, she cautioned her children, "Right now it seems it would be the wrong thing for him to do, this country is so unsettled and there is the element that tries to obstruct the white man." In 1950, Ethel assured Bill, "And you personally would be an asset to the Heald Lumber Co. because you instinctively know how to deal with these people. And if this govt were stable, and the Huks kept in control, it would be a good place to come to. But right now, and especially with this present strike, things are worse than ever."[40] They were worse than ever because the Cold War was starting to escalate.

The Korean War

The outbreak of the Korean War in June 1950 must have confirmed Ethel Herold's fears of instability in Asia. It also likely convinced her that the Democratic Party in the United States was incapable of effectively handling foreign affairs and keeping Americans safe. "We certainly hope the Democrats get the licking of their lives in the fall elections," she wrote to her children three months before the war started. "If I lived in the States, I'd surely have to go into politics and yell my head off about the way things are going. Let all (P.I. included) these foreign countries go jump in some lake, we have helped them enough already; there is never any gratitude for anything; and U.S. taxes are just going higher. There will be no Marshall Plan to help us."[41]

Like many American women involved in women's organizations after World War II, Ethel initially hoped that international cooperation would keep the peace. Just as she had promoted the League of Nations to her high school students in Lancaster, Wisconsin, after the Great War, she supported programs sponsored by the United Nations. For instance, in the fall of 1947, she wrote admiringly of the UN's Economic Commission for Asia and the Far East (ECAFE), which held a conference in Baguio beginning on November 24. The Herolds hosted several people who traveled to Baguio for the meeting, including Jim Halsema, who came in his capacity as a newspaper reporter. Ethel Herold was doubly pleased not only because Halsema was an old friend, but also because, as a journalist, he "always knows so much stuff that does not ever get into print." She labeled the conference "most interesting" and wished her children "could have witnessed how diplomacy works." Her views on the contributions of the United Nations put her at odds with most postwar conservatives, who considered it a threat to the American way of life, to democracy and freedom. Her work in women's organizations, particularly the Monday Club, had reinforced for her the benefits of people around the world reaching across borders to help each other.[42]

But international cooperation was not always successful. During the spring of 1946, under the Truman administration, the U.S.-Soviet Joint Commission had been unable to decide on the structure of government for a unified Korea, which had been artificially divided by the two countries at the end of World War II. The Republic of Korea, the democratic south, gained formal independence in 1948 following the election of Syngman Rhee as its president. By the next year, the United States had removed all of its occupying troops from the south. But North Korean leader Kim Il-sung sought help from his communist neighbors, China and the Soviet Union, to reunify the country. On June 25, 1950, North Korean troops invaded the south. Since the end of the Second World War, Americans had feared and tried to prevent the expansion of communism around the world. But now, despite the Truman Doctrine and the Marshall Plan, the United Nations, and NATO, communists were on the move again. And much like in 1941, when Americans had closely monitored fascist land grabs in Europe, another significant threat surfaced in Asia.[43]

"And now all this mess in Korea," Ethel Herold lamented. "No telling what the outcome will be." She worried about the safety of the Philippines, speculating that "Russia might just jump down here on the P.I. And maybe the Huks are far stronger than we think and are waiting for the signal from Russia to make a coup also." She advised her son, Bill, just graduated from Lawrence College and newly engaged, "not to burn your bridges there in the States; plenty can happen out here. We Americans might even be sent home." Thinking back to World War II and its bitter lessons, she wrote, "I surely hope none of this happens—but Pearl Harbor was so sudden and so awful." In early July 1950, Ethel still worried that the war would spread. Some American women and children living in Manila had gone home, although the army and navy families remained. Writing to her daughter, Betsy, Ethel noted that the U.S. ambassador to the Philippines, Myron Cowen, "continues to say that it is safe here in the P.I.; that we will not be invaded. I hope he is right. Your Dad and I surely do not want to get caught again." Yet once again she refused to leave the Philippines and for the same reasons: an American official did not advise evacuation, and Elmer Herold had no intention of leaving.[44]

In addition to her concerns about how the war would affect the Philippines, Ethel worried about Bill Herold's draft eligibility. She believed that her son should do his patriotic duty if summoned, but she hoped that the draft board would equate his World War II internment with military service and not call him up. He had already lived and suffered through one war, she argued, so he should not have to do so again. Bill Herold seemed to hold out little hope for this, though, so he and his fiancée Joanne Hamilton moved up their wedding to September 9, 1950. On such short notice, his parents were unable to attend. Bill received his draft notice about a month after the wedding, and however Ethel Herold took the news privately, she put on a brave face in a letter to her daughter: "Well, it's too bad Bill has been drafted, but it took a few million of other drafted boys to get us out of prison camp; so he must do his duty too."[45]

The legacy of World War I–era patriotic motherhood lived on in Ethel Herold. Though her children grew up outside of the United States, she had inculcated them with her patriotic beliefs and schooled them with an understanding of the superiority of the American political system. Bill and Betsy Herold had attended the Brent School, which before the war exclusively served the American and European population in Baguio, maintaining the colonial power structure. During internment, working around restrictions imposed by the Japanese, the children continued to take classes offered by their fellow prisoners, who always found ways to give instruction in the virtues of democracy. In their family quarters in the internment camps, Ethel Herold reinforced her belief in the supremacy of the United States by repeatedly telling her children that someday the Americans would come. Since she had raised her son to be a good citizen, he could now express his gratitude for that rescue through military service.

In November 1950, while Bill Herold trained for military police duty as part of the 45th Infantry Division at Camp Polk, Louisiana, the Chinese threw their troops into the Korean fray, aiding the north and raising the possibility for a widening war. "This awful war makes me actually sick," Ethel told Betsy in mid-December. Then she admitted her surprise over China's involvement: "And that China who has been weak all these many years—now killing off our American boys. Those Chinese have such hordes, they can last on and be killed off forever. . . . I wish Roosevelt were alive today to see this world mess." Ever the loyal Republican and echoing the sentiments of the party's conservative wing, Ethel blamed FDR and the Democrats for creating conditions that led to another war.[46]

Given her fears about the war in Korea, Ethel Herold's actions seem odd, as if she had not learned anything from her World War II experiences. Instead of taking preventive measures against the possibility of a widening war and leaving the Philippines for the United States just to be on the safe side, she once again remained in Baguio. But this time, because of official assurances and because of Elmer Herold's decision to stay, she must have had a feeling that history would not repeat itself. With her son on active military duty, she even encouraged her daughter to consider a career as an army nurse. If she joined the military, Betsy Herold might be posted to the Philippines, allowing her to see her parents on a more regular basis. Ruby Bradley, an army nurse who had been interned in Baguio, visited there in early 1951 while on leave from her duties in Korea, sparking an impromptu party at the Herold home. When she found out that Betsy was in nursing school, Bradley urged Ethel to convince her daughter to join the army for its "good pay, travel, fun, good retirement." As Ethel expected her son to do his patriotic duty with military service, she also expected Betsy to embrace similar notions of patriotism and service. Though she considered a stint in the military appropriate for both of them, she was not upset that Betsy ultimately decided against enlisting.[47]

Politics: Foreign and Domestic

As the war in Korea turned into a stalemate and it became clear that communists would not come pouring into the Philippines, Ethel Herold turned her attention to other matters. On December 10, 1952, she served as a fill-in speaker at a human rights program in Burnham Park, giving closing remarks on the subject of responsibility; it was similar to a speech she had given just the week before at a Rotary meeting. She pointed out that even though the constitutions of new democratic countries were full of promises about protecting human rights, this would never be achieved if the people in the government were not held responsible. She "emphasized how difficult is a democracy because ALL the people have to take part and know what to do. Freedom is not something to be talked about, but something to be attained. For democracies to succeed, all the people should be honest, strive for integrity, uphold the dignity of human labor, and be civic conscious." Ethel considered it a rather daring speech, especially as it was impromptu, but she felt strongly about the issue of responsibility, believing that too many people focused exclusively on rights.[48]

During the 1950s, politics continued to occupy her thoughts, especially the U.S. presidential elections. "Truman and all his democrats should be thrown out of office for good," she wrote to her daughter, Betsy, in early 1952. "We think Taft better than Eisenhower, as the latter would want too much military aid for Europe and elsewhere. Our own national debt should be considered and cut down and not enlarged any more." Though former general Dwight D.

Eisenhower won the Republican nomination over Senator Robert A. Taft, Ethel encouraged Betsy to "get around and do some electioneering" for the Republicans. She approvingly acknowledged that a Republican president would "slash ALL foreign aid by at least half" and would also "bring those 50,000 women and kids home from the armed forces of Europe and the 20,000 women and kids home from Japan."[49]

This affinity for Robert A. Taft was hardly surprising, given his conservative leanings, commitment to individual liberty, and connection to the Philippines. Taft's father, William Howard Taft, had come to Manila in 1900 as president of the Second Philippine Commission, charged with establishing a civilian government. Eight years later, he successfully ran for president of the United States. Robert Taft also spent some time in the Philippines, graduated from Harvard Law School, and moved through Ohio state government, then on to Washington, D.C. Despite his opposition to Roosevelt's New Deal, Taft proved to be an inconsistent conservative, supporting certain New Deal programs designed to help the poor and underprivileged. He ran for the Senate in the mid-1930s and served for fourteen years. In 1951, Taft was the ranking Republican on the Senate Foreign Relations Committee, and in 1953, shortly before his death, he became Senate majority leader.

Strongly antiwar, Taft also had a reputation as an isolationist, which may have cost him the Republican Party presidential nomination in 1948. Although he wielded considerable power on Capitol Hill, Taft came across as cold, delivering dry speeches that nonetheless often sparked controversy and revealed inconsistent positions. Extreme right-wing Republicans often found him too liberal. Taft lost the nomination bid to New York governor Thomas Dewey who famously lost the 1948 election to Harry Truman. Still, Republicans made significant gains in the 1950 congressional elections, including Taft's landslide Senate reelection, a reflection of the growing conservatism in the United States.[50]

Ethel Herold worried that as president, Dwight Eisenhower would commit too much money and too many American troops to Europe. The "Great Debate" over troop deployment had begun at the end of 1950 when the Truman administration announced that American troops would be sent to Europe to fulfill part of the country's commitment to the North Atlantic Treaty Organization (NATO). Conservative

Republicans, including Taft, could not understand why Truman decided to send troops to Europe when they were so badly needed in Korea. Taft questioned whether Congress or the president had the power to send U.S. troops abroad and concluded that Congress should have as much input as the president. Taft and his conservative supporters pushed for adoption of the Wherry Resolution, introduced on January 8, 1951, to prevent U.S. troops from being sent to Europe until Congress had created a policy about such actions. A compromise reached three months later set a ceiling on the number of troops that could be sent without Senate approval.[51]

By mid-October 1951, Taft once again began campaigning for the Republican presidential nomination, focusing on additional issues Ethel Herold believed in: individual liberty, economic freedom, and state and local control. He even had the support of top Republicans in her home state of Wisconsin, considered an important primary state for the party, and from General Douglas MacArthur, who had liberated the Philippines. However, it was General Dwight Eisenhower, the hero of D-Day and more recently the commander of NATO forces, who resigned his commission and challenged Taft for the Republican presidential nomination. Ultimately, Eisenhower's military record trumped Taft's decades of political service, and the former general won the nomination and the presidency.

If Ethel Herold felt disappointed that her particular candidate had not been chosen, she must have been pleased that the Republicans had retaken the White House. And Eisenhower, like Taft, had spent some time stationed in the Philippines. As the newly elected president prepared to take office in 1953, Ethel wrote to her daughter, Betsy, and her new son-in-law, Karl Heimke, "Power to him and may God help him to clean up our Washington mess. And cut down on . . . all foreign spending. Those foreign countries do not like us any better for our 'help.' The implementation has cost altogether too much. Let those lazy democrats who have been on the gravy wagon for so long, just get back to the States and really do an honest days [*sic*] work. That goes for the Philippines too." Although Ethel Herold did not directly advocate a Taft-like isolationism for the United States, her views on American involvement in world affairs seemed to be undergoing some kind of shift, which was likely influenced by both decolonization movements and fears of communist expansion.[52]

With Eisenhower's election came a renewed American interest in the stability of the Philippines. As president, he focused much of his attention on events in Asia, especially since the Korean War was still going on when he was inaugurated and would not be settled with a ceasefire until that July. Eisenhower, who had served with MacArthur in the Philippines, and John Foster Dulles, the secretary of state, were both dedicated to preventing the spread of communism in Asia. Indeed, the new president reflected the historical concerns of the Republican Party mainstream by focusing on the Pacific area. Besides, the Cold War in Europe appeared to have reached a stable stalemate while events in Asia and Africa seemed more volatile.

In 1953, the year Bill Herold finally moved his family to the Philippines when he took a job at the Bobok Saw Mill at Balatoc, Filipino politics heated up for the presidential election. American policy makers had little use for the Philippine president, Elpidio Quirino, who had had difficulty in suppressing the rebellious Huks without assistance from the Central Intelligence Agency. And at the end of April, Quirino recalled Carlos Romulo from his ambassador position at the United Nations. Ethel Herold speculated that Quirino wanted Romulo to stand for a senate seat as a member of the Liberal Party, but the ambassador resisted making any political commitment. After several conferences with Quirino, Romulo resigned his post to run against Quirino. Ramon Magsaysay, formerly Quirino's minister of defense, who had worked with CIA operatives to break the Huks, ran as the Nationalista's candidate. He enjoyed strong support from American officials.

Either Magsaysay or Romulo would make a good president, Ethel Herold believed, as they were both honest men. "But you can just imagine how rotten politics are here when Romulo even turns on Quirino," she wrote in a letter home. "If Quirino does get the nomination, we'll all lay low, as it will be a shooting election in November, as he'll try anything to control the ballot. Romulo would make a good president, but he has done more than anyone in the UN to put the P.I. on the map of the world and to give it a good name in so doing. We'd like for Romulo to be back on the UN." Elmer Herold did not believe that Romulo had a chance of winning the election but thought that Magsaysay would do a fine enough job. "Of course," he wrote his daughter Betsy in a rare letter, "we cannot make that statement out here or they would deport us. . . . We just watch the show and do not commit ourselves at all."[53]

This was an exaggeration likely sparked by the Herolds' growing belief that they were now outsiders in the Philippines. Still, there were ways they could show their political preferences. On June 28, 1953, when Carlos Romulo addressed the Rotary Club in Baguio, Elmer Herold, one of the senior Rotarians and one of the most prominent businessmen in the city, had "the privilege" of introducing him. Though their favorite candidate did not win, in November Ethel cheered, "Well hooray for Magsaysay!!! We did not ever think the vote would be so overwhelming in his favor. Our opinion of the Filipino people has risen—it shows they can think for themselves & not be led around by crooked politicians." The electoral outcome that boosted her opinion of Filipino voters in fact came courtesy of the CIA's Edward "Landslide" Lansdale, who orchestrated Magsaysay's impressive victory. The United States government apparently still believed that Filipinos required assistance in thinking for themselves.[54]

Though the Korean War ended with an armistice in the summer of 1953, the escalating war in Indochina raised new concerns for Ethel Herold. She declared in a letter in early April, "This damned war in Indochina surely has us worried. It could mean most anything. Billy is worried as he is on the reserve with a Manila outfit." Later she expressed hope that the Geneva Conference would settle the struggle between France and the Vietnamese people. "It will be the end of the world if our American soldiers are sent there as GROUND troops," Ethel Herold presciently predicted. "They should never have been sent to Korea in that capacity. And I don't see why France is having the cream of her manhood killed off there either—she has promised those countries their independence—what will she ever reap from their deaths?" She recognized that the fighting in Indochina had far-reaching consequences: "I can readily see why France does not back the war full force. And those damned Chinese Reds pouring in there by hordes. With Russia egging her on. The USA can't protect the whole world—and it does not want our protection—which all those countries think is backed by wicked USA capitalism. The USA just better begin looking to herself and let these other countries settle their own affairs."[55]

This opinion put Ethel Herold at odds with the U.S. government's desire to protect southeast Asia from communism. After much national and international wrangling, the South East Asia Treaty Organization (SEATO) was established in 1954 to help promote self-determination among the peoples in that region, backed by a U.S. pledge to provide assistance in halting the spread of communism. But Ethel Herold was very observant about other countries not wanting American help, at least not unilateral help, which was increasingly perceived as meddlesome and paternalistic. Still, her continued support of international diplomacy and international organizations like the United Nations indicate that she did not believe that the United States should totally withdraw from world affairs.[56]

As with other conservative Republicans, her willingness to leave other countries to their own devices did not mean that she was soft on communism. Ethel Herold had been closely following the Senate hearings of Wisconsin's most well-known red hunter, Joseph McCarthy, and she lauded his investigations. She did not approve of his attack on the army ("it is a wasted lot of bunk") but thought he was "really on the right track ferreting out those communists. He is ruthless at times—the Communists are always ruthless." In other words, harsh though it may seem, McCarthy used the correct kinds of tactics in dealing with communists.[57]

The Expatriate Experience Draws to a Close

After another world tour in 1956, complete with lengthy visits to Potosi and Missoula, the Herolds began their last round in the Philippines. Elmer Herold planned to retire in two and a half years when he turned sixty-five. A variety of illnesses had begun to plague them both, a combination of aging and the long-term affects of malnutrition from internment. And after four years with the Balatoc mine, Bill Herold had finally earned a paid vacation; thus, in April 1957 he flew his family back to the states for six months. They never returned. Bill called his parents in August to tell them that he had been offered a job in lime manufacturing in Strassburg, Virginia, so he and his wife Joanne had decided they should stay. "Their not coming back was a blow to us—but the states was the best place," Ethel conceded.[58]

She remembered her final years in Baguio as "a continuation of the others" as "time and life went on." By early 1957, she told her daughter Betsy, "As a matter of fact your Dad and I are looking forward to the time when he will be retired and living happily in the States. 3 years more. These Philippines continue to do dumber and dumber things." Ethel's dissatisfaction intensified after the death of President Magsaysay in a plane crash in March, and she wildly speculated that his death was the result of sabotage, "perhaps not of the plane—but of the personnel—knock-out drops could so easily have been put in their food—as Magsaysay had communist as well as political enemies in Cebu." She believed his vice president and successor, Carlos Garcia, was corrupt, "letting the old line of swindlers who Magsaysay had fired, get back on the gravy train."[59]

The "dumber and dumber things" that Ethel Herold attributed to Filipino politicians were policies designed, in the newly independent country, to privilege Filipinos over Americans. President Garcia implemented a Filipino First Policy to strengthen the islands' economy by limiting foreign business investment capital to 40 percent. If the Herolds could not prosper in the Philippines, it is no wonder that Ethel began thinking about returning to the states. Also, Garcia and members of his administration increasingly antagonized the United States by attempting to create a foreign policy independent of American influence, pushing for settlement of a $972 million "omnibus claim" involving damages from World War II and for the release of $125 million in promised credits and development funds, and resisting the continued presence of U.S. military bases in the Philippines. By early 1959, U.S.-Philippine relations had hit such an all-time low that Carlos Romulo, Philippine ambassador to the United States, was recalled to Manila.[60]

"I bet you got a kick out of TIME Feb. 2 on the Philippines," Ethel wrote to Bill and Betsy in 1959. "What a furor [President] Garcia made about it." *Time* had reported on the deterioration of the relationship between the Philippines and the United States, identifying recent grievances of the Philippine government but concluding that both countries were about equally responsible for the troubles. Still, the article enumerated certain excesses of the Garcia administration, infuriating the Philippine president to the point that he barred Jim Bell, *Time*'s Hong Kong bureau chief, from entering the country. Ethel Herold lauded the magazine for publicly standing by Bell in a February 16 editorial, and she praised Bell for an accurate article. "These Filipinos are really getting sassy these days," she observed of those who continued to criticize Jim Bell and *Time*.[61]

From the timing of the magazine pieces and the references to them in her letters, it appears that Ethel regularly read *Time.* By the mid-1950s, Henry Luce's weekly newsmagazine already commanded more than a million and a half readers. *Time* promoted internationalism, supported the "Modern Republicanism" of the Eisenhower administration, and endorsed anticommunist campaigns. So it is not surprising that Ethel would routinely turn to this magazine for the latest information of national and international events. *Time* reflected many of her own beliefs, though she would soon find much fault with Eisenhower's Modern Republicanism.[62]

In addition to all of the political wrangling, certain other aspects of Baguio life did not appeal to Ethel Herold any longer. The charity supper she planned for the Monday Club in October 1957 turned out to be a "yowling success," bringing in over two thousand pesos to pay Brent School tuition for some bright Igorot students. However, she did not approve of the school's becoming a melting pot. She thought its "high standard is falling fast" because it hired some Filipino teachers who "simply cannot discipline American kids" and because one of the female American students was going steady with a Filipino. As Ethel wrote to Betsy Herold Heimke, "Thank goodness Brent was not like that when you and Bill were there. And thank goodness Bill's kids are not there any more."[63]

Yet, her views on race were inconsistent. In March 1958, a group called Moral Re-Armament (MRA) held its second convention in Baguio, attracting two hundred people from twenty-six countries. Its founder, the former Lutheran minister Frank Nathan Daniel Buchman, believed in blending Christianity with moral absolutes and taking action to better the world. Buchman formulated his ideas into the MRA, which he established in 1938, partly in response to the growing international crisis. The organization stood as a bulwark against fascism and communism both during World War II and into the postwar period. At the 1958 convention, Ethel Herold listened to talks on "HONESTY, purity, unselfishness, love. All races, all classes of people. . . . And I think it is right." However, she believed that changes in race relations had to be approached slowly. Carefully monitoring developments in the civil rights movement in the United States, she deplored the actions of the Warren court because she believed they interfered with states' rights and because she believed that such changes had to take place slowly, with more consensus: "It has disgusted us all along the way Little Rock has been played up—think of the countless territory where things are going all right."[64]

Still, the enthusiasm for MRA illustrates Ethel Herold's commitment to human rights through international cooperation. This interest had been developing for several years, first manifesting itself in her speech at Burnham Park in 1952 during the Human Rights conference. There, Ethel had underscored governments' responsibilities in ensuring human rights, and six years later she acknowledged the international dimensions. As a young woman, she had not been particularly attracted to the social-justice programs of progressive reformers like Jane Addams or to Addams's vision of a "new internationalism" that worked for world peace and social justice through international cooperation. But Ethel's internment during World War II heightened her sensitivity to human-rights issues. She had experienced firsthand how cruel humans could be to one another, which may have convinced her of the value of international agreements on such issues. She retained a strong sense of nationalism, but it was one that allowed her to develop a world consciousness in which she could acknowledge the necessity of the United States working through international organizations.[65]

Tensions between the United States and Communist China over the status of Formosa helped firm up the Herolds' decision to leave the Philippines. Ethel wrote to her children, "Even if there is no shooting war in the near future, your Dad and I would like to get out of here by January or February of 1959. We have enough to retire on and we want to be back in God's country and near you kids." During September 1958, both the John Hay and Clark bases were on alert because of tensions between mainland China and Taiwan; thus, Ethel Herold made sure that she was "organized to get out fast." She never conquered her fear of being captured.[66]

Friends treated the Herolds to rounds of parties and awards prior to their departure in 1959. Ethel most highly valued the Baguio Woman of the Year Award from the Baguio Press Club. An article in the *Baguio Midland Courier* reported that the club chose her unanimously but that the award might "be a bit misleading in that it may give to mean that it was only during the past year that Mrs. Herold has done monumental work in public welfare and civic promotion. Undoubtedly one of the most civic-spirited American ladies in the community, Ethel has unassumingly but positively and effectively assisted in the promotion of well-chosen and worthwhile projects for social, economic and healthful wellbeing, not only this or the last year but through all the years she has been with us, before, during, and after the war." Ethel had a grand time at the awards dinner, describing it as "loads of fun," during which she was "quite the queen bee."[67]

On March 15, the Rotary Club of Baguio presented the Herolds with a special citation "in recognition of outstanding achievements and greatest appreciation for the unselfish services rendered to the people of Baguio." The Trinidad School feted the couple the following month in a Friday afternoon event, during which they met with a "whole lot of our old students, even one from Abra" and a group of farmers that the Monday Club had helped. Ethel "just cried when I saw all those old faces, and of course many of them cried too. And when I saw I had to say something on the program, I knew I just couldn't do it." After listening to many speeches "telling of the wonders of the Herolds," Elmer gave a "serious talk about Nationalism" before the superintendent presented them with an award listing all of their accomplishments. Ethel acquiesced to the students' request that she sing and gave a cappella renditions of "Rose Marie" and "The Bells of St. Mary's." When the superintendent told them about how tuition had been raised in an attempt to keep up with expensive purchases, Ethel and Elmer donated their piano because the school "was our first love out here."[68]

On July 1, 1959, Ethel Herold wrote what was "no doubt my last letter to you from dear old Baguio," telling her children that the Heald house had at last been packed up and that she hoped "our nerves, digestion, etc. hold out. Also our emotions." Five days later, the couple set sail on the *Pioneer Main* for a trip that took about six weeks, with eight stops and seventeen days on shore at various port cities. Bill Herold and his family met Ethel and Elmer in New York in mid-August, and from there they all traveled to Bill's home in Virginia. Although Ethel did spend a day in Washington, D.C., to report on the Monday Club at a business meeting of the General Federation of Women's Clubs, she and Elmer cut short their usual round of visits. They wished to hasten on to Illinois to meet their newest and final grandchild, Betsy and Karl Heimke's daughter Sally Ann. Finally, the Herolds arrived at the Bonn farm on the morning of October 2, 1959. This would be their final home.[69]

Ethel Clementine Herold, one year old, 1897.

Thomas family, 1901. Back row (l-r): Roscoe, Edna, Bart, Fred. Front row: Clem and Elizabeth seated, with Ethel standing.

Ethel, seated in the middle holding Jack, her pet rooster, 1904.

Ethel Thomas, valedictorian, Potosi High School, 1913.

Ethel and Elmer Herold's wedding day, June 24, 1920.

Ethel and Elmer Herold on horseback, Bangued, Philippines, 1922.

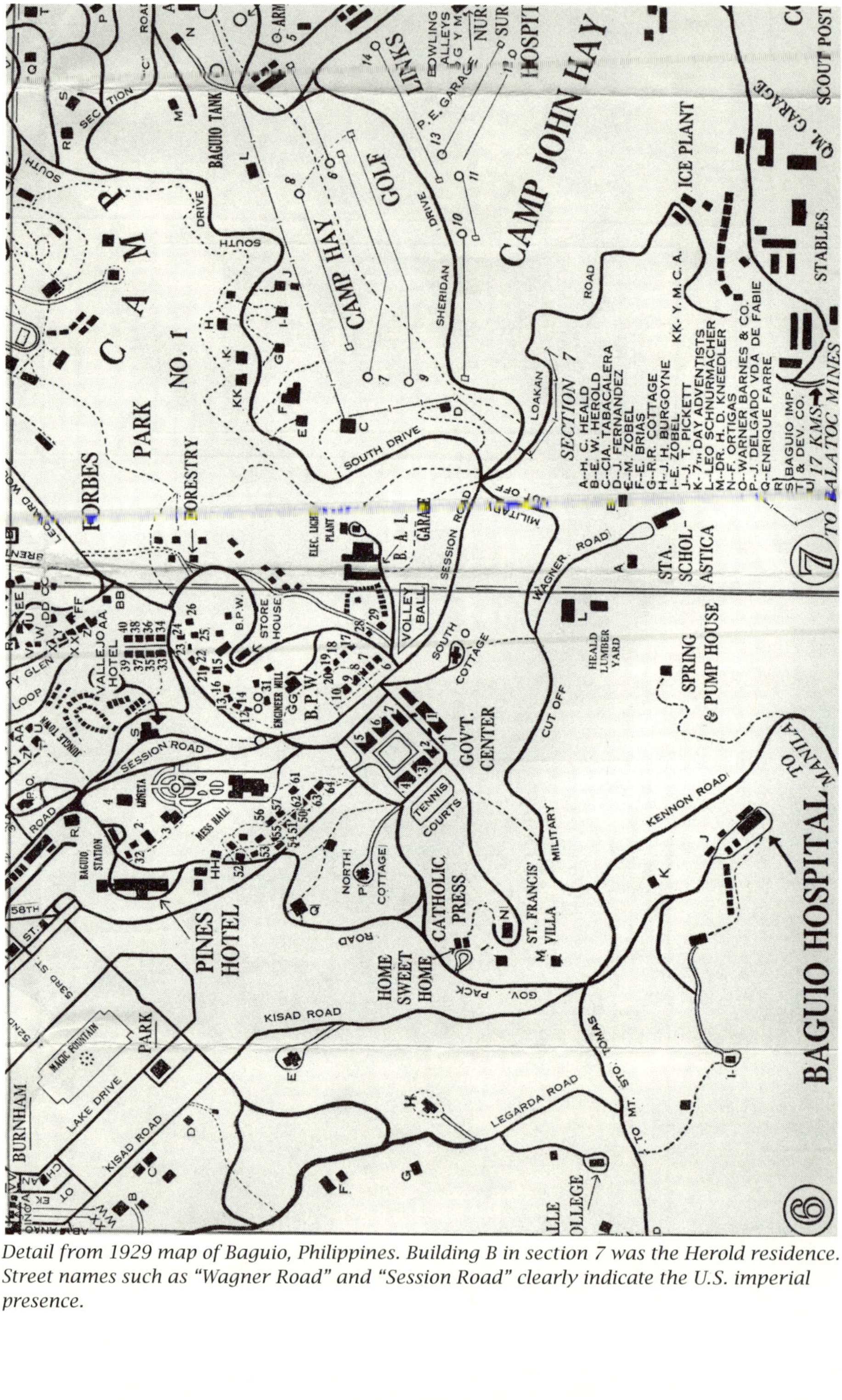

Detail from 1929 map of Baguio, Philippines. Building B in section 7 was the Herold residence. Street names such as "Wagner Road" and "Session Road" clearly indicate the U.S. imperial presence.

Ethel and Elmer Herold in Philippine dress, Bangued, Philippines, 1922.

Street scene, Baguio, Philippines, 1932. Courtesy of New York State Archives.

Ethel and Elmer Herold with Betsy (seated) and Billy, Baguio, Philippines, 1932.

Herold family passport photo, 1938.

Herold family Christmas card photo that was never sent, November 1941.

The Herold Family at an oil tank, Baguio, 1941. Elmer Herold destroyed this tank in December 1941 to prevent the Japanese from seizing it.

Ethel and Elmer Herold in the rubble of Manila, February 27, 1945. The Herolds had already gained more than ten pounds following their liberation from Old Bilibid Prison.

Ethel standing on the ruins of what used to be her kitchen steps, 1946.

Ethel standing on the front steps of destroyed home, 1946.

Bill and Betsy Herold visiting their parents at the ruins of their Baguio home, 1948.

Ethel Herold with Fred and Bart Thomas in Missoula, Montana, 1949.

Ethel and Elmer in their new Baguio home, Christmas 1958.

Chapter Six

The Return of the Expatriate

THE BONN FARMHOUSE "already seemed like home to us," Ethel Herold wrote of her arrival in southwestern Wisconsin. "During 3 previous vacations, we had done a lot of living there." She unpacked their freight, and "in no time, with the Persian rugs on the floors and things put to rights, it looked like a home—if not a museum." Of all the items Ethel Herold displayed, she felt especially proud of the various framed citations she hung to decorate the staircase wall: "The one we liked most commended our Philippine-American public relations for 38 years." This was how she described the work she had done in northern Luzon, both her public school teaching and her countless volunteer activities. Though friends and family members wondered how Ethel would get along on a farm near Potosi, an isolated, quiet place lacking servants, she claimed that she and Elmer welcomed the freedom from the "constant chaperonage" of household help and found that "it was just fun to be there *alone*" at the Bonn farm.[1]

Married for thirty-nine years, the parents of grown children with children of their own and survivors of two world wars, Ethel and Elmer looked forward to spending the bulk of their retirement years in their home state. Ethel Thomas Herold's life had come full circle. Refusing to use age as an excuse to withdraw from an active, vigorous citizenship, she quickly involved herself in community activities through women's clubs and the local Republican Party. This chapter examines her contributions to the political and cultural work of postwar American women's clubs and her increasing support of the conservative wing of the Republican Party, particularly during the 1964 Goldwater campaign. It also looks at how Ethel Thomas Herold chose to remember her life. In her seventies, after the death of her husband, she wrote an autobiography in which she portrayed herself as a patriotic American by reinforcing the romanticism and exceptionalism of U.S. imperialism.

The Politicized Club Woman

As much as she loved her new home and enjoyed living among old friends and family in southwestern Wisconsin, Ethel Herold could not bear to be too alone, too idle. Fixing up the farmhouse, rounds of visiting, and membership in a local bridge club occupied time in a way that was reminiscent of her first years in Baguio, and as they had then, these activities did not sufficiently exercise her intellect or provide a larger sense of accomplishment. So, within a few months of settling in at the Bonn farmhouse, Ethel began attending meetings of local women's clubs, including the Ladies' Aid and the General Federation of Women's Clubs. In May 1960, she drove to Lancaster, where she had taught high school history during the Great War, for the convention of the GFWC of southwestern Wisconsin. There she lectured about the Monday Club. Mrs. Norbert Kline, from the GFWC's Washington, D.C., office, heard the talk and encouraged Ethel to present similar ones to other clubs in the area. She took this advice, and during her first year of public speaking, she was in such high demand that she sent about five hundred dollars from her fees back to the Monday Club. She continued this practice for ten years though she noted that the club in Baguio "progressed so well without me . . . that it proved I was not so essential after all. I was almost jealous." Indeed, the Monday Club's community activities made such a difference in Baguio that the GFWC awarded it an international prize in its 1960 Community Achievement Contest.[2]

Since 1890, the GFWC had functioned as an umbrella organization, "a common fellowship and central bond of union" for the myriad women's clubs in the United States. Describing itself as an "international women's organization," it was also affiliated with women's groups outside of the United States. GFWC members in the United States tended to be white and comfortably middle class, with most living in suburban areas. If Ethel Herold represented the rural minority, she was right in step with those who felt disinclined to allow African American members—not because they were racists, they would insist, but because black women could join the National

Council of Negro Women. The GFWC also allowed her to interact with mostly professional, college-educated women who valued their own careers, had an interest in other cultures, and knew enough about politics to understand the communist threat. This was certainly Ethel's milieu, though she would go on to become more stridently anticommunist than most GFWC members.[3]

The GFWC had continued to promote a variety of national and international projects during the 1950s, many of them in support of anticommunism. Clubwomen helped relief efforts in Korea, organized programs for American soldiers serving in the Korean War, raised money for the Voice of America, and awarded scholarships to international students. In 1959, the year that the Herolds left the Philippines, the GFWC held its first Asian Conference in Manila, which attracted about five hundred women from fourteen Asian countries and the United States. By 1960, when Ethel Herold was still receiving many invitations for speaking engagements, the GFWC was advocating moving away from single-speaker events to roundtable discussions that could better foster an open dialogue. The women's club movement showed its willingness to change with the times, but it was not clear how much Ethel Herold would change along with it.[4]

At these various meetings, Ethel felt comfortable with women she had known decades ago growing up in Potosi and with some of her former Lancaster students, but she admitted, "I don't know just what I am in for." She complained that she found it "positively stupid" the way the women's clubs in Potosi conducted their business meetings, "so long & boring & no accomplishment." She long maintained that the "best attribute" of the Monday Club had been its short business meetings, during which she insisted she did not "railroad things" but "sure put on the pressure for speed." As a newcomer and as a seasonal member (she and Elmer intended to winter in the south), Ethel realized that though she felt at home, many of the other women probably considered her an outsider. She decided not to force change in the Potosi clubs, declining as well to seek leadership positions within them.[5]

She contented herself with participating as a member or as a guest, but when an interesting opportunity arose, particularly if she could talk about her life in Baguio, she took it. Ethel served as the Philippine representative to the GFWC's international meeting in

Milwaukee in June 1963 as the Monday Club's envoy. "This will be most enjoyable," she wrote to her children, "and I might as well go to one of these GFWC conventions being as it is so near." The GCWF chose as its theme for that year "Women's Role in a Changing World," and at least one of the conference speakers argued that the "changing world implies a growing interdependence." Others focused on equal rights and equal opportunity, especially for women in the work force and in politics. The front page of the *Milwaukee Journal* ran a photograph of four of the GFWC women wearing the national costumes of the countries they represented, including Ethel Herold, looking elegant in an off-the-shoulder Filipina dress, her white hair swept on top of her head. She lectured about the accomplishments of the Monday Club, highlighting the loan program that enabled farm school graduates to purchase their own land and proudly telling her children that the speech produced "a burst of applause." She did not take it all as personal glory, however. In this talk, as in others, she emphasized what the Monday Club had achieved rather than the actions of any one member (even herself) in particular.[6]

The more Ethel Herold's club speeches focused on her experiences in the Philippines, the more attention she paid to American politics, which in turn inspired increased political activity. During the last decades of her life, she directly exercised her citizenship rights through voting and by volunteering with the Republican Party. The state party needed her support. While Wisconsin voters had overwhelmingly supported President Eisenhower's reelection in 1956, two years later the Democrats controlled the Wisconsin state assembly and installed a Democratic governor, something the party had not achieved since 1932. Economics played a large role in Democratic victories both times: the depths of the Great Depression in 1932 and a big recession in the late 1950s that put around ninety-two thousand Wisconsinites out of work. But by 1960, state political issues like joblessness and a proposed sales tax were eclipsed by the presidential election.[7]

More conservative than either the liberal Republicanism of Nelson Rockefeller or even the Modern Republicanism offered up by President Dwight Eisenhower, Ethel Herold hoped that the party would select a conservative presidential candidate in 1960. She became one of thousands of grassroots activists whose contributions in 1960 helped pave the way for a more united conservative front in 1964. Also known as "kitchen-table" activists, women like Ethel helped shape the course of politics in the volatile decade of the 1960s, yet tended to get obscured by the more vocal New Left. The grassroots conservatives, far from being the overly emotional "kooks" or "nuts" usually portrayed in the mainstream media, were well educated and fairly affluent. They had a knack for blending traditionalism and modernity, which accounted for their longevity. These conservatives were both adaptable and tenacious, having been working since at least the 1930s to create a "modern conservative" agenda. It was Franklin Roosevelt's New Deal, not the liberalism of the 1960s, that first prompted their advocacy of a free market and a small federal government as the solution to the country's economic problems, beginning with the Great Depression. Ethel's conservatism could be traced back at least that far, as she never approved of FDR's activist use of the federal government, and the anticommunism of postwar conservatives kept her firmly anchored in their camp.[8]

In late March 1960, the Herolds attended a local Republican caucus in the Grant County seat of Lancaster. They "got a huge kick out of it. That was really Democracy featuring at the grass roots," Ethel Herold wrote admiringly. Yet she also found fault in the makeup and activities of the party: "But those Republicans all seemed of the bourgeoisie; there did not seem to be a laborer in the crowd." At a Republican fundraising dinner in Platteville the following month, she observed, "Those Republicans must wake up more. They don't even sing—not even one patriotic song." Apparently, Ethel Herold believed that politics should have a strong social component and that Republican ideology should appeal to all classes of citizens. Still, the Republican Party in Wisconsin proved organized and cohesive. Richard Nixon won the Republican primary there in April 1960; since he was the only Republican on the primary ballot, he would receive all of the Wisconsin delegates' votes at the national nominating convention that summer.[9]

News of Ethel Herold's voluntarist spirit quickly spread throughout the area. While attending a meeting of the Republican Party in Cassville in September 1960, she gave an impromptu talk about the Philippines. Ethel explained to her daughter, Betsy, that she "dragged in politics & evidently hit the nail on the head as now they want me to make tape-recording to be broadcast just before election in this district." Exactly how she hit the nail on the head with the audience is not entirely clear, but her speech likely had a politically conservative bent, with a strong dose of anticommunism fervor.[10]

This political activity was in service of that year's presidential election, which turned out to be one of the most dramatic in the nation's modern history, with Democrat John F. Kennedy winning by the slenderest of margins over Republican Richard M. Nixon. That summer, bowing to pressure from their children, Ethel and Elmer Herold purchased a television set, and after watching the Republican National Convention, Ethel declared that the television had "paid off already." The couple enjoyed all of the speeches, especially Senator Barry Goldwater's "conservative concession" and the acceptance speeches of Nixon and his running mate, Henry Cabot Lodge III. "It was a stroke of politics to have [Herbert] Hoover make the first speech," Ethel wrote, "which was a masterpiece of Americanism." The television also came in handy for watching the presidential debates. "Nixon looked better than the first time & wasn't so agreeable as the first time," she opined after the second debate in October, apparently pleased that Nixon spoke more forcefully that time around. "I'm scared of that Kennedy. He & that Bob are slick ones—in fact the whole family."[11]

At the end of the 1960s, the term "Americanism" would be embraced by neoconservatives to reassert American nationalism—or patriotism, as Ethel Herold preferred—and reaffirm American "exceptionalism." Ethel had long and proudly advocated the country's exceptionalism, believing in the essential goodness and superiority of the United States. This had influenced her support of empire back in the 1920s and would continue to make her feel at home with conservatives for the rest of her life.[12]

In the end, Vice President Richard Nixon secured the Republican nomination in 1960, but Arizona Senator Barry Goldwater emerged as the light of the party's conservative wing. His book, *The Conscience of a Conservative,* sold seven hundred thousand copies in 1960 and continued to rack up sales over the next few years. Goldwater clearly outlined the beliefs of the right wing of the party, from a rejection of federal-aid programs to "Better Dead than Red" anticommunism. He also condemned foreign-aid "giveaways," which he claimed only promoted anti-American sentiment among its recipients. Ethel Herold had supported the termination of American foreign aid since the end of World War II, and she found a lot to admire in Goldwater's brand of Republicanism. After the death of Robert Taft, she likely considered the Arizona senator the voice of reason within the party and the only hope for getting the United States on the right track both domestically and internationally.[13]

Richard Nixon carried the state of Wisconsin, which must have pleased Ethel, but he lost the election. Kennedy campaigned more often in Wisconsin than any other state; yet he still lost there by over sixty-four thousand votes. Of Kennedy's national victory, Ethel lamented in February 1961, "We listen to the news or see TV every day & *groan.* What is our world coming to? And who elected Kennedy? All the people we talk with are Republicans." In southwestern Wisconsin, a predominantly Republican area of the state, it would not have been unusual for her to encounter many Republicans, and the fact that Nixon carried the state would have guaranteed that she would find a lot of Nixon supporters.[14]

Ethel Herold had never been the kind of person to give in to disappointment, though, and she continued her work for the party. Because of concern about challenges to liberalism from the left, in the early 1960s conservatives such as she were overlooked as a significant political threat. This gave them crucial time to build support at the state and local levels with little meddling from liberals. In appreciation for the Herolds' campaigning that fall, the Republicans in Potosi and Lancaster paid their way to a state Republican dinner held in Madison in April 1961. Ethel thoroughly enjoyed the evening in the state capital, for many "intelligent Republicans" attended, no one gave a "dry" speech, and there were plenty of "take-offs on the Kennedy Administration." The couple also served as delegates to the state convention held in Eau Claire the following month. Ethel told her children that the Lancaster Republicans wanted her to serve as their president, but she declined since she and Elmer did not live in Potosi year-round. Still, she thought, "it would have been fun." Her efforts over the next few years would help strengthen conservative networks within the party, culminating in the nomination of Barry Goldwater in 1964.[15]

In addition to their contributions to the Republican Party, the Herolds maintained their political education by closely monitoring national and world events from the relative seclusion of the Bonn farm, continuing subscriptions to the major newsmagazines *Time* and *U.S. News and World Report,* which they had read while living in Baguio. In May 1960, they followed the story of Gary Powers's downed U-2 plane over the Soviet Union. Ever distrustful of communists, Ethel doubted the success of Yuri Gregarin's space flight in 1961, speculating that many Russians had probably gone before him and not returned. She hoped that countries in both North and South America would join together to "knock hell out of [Fidel] Castro and take over Cuba"; however, she was unsure of what the United States should do if that were to happen. The American government's recent attempt to force Castro's overthrow with the Bay of Pigs invasion had been a disaster, which Ethel perhaps viewed as another cautionary tale about unilateralism. During a curry dinner Ethel and Elmer hosted for Grant County Republicans in May 1961, everyone ate two platefuls of the main dish "and did we ever pan that inexperienced Kennedy. We just wonder what the world is coming to with him at the head of our great country. It is for sure that Nixon would never have got involved in this Cuba mess."[16]

Considering Richard Nixon's strong anticommunist stance and the fact that he served as vice president in the administration that originally planned the Bay of Pigs, Ethel may have been projecting her own beliefs on Nixon. And such beliefs only partially embraced the "new interventionism" of most conservatives that "emphasized unilateralism and a reliance on military solutions." Espousing the older anti-interventionism of Robert Taft, Ethel rejected the use of warfare to overthrow Castro's communist regime. "The USA can't protect the whole world," she had commented a decade earlier when the government first contemplated involvement in Vietnam. She saw no reason to change her mind but continued to oppose the use of American economic aid to developing countries, a belief shared by other conservative new interventionists.[17]

Ethel's opposition to economic aid came through clearly in her criticisms of the Peace Corps. In April 1961, she addressed the school teachers of Grant County at their annual banquet, discussing the role of American teachers in the Philippines. She "linked this in with their training to be an independent country. . . . The American emphasis on the Dignity of Labor, honesty, responsibility, etc. I also touched on Kennedy's 'Peace Corps.' I made them laugh and I made them cry. They sat there so interested that I talked an hour and 10 minutes." Though it is uncertain whether sincere interest or after-dinner lethargy kept the teachers sitting quietly for over an hour, the fact that many of them asked Ethel Herold to deliver a similar talk to their local PTAs suggests that they believed she had something important to say.[18]

Though she lectured about it and had participated in a program that could be considered its forerunner, Ethel did not approve of the Peace Corps. President Kennedy had launched the volunteer organization as part of his New Frontier program, as a way of modernizing "third world" countries by introducing American education and technology. The Peace Corps attracted a lot of young people who were about the same age Ethel had been when she went to the Philippines in 1922, eager to Americanize wherever they could. In August 1961, the *Chicago Daily News* ran a series of articles about the various places the volunteers would be sent, leading off with a piece called "Filipino Eden No Paradise." It explained that four Peace Corps members were going to Santo Domingo, a town of about fifteen thousand in Albay Province on the island of Luzon to engage in a "great new experiment in American foreign aid." The volunteers would teach English to children while living just like the other Filipino teachers there, in a nipa-roofed house with no electricity, gas, or running water. The two hundred pesos they would earn each month, paid by the U.S. government, equaled the salary of Filipino teachers. The article pointed out that Filipinos wanted to learn English and that they welcomed the help of the American volunteers, quoting Philippine president Carlos Garcia: "It is good."[19]

Ethel Herold wrote an unpublished letter to the newspaper's editor in response. She challenged the notion that a posting in Santo Domingo would work any hardship on the young people, describing the location as "one of the most delightful Provinces of the Philippines," where they would "have the most interesting and happiest two years of their lives." But most of all, Ethel Herold objected that the United States government would "pay for their fun." She sketched out a brief history of the Thomasites and American teachers in the Philippines, explaining that back then it did not cost three thousand dollars to "administer" each teacher. She suggested that if Kennedy intended to use the Peace Corps to make "Americans abroad to get closer to the common people," he could save a lot of money by instructing all U.S. employees in foreign countries to "get out of their air-conditioned comforts and Cadillacs and get to know the people."[20]

This statement about air-conditioned comforts suggests that Ethel Herold was familiar with William J. Lederer and Eugene Burdick's *The Ugly American,* the 1958 best-selling novel that instructed readers about the proper way to behave while living and working in an Asian country. This book, along with the popular periodicals *Reader's Digest* and the *Saturday Review,* functioned as guides "through a new international order of U.S. global expansion and Third World colonization" for middle-class American readers. The magazines in particular promoted a kind of cultural transnationalism by encouraging their readers to see the connections between themselves and people in other countries. Ethel's lectures around Wisconsin functioned in a similar manner, and she exemplified the qualities that Lederer and Burdick promoted in their novel for every American working in Asia: "(1) Know the area (before going). (2) Know necessary techniques. (3) Know U.S. policy. (4) Glorify in having a tough job—not just look for a luxury vacation."[21]

As her letter to the *Daily News* demonstrated, Ethel believed that her years of expatriate living in the Philippines qualified her as an expert, so she did not hesitate to criticize the Peace Corps program. "Filipino children do not need to be taught games," she pointed out, "they have many of their own invention. Nor do they need to be taught music, music and rhythm are born in them. 'Little seminars' in English could be classed as propaganda." Echoing Barry Goldwater's point about the limits of U.S. foreign aid, she argued that Filipinos, like other people in underdeveloped countries, needed "more and better food," not a "smattering of young people" sent in through a government program that "seems just another waste of American taxpayers' money." Her defense of Filipino culture nevertheless contains a hint of racism and is almost entirely undercut by her concern over the cost of the Peace Corps.[22]

The vast differences between the Philippines of the 1920s and of the 1960s, brought on by the end of colonialism, remained largely unacknowledged in this letter. The American education Ethel Herold had once so highly prized for Filipino students, considered by many to be the cornerstone of the imperial relationship, she now wrote off as inappropriate and wasteful. She did not admit that what had made her teaching experience so enjoyable—and indeed possible—was the elevated status associated with being a representative of colonial power: she earned a salary substantially higher than her Filipino counterparts, lived in a spacious home that had some modern conveniences of the time and was staffed with servants, and belonged to a country club. With the Peace Corps, American teachers would have none of these benefits; they would live like Filipinos, which, in Ethel's view, was unacceptable. Expatriate Americans should get out of their air-conditioned comforts, but they should not have to actually give them up.

Even so, Ethel Herold maintained an intellectual curiosity about other places and other cultures, and she traveled as extensively as possible. She prized her American citizenship and still believed in the exceptionalism of the United States, but she also continued to value the presence of Americans throughout the world. In 1963, she and Elmer planned an around-the-world trip, focusing on the Middle East and Africa. They prepared by reading as many books on these countries as they could, and Ethel gave reports on some of what she read to local women's groups, presumably to share what she had learned. The 1960s were volatile years for African countries as they struggled with their transition from colonial status to independence. Like many other Americans, Ethel expressed hope that these new governments would reject communism, and she praised South Africa as "one of the most anti-communistic countries in the whole world—we can't depend on the loyalty of any of those other African countries." Acknowledging the existence of apartheid, she nevertheless believed that the South African government treated blacks "all right" and that the United Nations ought not to interfere with its race relations.[23]

The Herolds left the United States in October 1963 and returned the following April, traveling from Cairo to Cape Town to Hong Kong, then on to the Philippines and Japan, making numerous stops between the main cities. After a late-night dinner in Luxor, Egypt, from which they retired early, Elmer Herold, now seventy years old, woke his wife, complaining of chest pains. Assuming that he might be coming down with pneumonia, she gave him two Bufferin tablets with a glass of water (which may have saved his life that night), used bath towels to soak up his perspiration, and covered him warmly. Even though he said he felt better, Ethel kept her husband in bed the following day where she "fed and petted him along" until they had to catch their train to Aswan in the early evening. Through Jim Halsema, now an officer with the U.S. Information Agency in Cairo,

Elmer had received permission to visit the building site of the Aswan Dam, and he had no intention of missing it. Although Elmer quickly recovered, he had not been on the brink of pneumonia; rather, he had experienced the first of the heart problems that would ultimately lead to his death.[24]

While in Nairobi, Ethel Herold encountered Kenya's first contingent of Peace Corps volunteers, observing firsthand the program she had so soundly criticized. She thought that they "look so youthful—especially the girls. They seem so very fair & helpless. The boys seem more capable. It's a great risk sending such young girls out into places like this . . . but I'm sure powerful few will stay here." Since volunteers had to be college graduates, these "young girls" could not have been much younger than Ethel Herold was when she and Elmer first went to the Philippines in 1922. And though she still did not approve of the Peace Corps, she lauded the actions of the British and other European powers that had colonized Africa or "it would all be back in the 16th century." She did not acknowledge any similarities between the projects of the Peace Corps and the intrusions of colonial powers.[25]

The trip culminated in a visit to the Philippines in February 1964, and for the first time the Herolds were visitors rather than residents. After five days of parties with friends in Manila—with the city still showing signs of wartime damage—they headed north, stopping first at one of their old favorite vacation spots, Juaquin's Beach Resort near Bauang, to spend some time relaxing and swimming. Then they took a converted jeep and drove on to Bangued, Abra. It had been forty-two years since they had made that trip for the first time, and Ethel must have been keenly aware of the passage of time, though she claimed that much was the same in Bangued, "only an abundance of children." The sight of Luisa Bersamin, now in her early eighties, startled Ethel, for the Filipina looked "shorter and more dried up than before." The Herolds stayed with Mrs. Bersamin, taking time to visit with their former servants, including Tuding, as well as many of their old students. They gave speeches at the high school assembly before finally heading up to Baguio.[26]

The Herolds stayed in the bishop's cottage on the grounds of the Brent School, an honor accorded perhaps as a thank you for Elmer's many years of service on the school's Board of Regents. Although they had been away for a few years and recognized that Baguio was no longer their home, the couple seemed to easily slide back into the colonial mindset. For example, the bishop employed a servant at the cottage, but the Herolds had one of their former servants accompany them because "she knew our likes and dislikes." They ate many of their meals in the common dining room, where Ethel noticed the change in the school's student body—the presence of many different nationalities and races as compared to before the war when only white students were admitted. It was a change that did not set well with her, as her "separate but equal" philosophy had been little changed by decolonization and by the growing civil rights movement. Brent's integration signaled to her yet again just how much the Philippines had changed without American influence—and not for the better.[27]

It was a whirlwind visit: "Every time we go to town or out anywhere—we are deluged with old friends. We are booked up with several parties in our honor." The couple traveled up to KM 102 so that Elmer could make a ceremonial inspection of the mill at Benguet. The workers and school children constructed a big welcoming arch over Halsema Road, and they all turned out to meet the couple and then treated the visitors to a grand feast, a ritual that was repeated at Bontoc. Back in Baguio, to honor their years of community service, the Rotary Club invited Elmer to a meeting, and the Monday Afternoon Club women asked Ethel to conduct a meeting. She declined, however, later admitting that she "would have been too near tears."[28]

She enjoyed their time in Baguio but concluded, "You can't go back to yesterday. It was so different not living in our own house, and not driving our own car. Our oldest and best friends were gone. Even on the streets and market it was different—we were stared at as strangers. This was our home town, we had grown up with it twice: once before the war and painfully after the war. We should not be looked at with surprise or even disdain." What Ethel recognized—and what she took as almost a personal affront—was the fact that, in their independence, the Filipinos had completely claimed their own country. Now Americans were tolerated but not revered, a climate much different from what she and her husband had encountered when they first arrived in 1922.[29]

The letters Ethel sent to her children while she and Elmer vacationed in Baguio spoke more of the past and of how old friends were getting along than of current political events. And the Herolds found the visit physically and emotionally exhausting. Now at the tail end of their long trip, they were anxious to get home. Ethel Herold described the farewell parties in Manila as "very nice—but all too nostalgic—too many tears," and in their haste to return to Potosi, the couple decided to fly rather than take a ship. They even cut short a stopover in Japan, which always had been, ironically, one of their favorite countries to visit.[30]

After returning from that around-the-world tour, Ethel Herold's interest in Philippine politics became intertwined with her overall concern with world affairs. By the early 1960s, Philippine politics were a jumbled knot of party factions, personal squabbles, and seemingly endless rivalries of every stripe. Since she no longer lived there and probably did not know many of the people involved, Ethel Herold did not keep up with the details of President Carlos Garcia's attempt to hold on to his position in the face of a rising challenge from his own vice president, Diosdado Macapagal, a member of the opposition Liberal Party. Even Presidents Eisenhower and Kennedy paid little attention to the Philippines' internal political struggles; still, the CIA apparently continued its attempts to influence the outcomes of the islands' legislative and presidential elections to ensure that communism did not take hold.[31]

If keeping track of Philippine politics had become too confusing for Ethel Herold, she was careful to maintain the social and cultural connections she had forged with the islands. As she had favored wearing jewelry and clothing from the Philippines and other countries she and Elmer had visited and as she continued to decorate their home with items from those places, she also cultivated personal ties whenever she could. For instance, in 1964, not long after returning from their world tour, the Herolds invited a group of thirty Filipino students studying at the University of Wisconsin in Madison to the Bonn farm. Ethel prepared a lunch of chicken salad and baked beans, and she arranged for the students to visit a nearby dairy farm. The visit culminated with a lawn supper at the church.

Middlebrow intellectuals of the time may have interpreted this event as Ethel Herold's acceptance of cultural variety among groups of human beings rather than as an expression of American superiority. And it is likely that she organized the outing as a form of cultural exchange: the Americans shared farming information and samples of local cuisine, and the students reciprocated by dressing in Filipino costumes and dancing. But at the end of the evening Ethel joined the students in singing the U.S. national anthem: "I sang with them for 3 verses, but cried out the last one." Though the song choice could be construed as a part of the cultural exchange, it also reflects her persistence in maintaining the old imperial ties. The song served as a reminder to the foreign guests about how they came to be where they were.[32]

The Conservative Republican

The 1964 presidential election raised Ethel Herold's hopes that conservative Republicans would finally gain control of the party and of the country and would, presumably, stop wasting taxpayers' money. Her participation in the Goldwater campaign suggests how the actions of anticommunist women helped redefine prevailing assumptions about women as political actors in the postwar period. Their extraordinary organizational abilities and keen grasp of the issues turned conservative women into influential political players. At the beginning of 1963, already planning ahead for the election, Barry Goldwater and other right-wing Republicans sensed that Kennedy might be vulnerable. Offering American voters a clear conservative alternative to a Kennedy-Johnson reelection just might bring Goldwater into the White House. After Kennedy's assassination in November, Goldwater briefly reevaluated his chances of securing the Republican nomination; he then made his candidacy official in January 1964. "I will offer a choice, not an echo," he promised voters.[33]

Goldwater's candidacy statement became a slogan for conservatives. In the summer of 1964, Ethel Herold read Phyllis Schlafly's book, *A Choice Not an Echo,* and immediately wrote to her son and daughter, asking if they had read it yet. "Who is she?" Ethel wondered about Schlafly. "We are all for her." Schlafly, the mother of six children with a master's degree in government from Washington University in St. Louis, had already lost an election for a congressional seat and had recently emerged as a powerhouse among Republican women. The president of the Illinois Federation of Republican Women in 1960, she went on four years later to become the first vice president of the National Federation of Republican Women. Schlafly self-published her book in 1964, a condemnation of the secret "kingmakers" who controlled the Republican national conventions from behind the scenes and who planned to dilute Republican ideology to the point where a merger with the Democrats would be possible. She was especially critical of a U.S. foreign policy that "allowed" for communist victories around the world.[34]

The only hope for the Republican Party, Phyllis Schlafly contended, was Barry Goldwater's nomination. Ethel Herold was just one of many Republican grassroots workers attracted to Schlafly's argument, which was plainly written in a popular style, free of academic jargon. And Ethel was one of many who helped Schlafly sell her book through word of mouth: Ethel wrote to her son and daughter at least one more time and asked if they had read it. It is easy to see why Schlafly's book so captivated her. While its message was, of course, the most important thing, Ethel could also closely identify with the author: a white, middle-class wife and mother, well-educated, politically aware, and involved in women's organizations. She was exactly the kind of woman who could help drum up so much support for Schlafly's publication that it sold three and a half million copies by election time.[35]

The fact that Ethel's letters to her grown children regularly contained commentary on American politics shows that she had not abdicated her role as maternal educator, that she continued to function, quite literally, as a Republican mother. This was especially true in 1964 during an election that seemed particularly important to her, but she routinely prodded her daughter, Betsy, about her political voluntarism and enthusiastically supported Betsy's husband, Karl Heimke, when he became interested in holding local office. According to Ethel, American citizens, male and female, should participate in politics.

Goldwater faced stiff challenges from Republican rivals Nelson Rockefeller and Henry Cabot Lodge during the primaries. Ethel closely followed all of them, wondering if the Republicans were trying to "commit suicide" with all of their infighting. She and her husband had become "disgusted" with Lodge mostly because of how he had acquitted himself as ambassador to Vietnam, but they lauded Goldwater as an "honest man." She wished the Republicans would "yell out against that slick Johnson and all the things the Democrats have done and are doing." Ethel Herold criticized the Democrats for putting too much emphasis on civil rights issues to "cover up all their foreign mistakes," presumably a comment about the deteriorating situation in Vietnam. Then she proposed, "Instead of foreign aid why not increase our police force and do away with crime in the USA?" This last comment suggests that Ethel represented the majority of conservatives whose overriding concern about the communist menace eventually dissolved into anxiety about domestic moral issues. Yet, in fact, her conservatism remained largely political, focused on the size of the federal government, economic policies, and the role of the United States in the world.[36]

The Herolds watched the Republican National Convention in mid-July of 1964, pulling for Barry Goldwater's nomination. "We listened to practically every word of the convention," Ethel wrote to her children. "We are thoroughly disgusted with Lodge and Rockefeller and Ike. Especially Rockefeller." She did not specifically mention Rockefeller's fairly recent divorce and remarriage, which cost him female supporters who disapproved of his "immoral" actions, an indication that she cared more about policy. However, she believed that Lodge's "laziness" and Rockefeller's "jealousy" of other GOP candidates were exacerbating the kinds of party and voter divisions which, along with "Chicago's crooked balloting," had led to Nixon's loss to Kennedy in 1960. Ethel and Elmer Herold lauded Goldwater's acceptance speech, in which he said, "I would remind you that extremism in the defense of liberty is no vice. And let me remind you that moderation in the pursuit of justice is no virtue." This led Ethel to muse, "What is so wrong about being extreme on some things?"[37]

Ethel Herold believed in and admired the Republican candidate, though that put her in the minority of Republican women. While Goldwater routinely praised women's important contributions to the party and focused on their interest in religion and morality, most Republican women simply did not like him. But though Goldwater emphasized female qualities in the political arena that Ethel Herold probably considered less important than an intellectual, educated understanding of the issues, she liked Goldwater, precisely for his positions on economics and the size and function of the federal government. And she was not complimentary about those who disagreed with her. "Now I'll have to get busy on Goldwater," she told her children right after the convention. "These stupid Americans. Letting that slick Johnson hoodwink them. If we don't battle this state socialism quick, it will be too late."[38]

She shared these opinions outside of her family as well, defending Barry Goldwater at every opportunity, and she was especially outraged by a 1964 *Saturday Evening Post* editorial titled "Why Lyndon Johnson Must be Elected." The magazine's editors claimed that the Republican Party had "shirked and betrayed its duty" to American voters by nominating a man "manifestly unqualified" to serve as President. The editorial described Goldwater as a man of the past, too single-minded in his pursuit to shrink the national government, "a grotesque burlesque of the conservative he pretends to be." For the good of the Republican Party, it concluded, "we hope that Goldwater is crushingly defeated." It was a brutally blunt piece.[39]

"Never in my forty years of reading the POST, have I read such a vile editorial," Ethel Herold wrote in an equally blunt letter to the magazine. "And this tirade is against Senator Barry Goldwater who has the courage to stand out for the freedom of the American people against the creeping socialistic government of President Johnson. Is the POST being influenced by the Kennedy or Johnson millions? It is for certain that the processes which produced this editorial were not intellectual." Ethel correctly predicted to her family that her letter would not be published, but this did not represent unwillingness by the *Post* to air opposing viewpoints. The first two October issues contained several letters about the editorial with a nearly equal balance of pro and con opinions. Ethel's was probably one of many expressing disappointment that the magazine chose to support Lyndon Johnson. Still, she pressed on to promote Goldwater. Whenever she gave talks that fall, she wore her "gold H2O pin boldly" and promoted his candidacy at every opportunity. (The Goldwater "droplet" jewelry—pins, earrings, and necklaces—had been designed by a Tennessee banker and quickly became popular fundraising items for the campaign.) Yet Ethel Herold became "so disgusted with the partiality of the press and the T.V. And even some protestant churches are against Barry because of his stand against foreign aid, civil rights, and the U.N."[40]

Though Ethel Herold must have been disappointed with President Johnson's election, this particular sentiment did not surface in any of her letters. But she seemed prepared for it. At the end of September, she admitted, "I don't see how there is hope for Goldwater—but we have not given up." She and Elmer continued to work on Goldwater's campaign right up until the end. Grassroots campaigners formed Citizens for Goldwater-Miller (the latter was U.S. Representative William E. Miller of New York, Goldwater's running mate) and proclaimed a "law and morality" crusade, mostly to draw in people who usually did not get involved in politics. Part of that effort included the formation of Mothers for a Moral America, which purported to promote "good government" through small government and individual initiative. Goldwater staffers hoped to tap into the vast women's organizational networks to present their candidate as the guardian of home and family. The tactic did not work. Contributing to Barry Goldwater's defeat were women voters who, for the first time since 1952, failed to vote in higher numbers than men for the Republican presidential candidate. Despite Goldwater's appeals to domesticity, most female voters were alienated by what they perceived as his extremism.[41]

Barry Goldwater's 1964 presidential campaign demonstrated the power of conservative Republicans to take control of their party; but they failed to effectively compromise with the more moderate factions of the party, and most of all they failed to present an appealing platform to American voters. The backlash against Goldwater conservatism surfaced as early as the end of the Republican National Convention that year. Concerns over his extremism survived well beyond the 1964 election and came close to obliterating what conservatives had worked so hard for in the 1950s and '60s. Although Ethel Herold had not objected to extremism and was a firm conservative, she had not been totally unrealistic about Goldwater's chances for success, at least initially. Alabama governor George Wallace, a dedicated segregationist, attracted 34 percent of the votes cast in the Wisconsin Democratic primary, indicating a conservative bent that cut across party lines. Still, presidential election results in Wisconsin showed that Goldwater did well only among the "hard-core" Republicans—those sixty-five or older with a college education and a continuing commitment to anticommunism. Democrat Lyndon Johnson swept the state with 62 percent of the vote. Like voters nationwide, Wisconsinites firmly rejected Goldwater conservatism, which must have been a huge disappointment to Ethel Herold.[42]

The Goldwater campaign marked the high tide of Ethel's political activism. During the mid-1960s, a variety of health problems (including glaucoma, which made reading and writing difficult) began to slow her down. Seventy-two years old in 1968, she kept close tabs on the presidential election news and the other traumatic events of that year. She pulled for Richard Nixon to become the Republican Party's presidential candidate and predicted that Robert Kennedy's challenge to Eugene McCarthy for the Democratic nomination would help Nixon's chances. She and her husband spent two hours watching the televised funeral of Martin Luther King on April 9, which she labeled "impressive." Carefully distinguishing his approach to civil rights from activists like Stokely Carmichael, she speculated, "If the Negro people as well as the whites follow King's philosophy of PEACE, our dear USA may get along with a minimum of violence. There are enough intelligent negros to carry on." She did not object to civil rights but rather to methods that provoked violence.[43]

Ethel labeled the televised Republican Convention of 1968 "sazzletazzle," criticized the boisterous entertainment that augmented the political speeches, and regretted sending a contribution to the party. Still, she supported Nixon, writing on the eve of the election, "We just hope NIXON makes it tomorrow. If he does not, we will feel very sorry for our dear United States." Nixon managed to beat Hubert Humphrey, bringing a Republican into the White House for the first time since Eisenhower. That alone must have given Ethel Herold hope for the immediate future—hope that the liberal agenda of the Johnson administration had not killed off conservatism in the United States and that conservatism would put the country back on the right path.[44]

Most of Ethel Herold's political involvement was directly with the Republican Party of Wisconsin, through fundraisers and caucuses she attended with Elmer. The Herolds represented the hundreds of married couples who organized their friendships and socializing around right-wing politics in the 1960s. These kinds of mixed-gender functions had always attracted her, going back to her days as a suffrage activist at Lawrence College. But she also interacted with the Republican Women of Grant County, attending monthly luncheons with them when she could. She was one of thousands of women who worked through the National Federation of Republican Women and the Women's Division of the Republican National Committee and made significant contributions to the party. In the postwar years, the National Federation, an organization semiautonomous from the party, embraced Republican right-wing ideology even as the majority of women who voted Republican expressed more moderate views that combined ideas of individualism and self-reliance with an activist government. Ethel Herold's conservative leanings, then, made her just the kind of activist the National Federation courted after the war to increase its membership.[45]

However, as Ethel and Elmer Herold aged, physical infirmities increasingly restricted even these volunteer activities. For thirteen "glorious summers" after Elmer's retirement, the couple entertained friends and family at the Bonn farm, participated in numerous Mason and Eastern Star functions, and joined a variety of other local groups. Elmer attended Rotary meetings in Dubuque, Iowa, and in Platteville, Wisconsin, while his wife gave so many talks that she was able to donate five hundred dollars from her fees to the Monday Club in the first stateside year alone. To Ethel, this was "perfect country living." Although sequestered on the Bonn farm, the Herolds were situated close enough to Potosi, Lancaster, Platteville, and Dubuque to participate in numerous activities, which they cut down on over the years. In the late winter of 1961, for instance, when Ethel was almost sixty-five years old, she was diagnosed with a duodenal ulcer and gallstones. But even burdened by age and illness, any length of inactivity caused her twinges of guilt. As she wrote to her children in 1962, "I really feel guilty having such a life of ease for so long. These retired people from the P.I. surely have a round of fun, etc. I don't want to lead that kind of life yet. I'm really anxious to get back to the farm & actually do something."[46]

The Herolds' unceasing contributions to their communities did not go unrecognized. Lawrence University in Appleton, Wisconsin, awarded Elmer its Alumni Distinguished Service Award at commencement on June 11, 1967, the fiftieth anniversary of his graduation. "We could both have dropped dead with surprise & glee," Ethel wrote to Bill and Betsy. The citation read in part, "Elmer Herold, your capacity for selfless good work has brought you international acclaim. You have labored with the Igorot people in the Philippines as teacher, author, businessman, public servant, and patron of the arts. Your dedication caused you to remain with your responsibilities during times of grave peril. Even internment by the Japanese forces during World War II did not halt your efforts on behalf of your Igorot and Filipino friends." Almost all of these things could have been said about Ethel Herold as well, of course, but she did not receive an award. Still, she loved and admired her husband, and she basked in the glory he received.[47]

This high point was soon followed by a low. In late August of that year, while attending a Republican Party picnic, Elmer was hit by a recurrence of the chest pains he had suffered in Luxor four years earlier. When a battery of tests at the local hospital could not pinpoint a cause, Ethel called Dr. Beulah Ream Allen, one of her friends from Baguio now living in California; she explained Elmer's symptoms and the results of his tests and asked for her opinion. Dr. Allen concluded that Elmer Herold had a dissecting aortic aneurysm and advised Ethel to take him to an artery specialist in Chicago. There Elmer learned that he could have another attack at any time, but there was nothing that could be done for him. A pair of operations might repair the problem, but the doctor believed that he could not survive one operation, telling Ethel Herold to take her husband home and "with care, he might live quite awhile." Despite the devastating news, she found "it was wonderful being home with Elmer. Even if he could not drive the car or do a lot of things, he was alive and we were happy. In fact he was quite sexy."[48]

But by early November 1967, Elmer Herold was back in Chicago, undergoing an operation that the doctors gave him a 5-percent chance of surviving. He did better than expected and remained in the hospital recuperating until after Thanksgiving. To his wife's great relief, "Elmer's constitution of iron had pulled him through." After convalescing at their daughter's home in Wheaton, Illinois, the couple flew to Apache Junction, Arizona, in January 1968 for the remainder of the winter, hoping that the sunshine would further speed Elmer's recovery.[49]

The pattern of quiet country living on the Bonn farm and winter vacations in warmer climates continued for the next two and a half years, despite another heart attack that Elmer suffered in early 1969 while the couple was in Arizona. A back injury put Ethel in the hospital for nineteen days late that summer, and in addition to glaucoma, her left retina was deteriorating. Still, she did not completely withdraw from community activities, though she scaled back her speaking engagements, spending most of her leisure time playing bridge and attending Republican Party, Ladies' Aid, and Eastern Star events.

On June 24, 1970, the Herolds celebrated their golden wedding anniversary at the old Thomas house on the hill in Potosi, and Ethel observed that "no poetry has ever been written to describe those 50 years." They would have little more than a year left together. By early 1971, it was clear that Elmer's health had begun its final, rapid decline. Yet the couple remained as active as possible, attending commencement festivities at Lawrence University and traveling to Elmer's hometown, Prairie du Chien, where he was honored for his fifty-year membership in the Masons. On August 29, after a houseful of guests departed, the couple "just monkeyed around doing nothing. . . . We sat on the cool terrace and talked of our travels, watched the wrens, watched busy Manang [the dog] policing the area. We didn't even care to hear the 10 o'clock news—it was just so nice to sit and hold hands and enjoy being together." But shortly after Elmer got into bed, he was hit with a terrific chest pain, and he died the next morning at the Lancaster hospital. Ethel Herold buried her husband with a small bouquet of flowers from his eight grandchildren, an American flag, his 32-degree Mason ring, his diamond Rotary pin, and a small handkerchief embroidered with "Ethel." On his tombstone were etched the words: "Humanitarian—Patriot."[50]

Widowhood

After the funeral, Ethel Herold first went to Overland Park, Kansas, where her daughter, Betsy, and son-in-law, Karl Heimke, were currently living; then she traveled to New Orleans to spend some time with her son, Bill, and his wife, Joanne. "With worn-out bones, worn-out digestive system, worn-out eyes, I just about fell by the wayside—often wishing I had," Ethel wrote. "Life without my husband of 51 years was almost unbearable."[51]

She lived for another seventeen years without her beloved husband. In the first year following his death, her eyesight and handwriting further deteriorated, causing her to rely more on the telephone as a means of communication; thus, her written correspondence dwindled. Television substituted for newspapers and magazines. Ethel watched the national news and the *Today* show but also enjoyed *All in the Family* and the *Lawrence Welk Show* for entertainment. Unable to drive, she found it impractical to live at the Bonn farmhouse, even in the summer, so she rented out both the house and the land and lived for part of the year with her niece in Potosi in the house in which she had grown up. Ethel spent more time away, though, visiting friends and relatives, increasing the amount of time with each of her children and with her favorite nephew, who owned and managed an apartment complex on a lake in Kirkland, Washington. During the summer of 1972, nearly a year after her husband's death, she recalled the happy way in which the previous summer had begun, but "little did I know what calamity lay ahead of me. Looking back I don't see how I ever stood it. Without Elmer, my world suddenly collapsed."[52]

Politics distracted her from some of her sorrow. She closely followed President Nixon's foreign policy, predicting that his trip to China in February 1972 would further negotiations with North Vietnam over the end to the war there and the return of American prisoners of war. She expressed shock over the assassination attempt on Alabama governor George Wallace. She found the "Eagleton affair interesting"—the disclosure that Democratic presidential nominee George McGovern's running mate had been treated for psychiatric problems—speculating that it would mean more votes for Nixon, regardless of whether or not Thomas Eagleton remained on the ticket. As usual, she watched the Republican Convention on television, praising speeches by Ronald Reagan and Spiro Agnew but expressing disappointment in Nixon's because "there was nothing left for him to say." Ethel admired the pageantry of Nixon's second inauguration and was optimistic that peace was in fact in hand in Vietnam.[53]

Revelations about the Watergate break-in did not change her mind about Nixon or the Republicans. A speech Nixon gave in April 1973 almost moved her to tears as she believed he was "entirely innocent of any of that Watergate stink pot." Ethel Herold blamed the *Washington Post* for creating the scandal and predicted that "there is no telling when it will stop and what a lot of innocent people will be drawn in to and be stained." As for Illinois senator Charles Percy, "I could choke him for even mentioning the word impeachment." While watching the televised Senate hearings, she came to the conclusion that "it is not exactly right to bug, but both parties have done it—we were just unfortunate to be caught." She followed the developments closely all spring and summer.[54]

"I am so useless" was Ethel Herold's biggest complaint. She was almost seventy-seven years old and various physical infirmities prevented her from participating in the kinds of organized activities on which she had thrived her entire life. She could only spend so many hours per day writing, watching television, and visiting. Although her family and friends had been most solicitous since her husband's death, she felt like a burden to them. In the spring of 1973, Ethel decided to move to the Beatitudes, a retirement community in Phoenix, Arizona: "I could see well enough to get my breakfast. . . . If I know where things are I can do a little cooking on electricity . . . [and] I can eat one or all of my meals there in the dining room." She assured her children that they had done everything possible to make her feel welcome in their homes but pointed out, "Your Dad always said we should not live with our children—even how good you are to me."[55]

She settled in her retirement apartment in November 1973 and told her children, "Oh, Oh, Oh you should see my apartment with the 6 Amorsolos [paintings], the map of Baguio, two of Bertha [Bonn's] pictures and some of Elmer's awards. Really it looks quite different and I just sit and admire it, even though I cannot see all very well. But I know those precious scenes are there." These Filipino and American items symbolized both her transpacific, imperial life and her enduring love for Elmer Herold. Ethel took two walks a day, attended various programs offered at the complex, joined bridge tournaments, sang with the BeatiTones, gave lectures, and listened to recorded books. In a burst of self-reflection, she admitted, "When it comes down to it, it might be a good thing that I can't see very well. It slows me down, makes me more careful with my opinions, and very selective with my friends. Otherwise, I might begin to run this place and people would not like me for being so assertive."[56]

Limiting her reading to the *National Geographic* and *U.S. News & World Report,* Ethel gave up on other magazines that focused too much on "Women's Lib, Negro problems, sex . . . [and] high finance." These particular issues never seemed to interest her as they did social conservatives. She cultivated a circle of friends ("All Republicans. However, not narrow minded.") with whom she discussed world and national events. Lula Detrick and Edna Ferguson, two women who had also lived in the Philippines and shared many of Ethel's views, quickly became her closest friends. As a loyal Republican, she still closely followed Watergate developments, and by early 1974 she realized that impeachment was a possibility. She wondered, "Why doesn't congress get on with the impeachment and get it over with.

No one has ever heard of such a minute investigation in this whole world. There is not enough evidence to impeach Nixon, and I hope to heaven he does not resign. The press says let's get the country going again, well when did it ever stop?" Interpreting the scandal as purely partisan politics, she claimed that Nixon was "not just sticking up for himself, but for PRESIDENCY as opposed to Congress and the Courts. If he gave in too easily all future presidents would criticize him for it." Perhaps because she had been expecting impeachment or had become wrapped up in her late-summer travel plans, Ethel did not comment on Nixon's resignation in August, only later lamenting, "When will TV stop persecuting Nixon?" Four years later, on a flight to St. Louis, she would defend Nixon to her seatmate, predicting (incorrectly thus far) that the former president "will go down in History as a great American."[57]

Death increasingly occupied Ethel Herold's thoughts. Seventy-eight years old in 1974, she had outlived her husband, her parents and siblings, and many of her friends. Although she mostly enjoyed her time at the Beatitudes because she could participate in its many activities and command good audiences when she gave talks about her travels, she worried about ending up in the nursing-home part of the facility, unable to care for herself. After a pleasant round of visits in Kansas and Wisconsin in 1974, she returned to the Beatitudes, only to have trouble settling back in as she "wondered why I had left the world of life to come back to a place where death is the only thing to look forward to."[58]

By the mid-1970s, most of Ethel Herold's letters were filled with information about her health, visits to the doctor, and visits from friends. She continued annual trips to see her children and to vacation in Potosi with her niece, but the arrangements became more complicated as she required more assistance. Ethel Herold still followed politics, however, commenting in late 1976, "I am almost staggered with the thought that Jimmy Carter is to begin to run our government. God help us and US too. I hope he has sense enough to keep on a lot of Republicans, especially Kissinger. And I hope Mrs. Carter does not try to run things. What does she know about anything? Mrs. Truman and Mrs. Eisenhower were wise to keep in the background and use their influence there." She came to view Carter as a moral man, and even as she despaired over the Iranian hostage crisis, she believed he was doing all he could. As Ronald Reagan became a frontrunner for the Republican presidential nomination in 1980, Ethel expressed lukewarm support, maybe more so from the fatigue of old age rather than from political conviction: "I hope he turns out better than I think he will. But he is the best we have to choose from." It would be the last presidential election that she would ever follow.[59]

Remembrance and Writing

More than twenty years after her liberation from a wartime internment camp, Ethel Herold expressed a wish to see the movie *Gone With the Wind,* which she had seen once in the Philippines, just before the war. The story of the destruction and rebuilding of the American South during the Civil War period had taken on a deeper personal meaning for her, one that was colored by the romance and sentimentality of U.S. imperialism. "Yes, our life was like that too," she observed. "Such heavenly bliss before the war and then never again." Baguio was to Ethel Herold as Tara was to Scarlett O'Hara, both women drawn back after the war to the land of her heart. And, like Scarlett at Tara, Ethel worked with all of her might to bring Baguio back to its former glory. But it could never be the same again, and Ethel devoted considerable time to thinking and writing about her experiences as a citizen of empire.[60]

Writing always had an important place in Ethel Thomas Herold's life. As a child, she first learned about the Philippines from her brother Bart Thomas's letters, and she understood the value of those letters in documenting his experiences. In the early twentieth century, letters served as the main form of communication between family and friends. Without them, personal news would not travel. When Ethel went off to the Philippines in 1922 with Elmer, she decided to write similar missives home because she remembered how much her parents enjoyed them. She also kept a diary to detail additional thoughts and observations.

After the Herolds returned to the United States in 1924, Ethel attempted to turn these personal writings into public stories. With Elmer settled back into a teaching job in Kankakee, Illinois, that September, she decided to spend her time writing a book about their travels in the Philippines. Since she was no longer teaching, she hoped to add to their income with her authorial earnings. She purchased a portable typewriter and checked out some travel books from the library. After reading through those books, Elmer told his wife that her diary "would be more interesting than any of those." She quite agreed. In fact, she pointed out that she "had purposely written my diary in such a way that about all it would need was careful copying" into story format.[61]

With her new typewriter, Ethel Herold banged out an original and two carbon copies of her travel book. Having identified three publishing houses that might be interested in the manuscript, she was so intent to finish it that "some days I typed so much that my hands ached." When the couple headed up to Prairie du Chien for Christmas, she brought along the portions of the book she had finished and read them to family members. "Elmer's dad thought it great," she boasted. Buoyed by these positive responses and time-pressed because of their decision to return to the Philippines, Ethel finished her book and sent it off to the three selected publishers at the beginning of March 1925.[62]

"I blush now when I think of how *awful* they were," Ethel Herold later wrote. "I don't see why the 2 carbon copies were not dumped in a waste basket and never returned." Still, at the time she was so confident that the book would be published that she felt "a little panic-stricken" that all three publishers would accept the manuscript and then start lawsuits over who owned the rights. "I could always find something to worry about," she admitted, but the two carbon copies "came right back C.O.D." Though she did not mention the names of the publishing houses to which they had been sent, the original copy of her manuscript went off to the *Saturday Evening Post.* That also came back C.O.D., but an editor had taken the time to tell her that she had "some interesting material" that she should carve up into short stories. While Ethel felt better about this rejection, she had no more time to work on the book because she and Elmer were off to the Philippines again. If she regretted this abrupt end to her fledgling literary career, she did not acknowledge it. Perhaps knowing that she would help her husband write his science textbook consoled her.[63]

Ethel's next attempt at writing came after the Japanese attacked the Philippines in December 1941. Using a blank copybook and various loose sheets of paper, she once again started keeping a journal in which she documented the family's experiences with internment and liberation. She began editing the diary after the war. In a parenthetical aside to her December 16, 1941, entry, Ethel wrote, "This tenth page was stopped purposely without punctuation in January 1946, now on September 24, 1946, I am 'back' and sincerely hope I have been doing what might have been implied in the last statement on the tenth page," a reference to returning to Baguio after the war. "Anyway," she continued, "with the urging of Billy and Betsy, I am going to copy the rest of the diary, but only for family consumption."[64]

By 1949, Ethel Herold had typed, edited, and expanded on the diary. She intended this as a legacy for her children, determined that they and their children should never forget the horrors of war. Florence Heald, the wife of Elmer's former boss and one of Ethel's closest friends, was among the first people to read the typed version of the diary. Ethel figured that because of Florence's many years in Baguio, she would be most curious about what had happened to her friends and neighbors during internment. Florence then passed the diary along to Bill and Betsy. Apparently, no one offered Ethel any negative criticism, which she took as a good sign about the truthfulness of her account. It would be another thirty years before she would regret not pursuing publication for a wider audience.[65]

While Ethel Herold restricted her diary's circulation, other former internees began to publish accounts of their wartime experiences. Perhaps the most famous was that of Agnes Newton Keith, an American woman who had been a journalist before the war. Agnes, her British husband, Harry, and their young son, George, had survived a grueling captivity by the Japanese on the isolated island of Borneo, a British colony. Keith crafted a spare but powerful narrative of their ordeal, which quickly became a bestseller in 1947 and was translated into many languages. Officials at Twentieth Century Fox studios had faith that the popularity of the memoir would translate into a successful film and cast Claudette Colbert, a highly regarded mature female film star, to portray Agnes Keith.[66]

In March 1950, Ethel Herold and her children discussed in their letters the just-released film version of *Three Came Home*. Ethel expressed skepticism that any movie could accurately depict the horrors of internment. "I don't see how the Fox outfit can ever find enough really THIN people to act in THREE CAME HOME. We who were in the prison camps will always think a picture of it supremely inferior. It simply could not bring out the constant pangs of hunger and the anxiety." But she felt compelled to take back these words after she saw the movie at the end of April, writing to her son Bill, "I saw it alone last Saturday and cried every minute of it; could hardly see to drive home. It is exceedingly well done; and how it brought back those godawful years; and then it is such a small portion of what really did happen."[67]

Agnes Keith and Ethel Herold met in February 1953, when the author visited Baguio, and Elmer had the honor of serving as Keith's dinner partner. "Those two really settled world affairs," Ethel wrote to Betsy Herold Heimke. "Her ideas on things agreed with your Dad's. Mr. Keith is a fine person too. The rest of us had a general conversation & good fun while your Dad & Mrs. Keith settled world affairs. They are coming up again & we'll have more good talk. George was also along, a fine well-mannered boy of 12." It is likely the second meeting never took place because Ethel did not mention it in subsequent letters. Still, this interaction with a professional writer and fellow internment-camp survivor must have reinforced for Ethel Herold the importance of written remembrances.[68]

"I try not to feel sorry for myself," Ethel insisted after her husband's death in 1971. "But it is frustrating that my eyes prevent my getting up and doing something worthwhile. My children, relatives, friends are all good to me. But to fill this awful gap of loneliness, I have quizzed my memory and written all this. While writing about Elmer, I felt I was with him again." This was how Ethel Herold described her "Memory Quiz," the massive autobiography that she set to work on, with the help of various family members, shortly after her husband's death. Bearing witness to the important events of the twentieth century provided her with another way to demonstrate her patriotism, to show that she had been an active and engaged citizen. Part personal recollection, part therapy, by early 1973 this "family history" had grown to nearly seven hundred pages and weighed five pounds. She allowed family members to read it, even though she considered it "very mediocre," and was pleased that so many people advised her to publish it.[69]

Work on the "Memory Quiz" prompted Ethel to think more deeply about her wartime experiences than she had since revising her war diary. A few years after completing the autobiography, she learned that Natalie Crouter's war diary was going to be published. The Herolds and Crouters had known each other in Baguio; but the two women had never been close friends, and the tight quarters of internment and opposing political philosophies had driven a wedge between them. "Someone wrote me that June and Bedie Crouter paid a publisher to publish their Mother's war diary," Ethel Herold informed her daughter Betsy in late 1978. "That would make Natalie happy, she had worked long and hard on it and was turned down by all publishers. One thing her book would be filled with minute details—she was always copying stuff. And I am sure I am one of the villains in the book." Ethel Herold believed that "everybody had their own private opinion of the war," but that did not prepare her for Natalie Crouter's public criticisms.[70]

In 1980, Burt Franklin & Company published *Forbidden Diary: A Record of Wartime Internment, 1941–1945* as part of its American Women's Diary series. Literary scholar Lynn Z. Bloom edited the diary to give it a strong narrative structure and put Crouter's narrowly focused story in historical context. Ethel Herold, intensely interested in what other Baguio residents wrote about internment, could not wait to read the finished product, but since she was virtually blind by this time, someone had to read portions of it to her. Crouter changed many of the names in her book, so it took a while for Ethel to recognize herself as "Enid." When she did, she wept over the criticisms. In one section, Crouter described "Enid" in a "rampage over flies and dysentery"; in another, she characterized her this way: "The woman chairman is severe, dogmatic, takes no criticism or suggestion, is high-handed, no one will stand up to her (with one or two exceptions) but she is not as unpopular because she does *mix* and tries to be just by her own standards and is a tireless worker." Natalie Crouter did not depict Ethel as a villain, but even the implied criticisms brought Ethel to tears.[71]

Ethel also disagreed with many of the facts Natalie Crouter recorded in her diary, which *Time* magazine repeated when it ran a short article about the book. The published diary received this brief bit of national attention because of the ongoing Iranian hostage crisis in which fifty-two American citizens would spend more than a year in captivity. In March 1980, Ethel wrote that "Betsy and Billy were as shocked as I" about the article, wondering, "I don't know how the writer of this TIME article read Natalie's book, and gave it the wrong interpretation." Though she objected to many things she read in the diary and fretted over "wrong" interpretations, Ethel ultimately held fast to her belief that everyone had a different perspective on internment, maintaining that she had the right to her own criticisms. By early 1981, Ethel declared that she was "more provoked than ever" that she did not work harder to get her "Memory Quiz" in shape for publication. She took a course in writing at the Beatitudes later that year, crafting vignettes of her life in the Philippines. The course kept her mind occupied, and she basked in the praise of her classmates. Though the teacher told her that her stories were worthy of publication, Ethel did not pursue it. Age was taking its toll.[72]

The chance for Ethel Herold to offer her version of internment finally came two years after the publication of Natalie Crouter's diary. The *Bulletin of the American Historical Collection,* a Manila-based quarterly journal that focuses on Philippine-American relations, published the "War Memories of Ethel Herold" in a two-part installment in 1982. World War I veteran Charles Vial, a resident of the Beatitudes, recorded the oral history. According the Ethel, Vial "was so impressed" when he heard her speak about the war "that he wants me to record on his cassette . . . anything I wish to have recorded." He was also willing to record anything she wanted from her "Memory Quiz," but she declined. Although she did not "know whether to be flattered or not" by his interest in her story, she agreed to the taping. When transcribed, the oral history stretched to seventy-four pages.[73]

Jim Halsema, a former Baguio internee and lifelong friend of the Herolds, forwarded a copy to Lewis Gleeck, editor of the *Bulletin.* Gleeck wrote to Ethel in 1981 asking for permission to publish, but by that time Ethel had evidently forgotten about Charles Vial's interview. She told her daughter Betsy, "I don't see where Gleeck ever got a copy of my diary. I had always guarded it closely. This is NOT the 'Memory Quiz.' I think maybe Jim Halsema has something to do with it." She allowed the publication to proceed, though she wrote Gleeck, "If I insisted on you sending me a copy of what you were about to print, I am sure I would have slashed it to pieces."[74]

Gleeck explained the value of this oral history in the July-September issue of the *Bulletin:* "Thanks to the redoubtable Ethel Herold, wife of the pre-war Baguio educator-turned-lumberman, we have a minute description of how the war come [*sic*] to Baguio and how the Americans and other Allied nationals were herded into internment there. Thus we now have a down-to-earth document to supplement Natalie Crowder's [*sic*] novel-length recital of events at Camp Holmes, apparently intended to serve as a vehicle for Women's as well as American Liberation."[75]

The tone of the editorial introduction may have soothed any lingering anxieties Ethel Herold had about making her wartime memories public. Gleeck clearly saw great value in her version of those events, describing the oral history as a "down-to-earth document" as opposed to Natalie Crouter's "novel-length recital." While that may have played well for Ethel's vanity, it is Gleeck's mention of women's liberation that is of particular historical interest. The national celebration of the United States Bicentennial in 1976 had sparked a flurry of attention to anything associated with the American Revolution. Perhaps because of the recent resurgence of the women's rights movement and because of women's participation in the Vietnam War and the antiwar movement, historians and other scholars paid particular attention to women's roles in that earlier revolutionary conflict. Understanding the complexities of war required an understanding that both men and women contribute to war efforts, and both Natalie Crouter's diary and Ethel Herold's wartime oral history clearly illustrated that.[76]

Ethel Herold always knew the importance of her World War II experiences, but it took decades for her to admit that anyone outside of her family might consider them of value. Worried that Natalie Crouter's diary might become the official story of the Baguio internment, she allowed the *Bulletin* to publish her oral history so that others would understand that there were multiple perspectives of this event. Though Lewis Gleeck alluded to this with his comment about women's liberation, Ethel Herold did not acknowledge that much of the value of her wartime reminiscences had to do with the fact that she was a woman, hardly surprising since she rarely viewed the world in gendered terms.

She also did not see that her wartime internment was actually a consequence of U.S. imperialism, the decision to colonize the Philippine Islands and thereby enter into a competition with the Japanese for control in the Pacific. Still, near the end of "Memory Quiz," Ethel Herold wrote, "We as individuals must always realize our responsibilities"; she then went on to explain what it meant to be an expatriate: "People have often asked us were we sorry we had gone to the P.I. 'No.' In the first place, besides adventure, we went as a patriotic duty. Even though we taught only 4 years, we aimed to be true Americans all the way. When I quit teaching, I lost my pay check, but I never ceased doing for the people. Our experience in teaching taught us to know the people and how to do for them. Elmer became a successful businessman—not aloof from the people. We had attained the height of luxury and were cut down by the Japanese to the depth of despair, hunger, squalor, drudgery, fear. This was a test of everything within us."[77]

That test had its roots in American imperialism, which Ethel Herold consistently described in "Memory Quiz" in sentimental terms, perpetuating the myth that Americans were benign protectors in what was in fact an intrusive program designed to alter the culture of entire groups of people. Because of her love for her country, Ethel could only see the benefits of the colonial system. Though in this passage she cast herself as a sort of servant to the Filipinos—"I never ceased doing for the people"—she could not have taken on those tasks had she not been part of the colonial elite. She determined what the people needed; she determined how those needs should be met. She was, after all, a supportive, enthusiastic citizen of the American empire.

Conclusion

BESIDES WRITING HER LIFE STORY, Ethel Herold turned to practical financial matters during the last years of her life. In 1980, eight years before she died, she reexamined her will, which she had not updated since 1956, when Elmer Herold was still alive. After revising the will, she sent a copy of it to her children, enclosing a letter that gave a synopsis of her final wishes and a basic breakdown of property distribution. "This letter is supposed to simplify matters for you when I die," she told them. The Bonn farm weighed heavily on her mind those last years as she dealt with renters and the reality that she would never live there again. Ethel encouraged Bill and Betsy to hold on to it, to consider it part of their family heritage.[1]

Now everything was settled. Ethel Herold lived another six years beyond the publication of her war memories, most of it at the Beatitudes; but because of her deteriorating health, she finally had to move in with her son, Bill, and his wife, Joanne, in Sylacauga, Alabama. Despite their best efforts, they could not adequately care for her at home and placed her in a nursing home, where she died quietly on March 30, 1988, at the age of ninety-two, mother of two, grandmother of eight, and great-grandmother of ten. Ethel Herold's body was cremated, and the ashes were taken back to Potosi where, after a memorial service at the Davies Memorial United Church of Christ, they were buried next to Elmer Herold in the British Hollow Cemetery.

At the end, we can return to the beginning—to the photograph described at the start of this book—to consider the historical importance of the life of Ethel Thomas Herold. The picture of her and Elmer standing in the ruins of Manila in 1945 indicates the main points: Ethel became a citizen of empire because of both love and war. The Spanish-American War at the turn of the twentieth century marked the United States' emergence as an imperial power. Replacing Spain as the colonizing power in the Philippine Islands, the United States exported its progressive ideals, certain that it could bring American-style democracy and freedom to Filipinos while advancing its own economic interests in Asia. And the United States was determined to practice its own style of imperialism, one vastly different from the harshness of European-style colonialism. American citizens were encouraged—even recruited—to travel to the Philippines, where they engaged in a kind of sentimental imperialism, taking jobs in business and government and the military to educate Filipinos in the best way to do things.

Bart Thomas, Ethel's eldest brother, influenced by the propaganda of the Spanish-American War and looking for a way to establish himself in a nonagricultural career, accepted a teaching position in the Philippines in 1901. Ethel would always view this as "doing a patriotic thing," and she admired her brother for it, taking away an understanding that patriotism requires action. Young Ethel's perceptions about citizenship and patriotism were also influenced by the various women's organizations that her mother and other neighbor women joined, especially the Woman's Relief Corps. Education helped shape her views as well. As a "new woman" of the early twentieth century, Ethel attended Lawrence College, where she studied history and politics alongside male students, which seemed to reinforce her assumption that men and women should work side by side. And at Lawrence, Ethel Thomas met Elmer Herold, the love of her life.

The Great War temporarily took Elmer away from her. While he was gone performing his patriotic duty as a soldier, Ethel demonstrated her patriotism through domestic duties like knitting, rolling bandages, and tending a victory garden. As a working woman with a career, she showed her loyalty to the American cause by teaching a government-approved history curriculum to her high school students in Lancaster, Wisconsin, and by promoting food conservation through the Grant County branch of the Food Administration.

Elmer Herold returned from the war safe and unharmed, and he and Ethel Thomas married in 1920. Determined to help spread American democracy in the world, in 1922 the young couple signed on to work as public school teachers in the colonial Philippines. There Ethel promoted Americanization first through her English-language schoolroom lessons and then through various charitable works in Baguio. During the 1930s, she wholeheartedly supported her husband's career with an American-owned lumber company, and the family reaped the economic benefits of American gold mining in northern Luzon. It was a busy, exciting, and luxurious life that Ethel nonetheless saw as patriotic because she was helping to support U.S. imperialism in the Philippines.

Then came the Japanese attack and occupation. By the end of 1941, American citizenship accorded Ethel Herold no special privileges. Along with the rest of the Allied nationals in the Philippines, now referred to by the Japanese as enemy aliens, she and her family endured years of internment under increasingly harsh circumstances. Ethel marshaled her considerable organizational skills to make the camps inhabitable, thereby ensuring the survival of the Baguio internees. Her battles with Major Musa Mukibo illustrate how she viewed the Japanese as an "alien political culture" that did not conceive of "good" and "evil" in the same way as Americans. By sticking to this belief, she continued to maintain, despite the wartime circumstances, that Americans were superior to Japanese. Within the confines of an internment camp, Ethel Herold expressed her patriotism by resisting Japanese rules, assisting the guerrilla forces, and sewing an American flag. Most of all she remained steadfast in her belief that the American military would rescue them and defeat the Japanese. It took until February 1945 for U.S. troops to liberate the Herolds and the other American captives, but Ethel never believed that her faith had been misplaced.

After the war, Ethel and Elmer Herold returned to Baguio. For Elmer, employment with the Heald Lumber Company offered the best opportunity for rebuilding his career and providing for the family's economic well-being. Ethel felt an obligation to the Filipinos who had assisted the internees during the war and wanted to help repay them by rebuilding Baguio to its prewar glory. She witnessed the official dismantling of U.S. colonialism in the Philippines when the islands gained independence in 1946, and her American citizenship once again put her in a less-than-privileged position. Though the Herolds prospered in postwar Baguio and though Ethel kept her promise and worked hard through the Monday Afternoon Club to rebuild Baguio, as Americans she and her husband were increasingly viewed as interlopers. Moreover, the Philippines seemed unsafe. Ethel was concerned about the spread of communism and worried that the

Philippines were not strong enough to resist; she never quite got over her fear of getting caught up in a war zone. Increasingly, she put her faith in the ideology and programs of conservative Republicans, whom she trusted to guide America's role in the postwar world.

In 1959, Ethel Thomas Herold once again became an American living on U.S. soil. Elmer Herold retired from Heald Lumber, and the couple took up residence on the old Bonn farm near Potosi, Wisconsin. Ethel immediately involved herself in a variety of organizations, including Wisconsin's Republican Party and a local group associated with the General Federation of Women's Clubs. Her connection with the GFWC maintained her transpacific tie to the Monday Afternoon Club in Baguio, which for years benefitted from the various speaker's fees that Ethel earned and donated to the club. Barry Goldwater's 1964 presidential campaign marked the high tide of Ethel Herold's political activism. Convinced that Goldwater's approach, favoring a small federal government, a free-market economy, and staunch anticommunism, was key to a healthy, democratic United States, she and Elmer promoted his candidacy around Wisconsin. Disappointed by Goldwater's defeat, Ethel nevertheless did not abandon her commitment to political conservatism.

After Elmer Herold's death in 1971, Ethel began work on "Memory Quiz," an autobiography that she conceived of as a way of working through her grief and keeping Elmer close to her. It was as much a work of love as it was a testament to the formation of a twentieth-century American citizen. The life story she believed would be of interest only to her family is in fact invaluable to understanding the ways in which American women have historically viewed their roles as patriots and as citizens. For Ethel Thomas Herold, that view was repeatedly informed by war—the Spanish-American War, World War I, World War II, and the Cold War—and caught up in American imperialism, turning her into a citizen of empire.

Notes

Introduction

1. Robert B. Westbrook, *Why We Fought: Forging American Obligations in World War II* (Washington, DC: Smithsonian Books, 2004), 13.

2. Ethel Thomas Herold, "Memory Quiz," unpublished autobiography, copy in the author's possession, 3; Lori D. Ginzberg, "Global Goals, Local Acts: Grass-Roots Activism in Imperial Narratives," *Journal of American History* 88, no. 3 (Dec. 2001): 870.

3. Linda K. Kerber, *No Constitutional Right to Be Ladies: Women and the Obligations of Citizenship* (New York: Hill and Wang, 1998), xx–xxi.

4. On gender and the Spanish-American War, see, for instance, Kristin L. Hoganson, *Fighting for American Manhood: How Gender Politics Provoked the Spanish-American and Philippine-American Wars* (New Haven: Yale Univ. Press, 1998), and Gail Bederman, *Manliness and Civilization: A Cultural History of Gender and Race in the United States, 1880–1917* (Chicago: Univ. of Chicago Press, 1995). Vicente L. Rafael, "Colonial Domesticity: White Women and United States Rule in the Philippines," *American Literature* 67 (Dec. 1995): 642.

5. Rafael, "Colonial Domesticity," 639.

6. Kerber, *No Constitutional Right To Be Ladies;* Rogers M. Smith, *Civic Ideals: Conflicting Visions of Citizenship in U.S. History* (New Haven, CT: Yale Univ. Press, 1997); John Bodnar, ed., *Bonds of Affection: Americans Define Their Patriotism* (Princeton, NJ: Princeton Univ. Press, 1996).

7. Quoted in Kimberly Jensen, *Mobilizing Minerva: American Women in the First World War* (Urbana: Univ. of Illinois Press, 2008), xi, and Francesca Morgan, *Women and Patriotism in Jim Crow America* (Chapel Hill: Univ. of North Carolina Press, 2005), 3.

8. Smith, *Civic Ideals,* 411.

9. Hoganson, *Fighting for American Manhood;* Bederman, *Manliness and Civilization;* Smith, *Civic Ideals;* Allison L. Sneider, *Suffragists in an Imperial Age: U.S. Expansion and the Woman Question, 1870–1929* (New York: Oxford Univ. Press, 2008), 9–10; Louise Michelle Newman, *White Women's Rights: The Racial Origins of Feminism in the United States* (New York: Oxford Univ. Press, 1999); Kristin L. Hoganson, "'As Badly Off as the Filipinos': U.S. Women's Suffragists and the Imperial Issue at the Turn of the Twentieth Century," *Journal of Women's History* 13, no. 2 (Summer 2001): 9–33.

10. Cecelia Elizabeth O'Leary, *To Die For: The Paradox of American Patriotism* (Princeton, NJ: Princeton Univ. Press, 1999), 3; Christopher Capozzola, *Uncle Sam Wants You: World War I and the Making of the Modern American Citizen* (New York: Oxford Univ. Press, 2008), 8; Kathleen Kennedy, *Disloyal Mothers and Scurrilous Citizens: Women and Subversion during World War I* (Bloomington: Indiana Univ. Press, 1999); Jensen, *Mobilizing Minerva.*

11. Westbrook, *Why We Fought,* 9, 17, 28; Marilyn E. Hegarty, *Victory Girls, Khaki-Wackies, and Patriotutes: The Regulation of Female Sexuality during World War II* (New York: New York Univ. Press, 2008), 5.

12. Wendy Kozol, "'Good Americans': Nationalism and Domesticity in *Life* Magazine, 1945–1960," in Bodnar, *Bonds of Affection,* 231–50; Helen Laville, *Cold War Women: The International Activities of American Women's Organisations* (Manchester: Manchester Univ. Press, 2002).

13. Kim Phillips-Fein, *Invisible Hands: The Making of the Conservative Movement from the New Deal to Reagan* (New York: W. W. Norton, 2009); Lisa McGirr, *Suburban Warriors: The Origins of the New American Right* (Princeton: Princeton Univ. Press, 2001); Catherine Rymph, *Republican Women: Feminism and Conservatism from Suffrage Through the Rise of the New Right* (Chapel Hill: Univ. of North Carolina Press, 2006); Mary C. Brennan, *Wives, Mothers, and the Red Menace: Conservative Women and the Crusade Against Communism* (Boulder: Univ. Press of Colorado, 2008), 2.

14. Robert Bickers, *Empire Made Me: An Englishman Adrift in Shanghai* (London: Allen Lane, 2003), 4–5; David Lambert and Alan Lester, eds., *Colonial Lives Across the British Empire: Imperial Careering in the Long Nineteenth Century* (Cambridge: Cambridge Univ. Press, 2006), 21; Linda Colley, *The Ordeal of Elizabeth Marsh: A Woman in World History* (New York: Pantheon Books, 2007), xix. Among books with an American focus, two of the best examples of this kind of biography are Melton A. McLaurin, *Celia: A Slave* (Athens: Univ. of Georgia Press, 1991) and Laurel Thatcher Ulrich, *A Midwife's Tale: The Life of Martha Ballard, Based on Her Diary, 1785–1812* (New York: Alfred A. Knopf, 1990).

15. David Thelen, "The Nation and Beyond: Transnational Perspectives on United States History," *Journal of American History* 86, no. 3 (Dec. 1999): 967. Transnational historiography is vast. See for instance, Michael McGerr, "The Price of the 'New Transnational History,'" *American Historical Review* 96, no. 4 (Oct. 1991): 1056–67; Laura Briggs, Gladys McCormick, and J. T. Way, "Transnationalism: A Category of Analysis," *American Quarterly* 60, no. 3 (Sept. 2008): 625–48; Laura Doyle, "Toward a Philosophy of Transnationalism," *Journal of Transnational American Studies* 1, no. 1 (Feb. 2009), available online at http://www.escholarship.org/uc/item/9vr1k8hk.

16. Linda K. Kerber, "The Meanings of Citizenship," *Journal of American History* 84, no. 3 (Dec. 1997): 854.

1. The Formative Years of a Female Citizen

1. Herold, "Memory Quiz," 3.

2. O'Leary, *To Die For,* 248n12; 7.

3. Morgan, *Women and Patriotism,* 3.

4. "Mrs. Thomas Dead," *Lancaster* [WI] *Weekly Teller,* 28 Feb. 1923, 11; Herold, "Memory Quiz," 21, 24. The obituary gives an incorrect marriage date for Lizzie and Clem.

5. "Potosi," *Grant County* [WI] *Herald,* 28 July 1906, 1; "Obituary—James Thomas," *Weekly Teller,* 2 Aug. 1906, 1; Herold, "Memory Quiz," 24.

6. "Town Officers," *Weekly Teller,* 9 Apr. 1896, 1.

7. Susan A. Brewer, *Why America Fights: Patriotism and War Propaganda from the Philippines to Iraq* (New York: Oxford Univ. Press, 2009), 13. For the kind of ideology Ethel Thomas Herold rejected, see Mary Ann Heiss, "The Evolution of the Imperial Idea and U.S. National Identity," *Diplomatic History* 26, no. 4 (Fall 2002): 511–40. Louis A. Perez Jr. also pulls apart the myth of the benevolent U.S. empire in *The War of 1898: The United States and Cuba in History and Historiography* (Chapel Hill: Univ. of North Carolina Press, 1998).

8. O'Leary, *To Die For,* 137, 147.

9. For a detailed argument about gender and masculinity in connection with imperialism, see Hoganson, *Fighting for American Manhood,* chap. 6. On the Thomasites, see Jo Anne Barker Maniago, "The First Peace Corps: The Work of the American Teachers in the Philippines, 1900–1910" (Ph.D. diss., Boston Univ., 1971). Information on Bart Thomas's appointment can be found in "To Hurry to Philippines," *Weekly Teller,* 20 June 1901, 3; "Lancaster Officials Pass Through Potosi Without the Smell of Smoke Upon Their Garments, *Weekly Teller,* 27 June 1901, 1; and "Potosi Passing Through a Hot Wave," *Weekly Teller,* 18 July 1901, 1.

10. This basic historical chronology can be found in Stanley Karnow, *In Our Image: America's Empire in the Philippines* (New York: Random House, 1989), and H. W. Brands, *Bound to Empire: The United States and the Philippines* (New York: Oxford Univ. Press, 1992).

11. Karnow, *In Our Image,* 201; O'Leary, *To Die For,* 172. Vicente Rafael also acknowledges the link between domestic reform in the United States and procolonization attitudes among Americans. See his "Colonial Domesticity," 639–66.

12. Judith Raftery, "Textbook Wars: Governor-General James Francis Smith and the Protestant-Catholic Conflict in Public Education in the Philippines, 1904–1907," *History of Education Quarterly* 38, no. 2 (Summer 1998): 146–48, 149; Jonathan Zimmerman, *Innocents Abroad: American Teachers in the American Century* (Cambridge, MA: Harvard Univ. Press, 2006), 84.

13. Maniago, "The First Peace Corps," 80; "Lancaster Officials Pass through Potosi without the Smell of Smoke upon Their Garments," *Weekly Teller,* 27 June 1901, 1.

14. Zimmerman, *Innocents Abroad,* 120–21; "Potosi Passing through a Hot Wave," *Weekly Teller,* 18 July 1901, 1; Herold, "Memory Quiz," 3; Bart

Thomas to Secretary of War, 7 Mar. 1905, Records of the Bureau of Insular Affairs, Record Group 350, National Archives and Records Administration (Archives II), College Park, MD; Maniago, "The First Peace Corps," 81. Subsequent citations of Bureau of Insular Affairs records will be abbreviated as RBIA.

15. Zimmerman, *Innocents Abroad,* 89; Maniago, "The First Peace Corps," 82.

16. Zimmerman, *Innocents Abroad,* 89, 91.

17. Smith, *Civic Ideals,* 429.

18. "New Supervisors," *Weekly Teller,* 4 Apr. 1907; "Potosi High School Notes," *Weekly Teller,* 13 June 1907; "Behold the Birds!" *Weekly Teller,* 13 June 1907; "Potosi Correspondence," *Weekly Teller,* 10 Oct. 1907; "Potosi Notes," *Weekly Teller,* 24 Oct. 1907.

19. For a full discussion of American women's interest in Asian items, see Mari Yoshihara, *Embracing the East: White Women and American Orientalism* (New York: Oxford Univ. Press, 2003), chap. 1. The concept of contact zones comes from Kristin L. Hoganson, *Consumers' Imperium: The Global Production of American Domesticity, 1865–1920* (Chapel Hill: Univ. of North Carolina Press, 2007), chaps. 1 and 2.

20. "Local Items," *Weekly Teller,* 4 Aug. 1910; Herold, "Memory Quiz," 15.

21. "Local Items," *Weekly Teller,* 1 Sept. 1910; "Potosi News," *Weekly Teller,* 8 Sept. 1910; "Railroad Laborer Murdered at Potosi," *Grant County Herald,* 31 Aug. 1910. The names of the Mexican workers were not spelled consistently from one newspaper to the next or even from one article to the next.

22. Herold, "Memory Quiz," 16; "Railroad Laborer Murdered at Potosi," *Grant County Herald,* 31 Aug. 1910; "Mexican Murderer Gets Twenty Years," *Grant County Herald,* 26 Oct. 1910.

23. "Rural Carriers Examination," *Weekly Teller,* 24 Mar. 1904; "Potosi's New Rural Routes," *Weekly Teller,* 22 Sept. 1904.

24. "Completed Census of Grant County," *The Weekly Teller,* 3 Aug. 1905; "Potosi," *Grant County Herald,* 17 Jan. 1906; "Potosi," *Grant County Herald,* 27 Jan. 1906.

25. Herold, "Memory Quiz," 13.

26. Morgan, *Women and Patriotism,* 38.

27. Ibid., 38–39; O'Leary, *To Die For,* 76.

28. O'Leary, *To Die For,* 99.

29. Morgan, *Women and Patriotism,* 70, 76–77.

30. Anne Firor Scott, *Natural Allies: Women's Associations in American History* (Urbana: Univ. of Illinois Press, 1991), 2.

31. Anne Ruggles Gere, *Intimate Practices: Literacy and Cultural Work in U.S. Women's Clubs, 1880–1902* (Urbana: Univ. of Illinois Press, 1997), 3, 145; Rafael, "Colonial Domesticity," 642.

32. "Lancaster Base Ballers and Other Important Locals," *Weekly Teller,* 9 May 1901, 1; "Come Unto Me," *Weekly Teller,* 21 Mar. 1907, 1; "Them That Love Us," *Weekly Teller,* 11 Apr. 1907, 1.

33. Gere, *Intimate Practices,* 145.

34. Lynn D. Gordon, *Gender and Higher Education in the Progressive Era* (New Haven, CT: Yale Univ. Press, 1990), 2, 5; Betty A. DeBerg, *Ungodly Women: Gender and the First Wave of American Fundamentalism* (Minneapolis: Fortress Press, 1990), 27. The concept of the "New Woman" is also discussed in Carroll Smith-Rosenberg, "The New Woman as Androgyne: Social Disorder and Gender Crisis, 1870–1936," in *Disorderly Conduct: Visions of Gender in Victorian America* (New York: Alfred A. Knopf, 1985); William H. Chafe, *Women and Equality: Changing Patterns in American Culture* (New York: Oxford Univ. Press, 1977); Jane H. Hunter, *How Young Ladies Became Girls: The Victorian Origins of American Girlhood* (New Haven, CT: Yale Univ. Press, 2002).

35. Barbara Miller Solomon, *In the Company of Educated Women: A History of Women and Higher Education in America* (New Haven: Yale Univ. Press, 1985), 63.

36. Ibid., 80–81.

37. These descriptions of Appleton and Lawrence College are taken from the *Lawrence College Bulletin,* Feb. 1914 and 15 Oct. 1914. Copies of these bulletins can be found in the Lawrence Univ. Archives, Appleton, WI.

38. *Lawrence College Bulletin,* 15 Oct. 1914, 11.

39. For a discussion of this second generation, see Diana B. Turk, *Bound by a Mighty Vow: Sisterhood and Women's Fraternities, 1870–1920* (New York: New York Univ. Press, 2004), chap. 2.

40. Herold, "Memory Quiz," 32.

41. Ibid., 39–40; Sneider, *Suffragists in an Imperial Age,* 13.

42. On the role of Wisconsin women in the suffrage campaign, see Genevieve G. McBride, *On Wisconsin Women: Working for Their Rights from Settlement to Suffrage* (Madison: Univ. of Wisconsin Press, 1993).

43. Solomon, *In the Company of Educated Women,* 112–14.

44. Sneider, *Suffragists in an Imperial Age,* 14; Gere, *Intimate Practices,* 145.

45. Herold, "Memory Quiz," 40; Sneider, *Suffragists in an Imperial Age,* 9.

46. Hoganson, "'As Badly Off as the Filipinos,'" 11, 14.

47. Sneider, *Suffragists in an Imperial Age,* 87; Hoganson, "'As Badly Off as the Filipinos,'" 13–14.

48. Herold, "Memory Quiz," 40. Ethel had her years mixed up, as she remembered these suffrage events taking place during her sophomore year.

49. "Stand Up for Women's Rights," *Lawrentian,* 3 May 1916; Editorial, *Lawrentian,* 10 May 1916.

50. Herold, "Memory Quiz," 52–53.

51. June Purvis, *Emmeline Pankhurst: A Biography* (New York: Routledge, 2002), 285.

52. "Famous Suffragette to Speak Here," *Lawrentian,* 10 May 1916; "Mrs. Pankhurst Not the Brusque, Bold Woman That Reputation Might Indicate," *Appleton* [WI] *Daily Post,* 12 May 1916; Herold, "Memory Quiz," 52–53. The 11 May 1916 issue of the *Appleton Daily Post* is not extant.

53. "Gives Money for British War Baby Fund," *Lawrentian,* 17 May 1916.

54. Herold, "Memory Quiz," 53.

55. Ibid., 54–55.

56. "Co-Eds March in Chicago Parade," *Lawrentian,* 13 June 1916, 3, 14; Herold, "Memory Quiz," 55–56. See also McBride, *On Wisconsin Women,* 266.

57. Herold, "Memory Quiz," 62; "?" *Appleton Daily Post,* 20 Sept. 1916.

58. "Prairie du Chien," *LaCrosse* [WI] *Tribune,* 9 June 1913.

59. "Preparations Completed for All-College Day," *Lawrentian,* 22 Sept. 1913; Herold, "Memory Quiz," 29.

60. Beth L. Bailey, *From Front Porch to Back Seat: Courtship in Twentieth-Century America* (Baltimore: Johns Hopkins Univ. Press, 1988), 15–16, 18–19.

61. Herold, "Memory Quiz," 30.

62. Ibid., 34.

63. Ibid., 39, 41.

64. Ibid., 51.

65. Ibid., 51.

2. Citizenship and Patriotism during the Great War

1. Herold, "Memory Quiz," 36.

2. Morgan, *Women and Patriotism,* 104.

3. Ibid., 108.

4. Kathleen Kennedy, *Disloyal Mothers and Scurrilous Citizens,* 1. Kennedy's discussion of "patriotic motherhood" and, by extension, mine, is based on Barbara Steinson, *American Women's Activism in World War I* (New York: Garland Publishing, 1982). For an argument that conservative women embraced "patriotic maternalism" through the 1920s and 1930s, see Christine Kimberly Erickson, "Conservative Women and Patriotic Maternalism: The Beginnings of a Gendered Conservative Tradition in the 1920s and 1930s" (Ph.D. diss., Univ. of California, Santa Barbara, 1999).

5. On the link between gender and citizenship, see Kerber, *No Constitutional Right to Be Ladies;* Hoganson, *Fighting for American Manhood;* Jensen, *Mobilizing Minerva,* 21. See also Bederman, *Manliness and Civilization.*

6. Edward M. Coffman, *The War to End All Wars: The American Military Experience in World War I* (Madison: Univ. of Wisconsin Press, 1986), 17.

7. Herold, "Memory Quiz," 59.

8. Kennedy, *Disloyal Mothers and Scurrilous Citizens,* 3.

9. Erickson, "Conservative Women and Patriotic Maternalism," 21. See also Stuart McConnell, "Reading the Flag: A Reconsideration of the Patriotic Cults of the 1890s," in Bodnar, *Bonds of Affection,* 102–19 (Princeton, NJ: Princeton Univ. Press, 1996).

10. "Break with Austria Over U-Boat Affair Seems Unavoidable," *Appleton Daily Post,* 17 Feb. 1917; "Suspect German Consul Having a Hand in Mexico," *Appleton Daily Post,* 19 Feb. 1917; "Armed Neutrality for United States," *Appleton Daily Post,* 26 Feb. 1917; "Intercepted Letter Reveals War Plot," *Appleton Daily Post,* 1 Mar. 1917; "Wilson Sounds New Doctrine of Peace," *Appleton Daily Post,* 5 Mar. 1917; "Germany and United States Are

at War," *Appleton Daily Post,* 2 Apr. 1917; "War Declared on Germany at 1:13 Today," *Appleton Daily Post,* 6 Apr. 1917.

11. Herold, "Memory Quiz," 63; "Lawrence Co-Eds Show Patriotism by Forming Red Cross Association," *Lawrentian,* 12 Apr. 1917; "Appleton Chapter Red Cross Will Begin Active Work in a Short Time—Fifty Members Now," *Appleton Daily Post,* 11 Apr. 1917.

12. O'Leary, *To Die For,* 220.

13. "Indications Are That at Least 10,000 Will Participate in Giant Loyalty Parade Planned to Be Held in This City on Monday Afternoon," *Appleton Daily Post,* 6 Apr. 1917; "More Than 5,000 Participate in the Loyalty Day Parade," *Appleton Daily Post,* 10 Apr. 1917; "Lawrence Joins Appleton in Biggest Demonstration in History of City," *Lawrentian,* 12 Apr. 1917.

14. "Lawrence Men Prepare for War—Organize as a Military Company," *Lawrentian,* 5 Apr. 1917; David M. Kennedy, *Over Here: The First World War and American Society* (New York: Oxford Univ. Press, 1980), 147.

15. "College Students May Join Training Camps or Company and Receive College Credit," *Appleton Daily Post,* 17 Apr. 1917; "No Athletics and Fewer Functions in College Social Set," *Appleton Daily Post,* 19 Apr. 1917.

16. Kennedy, *Over Here,* 148–49.

17. Capozzola, *Uncle Sam Wants You,* 6–8.

18. "Men Leave Lawrence for Fort Sheridan," *Lawrentian,* 17 May 1917; "Men Arriving Fast at Fort Sheridan," *Lawrentian,* 17 May 1917; Herold, "Memory Quiz," 64.

19. Herold, "Memory Quiz," 65.

20. "Liberty Bonds," "3,272 Men Register for Draft," "Red Cross Add 250 in Lancaster," *Weekly Teller,* 7 June 1917; "Old Vets Met at Potosi Last Week and Celebrated," *Grant County Herald,* 4 July 1917.

21. "Women's League Meets Saturday," *Weekly Teller,* 7 June 1917; "Potosi Items," *Grant County News* (Platteville, WI), 3 May 1918; R. B. Pixley, *Wisconsin in the World War* (Milwaukee: Wisconsin War History Company, 1919), 70, 391; John M. Barry, *The Great Influenza: The Epic Story of the Deadliest Plague in History* (New York: Viking, 2004), 129–30; Jensen, viii.

22. Morgan, *Women and Patriotism,* 107–8. Anne Ruggles Gere makes a similar point in *Intimate Practices,* 153.

23. Pixley, *Wisconsin in the World War,* 243.

24. Capozzola, *Uncle Sam Wants You,* 85.

25. Ibid., 83.

26. Herold, "Memory Quiz," 65–66.

27. Ibid.; Lewis Paul Todd, *Wartime Relations of the Federal Government and the Public Schools, 1917–1918* (New York: Arno Press and The New York Times, 1971), 151.

28. Job Application, 5 May 1922, RBIA; Todd, *Wartime Relations,* 201–7. The Bureau of Education reported an average annual salary for high school teachers of $1,031 in 1918; the lowest salaries ($652) came from Maine.

29. Advertisement for Lancaster High School, *Weekly Teller,* 30 Aug. 1917; "U.S. Language for Americans Says School Meeting," *Grant County Herald,* 3 July 1918; "Patriotic Send-Off on Sept. 18," *Weekly Teller,* 6 Sept.

1917; "Thousands Attend Send-Off for Soldiers— Every Section of County is Represented," *Weekly Teller,* 20 Sept. 1917; "Elaborate Plans for Second Send-Off for Drafted Boys at Lancaster Next Week," *Weekly Teller,* 27 Sept. 1917.

30. Editorial, "More American History in the Schools," *Weekly Teller,* 20 Sept. 1917; Herold, "Memory Quiz," 67.

31. Kennedy, *Over Here,* 55. For an explanation of the National Board for Historical Service, see Todd, *Wartime Relations,* 46n15.

32. Kennedy, *Over Here,* 56; Samuel Bannister Harding, *The Study of the Great War: A Topical Outline, with Extensive Quotations and Reading References* (Washington, DC: Committee on Public Information, 1918), 5; Todd, *Wartime Relations,* 36–37.

33. Maurine Weiner Greenwald, *Women, War, and Work: The Impact of World War I on Women Workers in the United States* (Westport, CT: Greenwood Press, 1980), 12–13; Robert H. Zieger, *America's Great War: World War I and the American Experience* (New York: Rowman & Littlefield, 2000), 144. On women's work patterns during the war, see also Alice Kessler-Harris, *Out to Work: A History of Wage-Earning Women in the United States* (New York: Oxford Univ. Press, 1982), chap. 8, and Carrie Brown, *Rosie's Mom: Forgotten Women Workers of the First World War* (Boston: Northeastern Univ. Press, 2002), chap. 5.

34. "Lancaster High School Graduates 21," *Weekly Teller,* 13 June 1918; "Public School Teachers Named," *Weekly Teller,* 13 June 1918.

35. Quoted in Capozzola, *Uncle Sam Wants You,* 91.

36. On public school teachers and the war, see Susan Zeiger, "The Schoolhouse vs. the Armory: U.S. Teachers and the Campaign Against Militarism in the Schools, 1914–1918," *Journal of Women's History* 15, no. 2 (2003): 166.

37. Kennedy, *Over Here,* 118; Todd, *Wartime Relations,* 65–67.

38. Capozzola, *Uncle Sam Wants You,* 96–97.

39. "Wilson County Food Agent," *Weekly Teller,* 21 June 1917; "Hoover Gives Rules for Saving Our Food," *Weekly Teller,* 12 July 1917.

40. Quoted in Hoganson, *Consumers' Imperium,* 209–10.

41. Capozzola, *Uncle Sam Wants You,* 97–98.

42. Pixley, *Wisconsin in the World War,* 209–11; Herold, "Memory Quiz," 68.

43. Capozzola, *Uncle Sam Wants You,* 101.

44. Herold, "Memory Quiz," 70; Wisconsin Cartographer's Guild, *Wisconsin's Past and Present: A Historical Atlas* (Madison: Univ. of Wisconsin Press, 1998), 31.

45. "Find Yearous Guilty," *Grant County Herald,* 31 July 1918; "Potosi Department," *Grant County Herald,* 7 Aug. 1918; "C. Yearous Draws $1,000 Fine and Year's Sentence," *Grant County Herald,* 14 Aug. 1918.

46. Kennedy, *Disloyal Mothers and Scurrilous Citizens,* 93, 101, 103.

47. Herold, "Memory Quiz," 66.

48. Dale E. Wilson, *Treat 'Em Rough!: The Birth of American Armor, 1917–20* (Novato, CA: Presidio Press, 1989), 1, 10, 26. For a more detailed account of the origins of tanks, see Patrick Wright, *Tank: The Progress of a Monstrous War Machine* (New York: Viking, 2002), chap. 2.

49. Coffman, *The War to End All Wars,* 64. The Tank Corps actively recruited during the war. For a lively firsthand account from an officer who joined the corps after he had already gone to France, see Harvey L. Harris, *The War as I Saw It: 1918 Letters of a Tanks Corps Lieutenant* (St. Paul, MN: Pogo Press, 1998).

50. Wilson, *Treat 'Em Rough!,* 63. Movements of the 337th are documented on pp. 71 and 129.

51. Kennedy, *Over Here,* 169.

52. Barry, *The Great Influenza,* 135; Carol R. Byerly, *Fever of War: The Influenza Epidemic in the U.S. Army during World War I* (New York: New York Univ. Press, 2005), 8.

53. "Potosi," *Weekly Teller,* 29 Aug. 1918, 8; "Potosi," *Weekly Teller,* 22 Aug. 1918, 8; Barry, *The Great Influenza,* 169; Alfred W. Crosby, *America's Forgotten Pandemic: The Influenza of 1918* (New York: Cambridge Univ. Press, 1989), 17, 21. Crosby notes that the flu got its name because Spain, which was not involved in the war and therefore did not practice censorship, honestly reported its health problems that spring when about eight million Spaniards came down with the flu. The Spanish believed that the disease had been imported from France. See p. 26.

54. Barry, *The Great Influenza,* 232; Wilson, *Treat 'Em Rough!* 72–73.

55. Barry, *The Great Influenza,* 305; Herold, "Memory Quiz," 76.

56. Herold, "Memory Quiz," 77; Zieger, *America's Great War,* 100–101.

57. Herold, "Memory Quiz," 77; "Miss Trainor Dies Suddenly," *Weekly Teller,* 19 Sept. 1918; "Potosi," *Weekly Teller,* 19 Sept. 1918; "Spanish 'Flu' Spreads in State," *Weekly Teller,* 10 Oct. 1918; "Public Meetings Ordered Closed," *Weekly Teller,* 17 Oct. 1918; "Potosi," *Weekly Teller,* 17 Oct. 1918; "Potosi," *Weekly Teller,* 24 Oct. 1918; "Doctors Called without Cause," *Weekly Teller,* 24 Oct. 1918; "Potosi," *Weekly Teller,* 31 Oct. 1918. The *Grant County Herald* ran similar stories.

58. "Armistice Declared," *Weekly Teller,* 7 Nov. 1918; "City Celebrates Early and Late," *Weekly Teller,* 14 Nov. 1918; Herold, "Memory Quiz," 78.

59. "City Dads Put 'Flu Lid' Down," *Weekly Teller,* 5 Dec. 1918.

60. "Potosi," *Weekly Teller,* 12 Dec. 1918, 8; Herold, "Memory Quiz," 80.

61. Herold, "Memory Quiz," 78–79; Coffman, *The War to End All Wars,* 355–56.

62. Herold, "Memory Quiz," 78–79; Coffman, *The War to End All Wars,* 357–58.

63. "Flu Ban has Been Lifted," *Weekly Teller,* 9 Jan. 1919; "School Notes," *Weekly Teller,* 13 Mar. 1919, 10 Apr. 1919, and 3 Apr. 1919.

64. "City Goes Over the Top," *Weekly Teller,* 24 Apr. 1919; "The Army Tank to Platteville" and "School Notes," *Weekly Teller,* 1 May 1919; "Tank Day Drizzles," *Grant County Herald,* 7 May 1919; Herold, "Memory Quiz," 78. Ethel mistakenly remembered the tank arriving in Lancaster on Armistice Day.

65. "School Teachers Employed for Coming Session," *Weekly Teller,* 26 June 1919; Herold, "Memory Quiz," 80.

66. "Potosi," *Grant County Herald,* 23 July 1919; "Potosi," *Weekly Teller,* 17 July 1919; "Potosi News," *Weekly Teller,* 24 July 1919; Herold, "Memory

Quiz," 83. Ethel remembered this first reunion taking place in August, but she was off by about a month.

67. Jennifer D. Keene, *Doughboys, the Great War, and the Remaking of America* (Baltimore: Johns Hopkins Univ. Press, 2001), 161.

68. "Potosi Items," *Weekly Teller,* 31 July 1919; "News Reviews of Current Events," *Weekly Teller,* 7 Aug. 1919; "Potosi Items," *Weekly Teller,* 14 Aug. 1919, 21 Aug. 1919; Herold, "Memory Quiz," 84.

69. Keene, *Doughboys,* 164-65.

70. Herold, "Memory Quiz," 84.

71. "School Notes," *Weekly Teller,* 11 Mar. 1920; "Lancaster School Notes," *Weekly Teller,* 18 Mar. 1920; "Potosi," *Weekly Teller,* 8 Apr. 1920; "Lancaster Wins in Big Contest," *Weekly Teller,* 6 May 1920; "Commencement Exercise Held," *Weekly Teller,* 3 June 1920.

3. An American Citizen in the Colonial Philippines

1. "Herold-Thomas Wedding," *Grant County Herald,* 30 June 1920; Herold, "Memory Quiz," 87.

2. Karnow, *In Our Image,* 12-13.

3. Herold, "Memory Quiz," 87-88; "Potosi," *Weekly Teller,* 29 Dec. 1920; Herold, "Memory Quiz," 95; Job Application, 5 May 1922, RBIA; "Potosi," *Weekly Teller,* 19 Jan. 1921. For a discussion of the popularity of commercial education, see John L. Rury, *Education and Women's Work: Female Schooling and the Division of Labor in Urban America, 1870-1930* (Albany, NY: State Univ. of New York Press, 1991), 147-53.

4. Memorandum, June 16, 1920, Walter W. Marquardt papers, Box 7, Bentley Historical Library, Ann Arbor, MI.

5. W. W. Marquardt to Mr. and Mrs. Elmer Herold, 18 Jan. 1922, RBIA; Herold, "Memory Quiz," 97-98; "Sixty Teachers to Be Imported for Provinces," *Manila Daily Bulletin,* 4 Apr. 1922; Job Application, 5 May 1922, RBIA.

6. Herold, "Memory Quiz," 98; Rafael, "Colonial Domesticity," 643; Alan Dawley, *Changing the World: American Progressives in War and Revolution* (Princeton, NJ: Princeton Univ. Press, 2003), 78.

7. Maureen A. Flanagan, *America Reformed: Progressives and Progressivisms, 1890s-1920s* (New York: Oxford Univ. Press, 2007), 200, 205; Dawley, *Changing the World,* 77, 297, 311-12.

8. W. W. Marquardt to E. W. Herold, 17 Feb. 1922, RBIA; [W.W. Marquardt], *The Philippine Islands: Information for Americans Thinking of Entering the Philippine Teaching Service* (Manila, PI: Bureau of Education, 1925), 4.

9. Marquardt, *Philippine Islands,* 10-11, 14.

10. Ibid., 28; Herold Job Application File, 5 May 1922, RBIA.

11. Herold, "Memory Quiz," 99; E. W. Herold to W. W. Marquardt, 7 Mar. 1922, RBIA.

12. "Transport Thomas Makes Quick Trip," *Manila Daily Bulletin,* 10 June 1922, 4; Herold, "Memory Quiz," 101; Rafael, "Colonial Domesticity," 649.

13. Theodore Friend, *Between Two Empires: The Ordeal of the Philippines, 1929–1946* (New Haven, CT: Yale Univ. Press, 1965), 17–18; Brands, *Bound to Empire,* 114–16, 119–20.

14. Brands, *Bound to Empire,* 125; Karnow, *In Our Image,* 250; Zimmerman, *Innocents Abroad,* 54.

15. Herold, "Memory Quiz," 102.

16. Ibid., 106, 109, 112, 113. On the hiring of servants for European colonial homes, see Elsbeth Locher-Scholten, "So Close and Yet So Far: The Ambivalence of Dutch Colonial Rhetoric on Javanese Servants in Indonesia, 1900–1942," in *Domesticating the Empire: Race, Gender, and Family Life in French and Dutch Colonialism,* ed. Julia Clancy-Smith and Frances Gouda, 135 (Charlottesville: Univ. Press of Virginia, 1998).

17. Rafael, "Colonial Domesticity," 646; Herold, "Memory Quiz," 112.

18. Herold, "Memory Quiz," 110–13. For an example of the complaints, see Zimmerman, *Innocents Abroad,* 123.

19. Herold, "Memory Quiz," 283; Foley, "Autobiography," 38–39.

20. Herold, "Memory Quiz," 121, 132.

21. Ibid., 137.

22. Rafael, "Colonial Domesticity," 646.

23. Herold, "Memory Quiz," 141. A good example of contemporary attitudes can be found in Felix M. Keesing and Marie Keesing, *Taming Philippine Headhunters: A Study of Government and of Cultural Change in Northern Luzon* (Stanford, CA: Stanford Univ. Press, 1934).

24. Rafael, "Colonial Domesticity," 644.

25. Herold, "Memory Quiz," 157, 134.

26. Karnow, *In Our Image,* 212.

27. Hoganson, *Consumers' Imperium,* 165–71, 185–86.

28. Herold, "Memory Quiz," 180.

29. Ibid., 195, 211.

30. Ibid., 216; "22 New Teachers in the Kankakee Public School," *Kankakee* [IL] *Daily News,* 11 Sept. 1924.

31. Herold, "Memory Quiz," 222; Raftery, "Textbook Wars," 151.

32. Herold, "Memory Quiz," 222; E. W. Herold to Bureau of Insular Affairs, 16 Sept. 1924, William Lay Patterson to E. W. Herold, 19 Sept. 1924 and 6 Oct. 1924, Orval P. Townsend to Elmer W. Herold, 10 Dec. 1924 and 7 Jan. 1925, War Department Telegram to E. W. Herold, 21 May 1925, RBIA; Herold, "Memory Quiz," 225, 228.

33. *Baguio Directory and Visitors' Guide* (Baguio, PI: Catholic School Press, 1937), 36–39; Herold, "Memory Quiz," 228, 230.

34. Herold, "Memory Quiz," 233; James J. Halsema, *E. J. Halsema: Colonial Engineer* (Quezon City, PI: New Day Publishers, 1991), 219–20.

35. George F. Nellist, ed., *Men of the Philippines,* vol. 1 (Manila: Sugar News Company, 1931), 133; Herold, "Memory Quiz," 245.

36. Alice L. Conklin, "Redefining 'Frenchness': Citizenship, Race Regeneration, and Imperial Motherhood in France and West Africa," in Clancy-Smith and Gouda, *Domesticating the Empire,* 81.

37. "Trinidad Riot Investigation Helps Wright," *Manila Daily Bulletin,* 16 Mar. 1927; Herold, "Memory Quiz," 246–48.

38. Herold, "Memory Quiz," 248–49; "Trinidad Riot Investigation Helps Wright," *Manila Daily Bulletin,* 16 Mar. 1927.

39. Herold, "Memory Quiz," 250; Jack C. Lane, *Armed Progressive: General Leonard Wood* (San Rafael, CA: Presidio Press, 1978), 262; Brands, *Bound to Empire,* 129–32; Herold, "Memory Quiz," 241–42; Halsema, *E. J. Halsema,* 189–90.

40. Interview with James J. Halsema, 19 May 2001, Glenmoore, PA.

41. Herold, "Memory Quiz," 252; "Student Riot Causes Stir," *Manila Daily Bulletin,* Mar. 7, 1927; Leonard Wood Diary, Mar. 8 and 15, 1927, vol. 3 (Jan. 1, 1927–May 27, 1927), Papers of Leonard Wood, Boxes 24–25, Library of Congress.

42. "Trinidad Riot Investigation Helps Wright," *Manila Daily Bulletin,* Mar. 16, 1927; Leonard Wood Diary, Mar. 22–25, 1927.

43. Herold, "Memory Quiz," 254.

44. Ibid., 255.

45. Ibid., 255–56.

46. Note [n.d.], RBIA.

47. Herold, "Memory Quiz," 324.

48. Locher-Scholten, "So Close and Yet So Far," 131; Rafael, "Colonial Domesticity," 642. Helen Callaway makes similar points about white women in Africa in *Gender, Culture and Empire: European Women in Colonial Nigeria* (Urbana: Univ. of Illinois Press, 1987).

49. Halsema, *E. J. Halsema,* 204, 194–95, 172; Robert Reed, *City of Pines: The Origins of Baguio as a Colonial Hill Station and Regional Capital* (Baguio City, PI: A-Seven Publishing, 1999), 66–71; *Memoirs of Baguio* (Baguio City, PI: Summer Capital Publishing House, 1960), n.p.

50. Ann Laura Stoler, "Tense and Tender Ties: The Politics of Comparison in North American History and (Post) Colonial Studies," *Journal of American History* 88, no. 3: 3, available online at http://www.historycooperative.org/journals/jah/88:3/stoler.html. See also Stoler and Karen Strassler, "Castings for the Colonial: Memory Work in 'New-Order' Java," *Comparative Studies in Society and History* 42 (Jan. 2000): 4–48.

51. Herold, "Memory Quiz," 268.

52. Ibid., 288–89. Dutch women held similar views of their Javanese servants. See Locher-Scholten, "So Close and Yet So Far," 139.

53. Herold, "Memory Quiz," 289; Locher-Scholten, "So Close and Yet So Far," 134.

54. Herold, "Memory Quiz," 294–95.

55. "Philippine Symphony," *Time,* 18 Aug. 1941, available online at http://www.time.com/time/magazine/article/0,9171,802142,00.html; Hyman Goldberg, "Dr. Zipper," *Yank,* 2 Nov. 1945, available online at http://www.oldmagazinearticles.com/pdf/YANK%20Zipper.pdf.

56. Herold, "Memory Quiz," 351.

57. Mina C. Roces, "Women in Philippine Politics and Society," in *Mixed Blessing: The Impact of the American Colonial Experience on Politics and Society in the Philippines,* ed. Hazel M. McFerson, 173 (Westport, CT: Greenwood Press, 2002); Herold, "Memory Quiz," 121.

58. Lori D. Ginzberg, "Global Goals, Local Acts: Grass-Roots Activism in Imperial Narratives," *Journal of American History* 88, no. 3 (Dec. 2001): 871.

59. [Ethel Thomas Herold], *Greetings from the Monday Afternoon Club, Baguio, Philippines: Our History, July 1933-November 1954,* privately printed pamphlet (photocopy in possession of the author); "Monday Afternoon Club Organized in Baguio," *Baguio Bulletin Supplement of the Manila Daily Bulletin* (hereinafter abbreviated as *BBS*), 25 Aug. 1933, 1; Herold, "Memory Quiz," 303.

60. Herold, "Memory Quiz," 303.

61. Ibid., 305, 311.

62. Margit Misangyi Watts, *High Tea at Halekulani: Feminist Theory and American Clubwomen* (Brooklyn, NY: Carlson Publishing Inc., 1993). While Watts analyzes the Outdoor Circle in connection with the club movement, she mostly ignores the imperialist aspects of these women's activities.

63. Herold, "Memory Quiz," 324, 303.

64. Brands, *Bound to Empire,* 153–54, 156–57.

65. Jose A. Cabranes, *Citizenship and the American Empire: Notes on the Legislative History of the United States Citizenship of Puerto Ricans* (New Haven, CT: Yale Univ. Press, 1979), 6n12. See also Julian Go, "Introduction: Global Perspectives on the U.S. Colonial State in the Philippines," in *The American Colonial State in the Philippines: Global Perspectives,* ed. Julian Go and Anne L. Foster, 6–8 (Durham: Duke Univ. Press, 2003).

66. Brands, *Bound to Empire,* 163.

67. F. Ryan Duffy, "Trip to the Philippines, 1935," F. Ryan Duffy Collection, Box 7, Folder 9, State Historical Society of Wisconsin, Madison.

68. Karnow, *In Our Image,* 255–56; Halsema, *E. J. Halsema,* 256–57; Philippine Commonwealth Committee Baguio Trip for the Congressional Party, "Our Trip to Baguio and Return," Nov. 9-10, 1935, F. Ryan Duffy Collection, Box 7, Folder 9, State Historical Society of Wisconsin, Madison; Herold, "Memory Quiz," 301-2.

69. Herold, "Memory Quiz," 301–2.

70. Duffy, "Trip to the Philippines, 1935," 8, 11.

71. Herold, "Memory Quiz," 348–49.

72. Ibid., 355.

73. Carol Morris Petillo, *Douglas MacArthur: The Philippine Years* (Bloomington: Indiana Univ. Press, 1981), 170–73. The quotation is from Richard Connaughton, *MacArthur and Defeat in the Philippines* (New York: Overlook Press, 2001), 43.

74. Herold, "Memory Quiz," 364.

75. Brands, *Bound to Empire,* 179–81.

76. P. Scott Corbett, *Quiet Passages: The Exchange of Civilians between the United States and Japan during the Second World War* (Kent, OH: Kent State Univ. Press, 1987), 10–11, 15–16. See also Frances B. Cogan, *Captured: The Japanese Internment of American Civilians in the Philippines, 1941–1945* (Athens: Univ. of Georgia Press, 2000), 26–27.

77. Herold, "Memory Quiz," 356. Ethel is vague about when this trip took place, but a newspaper story puts it in late 1940. See "In Baguio Social Circles," *BBS,* 3 Jan. 1941.

78. Herold, "Memory Quiz," 364.

79. "Sell Concert Memberships," *BBS,* 17 Jan. 1941; "Sing for Roosevelt," *BBS,* 7 Feb. 1941; "Meris Says City Should Build Air Raid Shelters," *BBS,*

3 Jan. 1941; "Organize Home Guard in City Defense Plan" and "Evacuation to City Possible," *BBS,* 26 Apr. 1941; "Mayor Appeals for Recruits in Home Guard," *BBS,* May 10, 1941.

80. "In Baguio's Social Circles," *BBS,* 3 May 1941; "Baguio Women of All Nations Aid in Setting Red Cross Work Record," *BBS,* 10 May 1941.

81. Brands, *Bound to Empire,* 185–87; Connaughton, *MacArthur and Defeat,* 113, 117; "Baguio's First Blackout Held Last Evening," *BBS,* Sept. 13, 1941; "Soldiers in P.I. Training Intensively in Every Phase of Modern Warfare," *BBS,* Sept. 5, 1941; Halsema, *E. J. Halsema,* 278–80.

82. Herold, "Memory Quiz," 370–71; Halsema, *E. J. Halsema,* 280–81. For a similar account of this meeting, see Natalie Crouter, *Forbidden Diary: A Record of Wartime Internment, 1941–1945* (New York: Burt Franklin & Co., 1980), 2.

83. Herold, "Memory Quiz," 372; Halsema, *E. J. Halsema,* 281–82. See also Crouter, *Forbidden Diary,* 2.

4. Enemy Alien

1. Herold, "Memory Quiz," 373; Betsy Herold Heimke, *Bring Cup, Plate, and Spoon* (Laguna Vista, TX: River Road Press, 2008), 3. Ethel remembered hearing the news shortly after 5:00 a.m., and Betsy recalled that her father always listened to the world news on the radio after he got up at 5:00. However, James Halsema points out that the first news broadcast from Manila (Baguio did not have its own radio station) came on at 6:00. See Halsema, *E. J. Halsema,* 283.

2. Brewer, *Why America Fights,* 88, 13.

3. Westbrook, *Why We Fought,* 14–15.

4. Herold, "Memory Quiz," 373; Ethel Herold, "War Diary, December 8, 1941–May 9, 1945" (unpublished copy in author's possession), 3.

5. Herold, "War Diary," 4, 6; Halsema, *E.J. Halsema,* 285; Herold, "Memory Quiz," 375.

6. Herold, "War Diary," 10.

7. Ibid., 11–12.

8. Ibid., 15–16, 18, 20.

9. Ibid., 20.

10. Herold, "War Diary," 24; Halsema, *E. J. Halsema,* 291–93; Foley, "Autobiography," 73; Crouter, *Forbidden Diary,* 8. Horan had phoned the Halsema house first and asked Betty Halsema Foley if she knew where his men had gone.

11. Herold, "War Diary," 24; Halsema, *E. J. Halsema,* 292.

12. Herold, "War Diary," 25–26; Herold, "Memory Quiz," 388.

13. Herold, "Memory Quiz," 390; Halsema, *E. J. Halsema,* 293. Bernard Norling credits Technical Sergeant William Bowen of the 228th Signal Service Company at Camp John Hay with sending those supplies to Horan. See Norling, *The Intrepid Guerrillas of North Luzon* (Lexington: Univ. Press of Kentucky, 1999), 52. Other civilian accounts confirm Ethel Herold's participation, along with that of other civilians. See James J. Halsema, unpublished wartime memoir, 1941–1942, 10 (copy in possession of author).

14. Herold, "War Diary," 31.

15. Ibid., 29–30.

16. Halsema, *E. J. Halsema,* 296; Herold, "Memory Quiz," 390.

17. Herold, "Memory Quiz," 390–91.

18. Herold, "War Diary," 33; Herold, "Memory Quiz," 394; Fern Harrington Miles, *Captive Community: Life in a Japanese Internment Camp, 1941–1945* (Jefferson City, TN: Mossy Creek Press, 1987), 36.

19. Corbett, *Quiet Passages,* 57–59.

20. Herold, "War Diary," 252, 269–71; Corbett, *Quiet Passages,* 97. On the repatriation rumors and camp voting, see Crouter, *Forbidden Diary,* 250–51.

21. Herold, "Memory Quiz," 394; Halsema, *E. J. Halsema,* 298; Philippe Burrin, *France under the Germans: Collaboration and Compromise* (New York: New Press, 1996), 1.

22. Herold, "Memory Quiz," 395. See also Halsema, *E. J. Halsema,* 297; Foley, "Autobiography," n.p.; Miles, *Captive Community,* 27.

23. Corbett, *Quiet Passages,* 3–4, 18; "Convention between the United States of America and Other Powers, Relating to Prisoners of War; July 27, 1929," Avalon Project at Yale Law School, http://www.yale.edu/lawweb/avalon/lawofwar/geneva02.htm, 3; Van Waterford, *Prisoners of the Japanese in World War II: Statistical History, Personal Narratives and Memorials Concerning POWs in Camps and on Hellships, Civilian Internees, Asian Slave Laborers and Others Captured in the Pacific Theater* (Jefferson, NC: McFarland and Co., 1994), 48n6.

24. "War Diary," 71; Corbett, *Quiet Passages,* 170; Cogan, *Captured,* 111, 121; Ryuzo Sato, *The Chrysanthemum and the Eagle: The Future of U.S.-Japan Relations* (New York: New York Univ. Press, 1994), 75.

25. Cogan, *Captured,* 569–60.

26. Herold, "War Diary, 55; "Convention," 5.

27. Herold, "War Diary," 55–56.

28. Ibid., 56.

29. Ibid., 56–57.

30. Heimke, *Bring Cup, Plate, and Spoon,* 65.

31. Cogan, *Captured,* 247; Herold, "War Diary," 66. Cogan writes that classes did not convene until the internees moved to Camp Holmes in the spring of 1942.

32. Herold, "War Diary," 274, 276; Crouter, *Forbidden Diary,* 258, 260; Cogan, 182. Red Cross parcels reached the Philippines prior to this, but the Baguio internees did not receive them.

33. Herold, "War Diary," 278, 280; Crouter, *Forbidden Diary,* 260.

34. Crouter, *Forbidden Diary,* 286, 288, 291; Herold, "War Diary," 286–87, 306–7; Herold, "Memory Quiz," 479.

35. Herold, "War Diary," 320; "Convention," 12.

36. Herold, "War Diary," 35–36.

37. Ibid., 36–38; Miles, *Captive Community,* 33–34.

38. Westbrook, *Why We Fought,* 28.

39. Herold, "War Diary," 59, 42. Some Baguio internees also referred to this as the General Committee.

40. Herold, "War Diary," 42; Halsema, unpublished memoir, 13; Herold, "Memory Quiz," 399.

41. Herold, "War Diary," 70.

42. Cogan, *Captured,* 127; Herold, "War Diary," 114.

43. Herold, "War Diary," 124–25.

44. Ibid., 132, 135.

45. Ibid., 159.

46. Ibid.; Crouter, *Forbidden Diary,* 81.

47. Herold, "War Diary," 180; Crouter, *Forbidden Diary,* 84.

48. Westbrook, 9, 17, 28; Cogan, *Captured,* 126–27.

49. Herold, "War Diary," 181; Herold, "Memory Quiz," 429; Crouter, *Forbidden Diary,* 149, 153. See also Theresa Kaminski, *Prisoners in Paradise: American Women in the Wartime South Pacific* (Lawrence: Univ. Press of Kansas, 2000), 61.

50. Herold, "War Diary, 230–31, 234, 266–67, 289; Kaminski, *Prisoners in Paradise,* 62.

51. Herold, "War Diary," 75, 159.

52. Ibid., 47, 76.

53. Ibid., 43.

54. Ibid., 57, 107.

55. Herold, "Memory Quiz," 460.

56. Ibid., 437–38, 452.

57. Herold, "War Diary," 163.

58. Herold, "Memory Quiz," 456.

59. Herold, "War Diary," 350, 367.

60. Ibid., 172.

61. David Joel Steinberg, *Philippine Collaboration in World War II* (Ann Arbor: Univ. of Michigan Press, 1967), 29, 92–93.

62. Herold, "War Diary," 16–17, 145.

63. Herold, "War Diary," 109–10; Jim Halsema to author, e-mail, 15 Feb. 1996; R. W. Volckmann, *We Remained: Three Years Behind the Enemy Lines in the Philippines* (New York: W. W. Norton, 1954), 103.

64. Herold, "War Diary," 137, 139.

65. Ibid., 176. In his unpublished memoir (p. 41), Jim Halsema says this happened on the twelfth. Natalie Crouter, however, notes Elmer's return to the camp on Aug. 15, and Ethel writes that he came back the day after he was taken. See Crouter, *Forbidden Diary,* 82.

66. Felisa A. Syjuco, *The Kempei Tai in the Philippines: 1941–1945.* (Quezon City, PI: New Day Publishers, 1988), 5–6; "Convention," 3–4.

67. Herold, "War Diary," 177.

68. Ibid., 178; Halsema, unpublished memoir, 41.

69. Crouter, *Forbidden Diary,* 82–83; Herold, "War Diary," 184.

70. Volckmann, *We Remained,* 111–12; Crouter, *Forbidden Diary,* 143.

71. Herold, "War Diary," 226; Crouter, *Forbidden Diary,* 143.

72. Herold, "War Diary," 226; Steinberg, *Philippine Collaboration,* 94; Crouter, *Forbidden Diary,* 535n31; Robert Lapham and Bernard Norling, *Lapham's Raiders: Guerrillas in the Philippines, 1942–1945* (Lexington: Univ. Press of Kentucky, 1996), 78–79, 82.

73. Crouter, *Forbidden Diary,* 145; Lapham and Norling, *Lapham's Raiders,* 137. See also Steinberg, *Philippine Collaboration,* 95.

74. Herold, "War Diary," 226.

75. Ibid., 229–30, 234–35; Crouter, *Forbidden Diary,* 179; Jim Halsema to author, e-mail, 15 Feb. 1996; Volckmann, *We Remained,* 112. Volckmann reported a rumor about Herman Kluge's death but never explained what happened to him.

76. Lapham and Norling, *Lapham's Raiders,* 35; Volckmann, *We Remained,* 62–65; Bernard Norling, *The Intrepid Guerrillas of Northern Luzon* (Lexington: Univ. Press of Kentucky, 1999), 105; Volckmann, *We Remained,* chaps. 5 and 6.

77. John F. Ream, "An Interview with Lt. Col. Herbert Swick," http://www.militaryphotos.net/forums/archive/index.php, 1; Crouter, *Forbidden Diary,* 136, 150–51; Volckmann, *We Remained,* 79–85; Herold, "War Diary," 223, 295. Herbie Swick remained a friend of the Herolds and served as a pallbearer at Elmer's funeral. See Herold, "Memory Quiz," 473.

78. Crouter, *Forbidden Diary,* 318–19, 322; Rokuro Tomibe, "The Secret Story of the War's End," *Bulletin of the American Historical Collection,* Oct.–Dec. 1979, 37–45; Herold, "War Diary," 296; Ream, "Interview with Lt. Col. Herbert Swick," 2.

79. Herold, "Memory Quiz," 482. For information on MacArthur's return, see Ronald H. Spector, *Eagle against the Sun: The American War with Japan* (New York: Free Press, 1985), 519.

80. Herold, "War Diary," 352–54, 357, 361, 365.

81. Ibid., 366, 369; Herold, "Memory Quiz," 495.

82. Herold, "War Diary," 389; Herold, "Memory Quiz," 507–8.

83. Herold, "Memory Quiz," 508; Herold, "War Diary," 399.

84. Herold, "War Diary," 393–94, 397.

85. Ibid., 425, 427, 437.

86. Ibid., 427, 438–40; Herold, "Memory Quiz," 514.

87. Herold, "War Diary," 447–48.

5. Postcolonialism

1. Herold, "Memory Quiz," 524–27.

2. Kozol, "'Good Americans,'" 234.

3. Benedict Anderson, *Imagined Communities: Reflections on the Origin and Spread of Nationalism* (London: Verso, 1991), 6–7.

4. Herold, "Memory Quiz," 526.

5. Ibid., 527.

6. Ibid., 527–28.

7. Ibid., 529–30.

8. Ibid.

9. Ibid., 532. The legal technicalities of the will were complicated. Bertha Bonn had to make numerous provisions concerning the farm because at the time she had the will drawn up during the war, she did not know for certain that any of the Herolds were still alive. Apparently, she never had time to change the will between the Herolds' repatriation and her death.

10. Karnow, *In Our Image,* 333–34; Brands, *Bound to Empire,* 220–23.

11. Quoted in Christina Klein, *Cold War Orientalism: Asia in the Middlebrow Imagination, 1945-1961* (Berkeley: Univ. of California Press, 2003), 62. Klein discusses the connection between U.S. foreign policy in Asia and postwar education on pp. 61-63.

12. Herold, "Memory Quiz," 535–36.

13. Ibid., 537; Ethel Herold (hereinafter EH) to Bart and Florence Thomas, 28 June 1946, 1; Karnow, *In Our Image,* 333.

14. EH to Bart and Florence Thomas, 28 June 1946, 2, 3; Herold, "Memory Quiz," 541; EH to the Montana People [Bart and Florence Thomas, Bill and Betsy Herold], 6 July 1946, 1. Ethel frequently wrote letters addressed to more than one person, expecting that they would be passed along.

15. Laville, *Cold War Women,* 2.

16. Herold, "Memory Quiz," 548. On the importance of home and domesticity in the Cold War period, see especially Elaine Tyler May, *Homeward Bound: American Families in the Cold War Era* (New York: Basic Books, 1988).

17. Laville, *Cold War Women,* 43–44.

18. [Herold], *Greetings,* 6–7. For more on the roles of overseas military wives and their contributions to Americanization, see Donna Alvah, *Unofficial Ambassadors: American Military Families Overseas and the Cold War, 1946–1965* (New York: New York Univ. Press, 2007).

19. [Herold], *Greetings,* 8; Mary Jean Houde, *Reaching Out: A Story of the General Federation of Women's Clubs* (Chicago: Mobium Press, 1989), 138.

20. EH to the Montana People, 28 June 1946, 4; Herold, "Memory Quiz," 549; "Seeds for Democracy Reach Down to Common Man in Philippines," *Albuquerque Tribune,* 28 Apr. 1952.

21. Robert Blum, "The Work of The Asia Foundation," *Pacific Affairs* 29, no. 1 (Mar. 1956): 46–56.

22. EH to Betsy Herold, 13 Sept. 1951, 23 Sept. 1951 (p. 2), New Years Day 1952.

23. EH to Betsy Heimke, 6 May 1958; EH to Children All [Bill Herold and Betsy Heimke], 11 June 1958, p. 1; Resolution No. 1173, Republic of the Philippines, Mountain Province, Bontoc, Office of the Provincial Board, 19 Dec. 1958 (copy in possession of author).

24. Douglas MacArthur, *Reminiscences* (New York: McGraw-Hill Book Company, 1964), 251–52.

25. Karnow, *In Our Image,* 323–324; Brands, *Bound to Empire,* 230–31; MacArthur, *Reminiscences,* 316. On postwar colonial struggles in Asia, see Spector, *In the Ruins of Empire.*

26. EH to the Montana People, 6 July 1946, 1; EH to Marie Halsema, 5 Nov. 1946, 1; Kozol, "'Good Americans,'" 234.

27. Kozol, "'Good Americans,'" 243.

28. Brands, *Bound to Empire,* 227, 233.

29. EH to the Montana People, 6 July 1946, 1.

30. Brands, *Bound to Empire,* 221-22.

31. EH to Florence and Herbert Heald, n.d. [1946], 2.

32. EH to Florence and Herbert Heald, n.d. [1946], 2; EH to Bill Herold, Feb. 21, 1947, 1.

33. Karnow, *In Our Image,* 310, 336–37.

34. EH to Florence Heald and Bill and Betsy Herold, 14 Feb. 1950, 1; EH to Bill and Betsy Herold, 28 Mar. 1950, 1; EH to [no salutation] 19 Feb. 1959.

35. EH to Bill and Betsy Herold, 11 Dec. 1949.

36. EH to Marie Halsema, 22 May 1950.

37. EH to Bill Herold, 2 May 1950, 1-2.

38. Brands, *Bound to Empire,* 261; Karnow, *In Our Image,* 345.

39. EH to Bill and Betsy Herold, 11 Dec. 1949.

40. Ibid.; EH to Bill Herold, 2 May 1950, 2.

41. EH to Bill and Betsy Herold, 30 Mar. 1950.

42. EH to Marie Halsema, 19 Nov. 1947, 2; EH to Marie Halsema, 13 Dec. 1947, 1; McGirr, *Suburban Warriors,* 177. Helen Laville discusses American women's growing disenchantment with internationalism in *Cold War Women,* chap. 4.

43. Spector, *In the Ruins of Empire,* 268–75.

44. EH to Bill and Betsy Herold, 25 June 1950; EH to Betsy Herold, 7 July 1950.

45. EH to Bill and Betsy Herold, Ganny Herold, and Sarah Herold, 30 July 1950; EH to Betsy Herold, 17 Oct. 1950; C. William Herold to author, e-mail, 20 Mar. 2001.

46. EH to Betsy Herold, 19 Dec. 1950; David W. Reinhard, *The Republican Right since 1945* (Lexington: Univ. Press of Kentucky), 68.

47. EH to Betsy Herold, 19 Jan. 1951; EH to Joanne and Bill Herold and Betsy Herold, 23 Feb. 1951, 2.

48. EH to Betsy and Karl Heimke, 8 Dec. 1952, 1-2.

49. EH to Betsy Herold, 15 Feb. 1952, 12 Mar. 1952.

50. Reinhard, *Republican Right,* 38–40.

51. Ibid., 72–73.

52. EH to Betsy and Karl Heimke, 19 Jan. 1953, 1.

53. EH to Betsy and Karl Heimke, 21 May 1953; Elmer Herold to Betsy Heimke, 31 May 1953.

54. EH to Betsy and Karl Heimke, 7 June 1953, 12 Nov. 1953; Brands, *Bound to Empire,* 253–54.

55. EH to Betsy, Susan, Karl, and Duffy [the dog] Heimke, 9 Apr. 1954; EH to Sarah Herold and Betsy, Susan, Karl, and Duffy Heimke, 26 Apr. 1954, 2.

56. Brands, *Bound to Empire,* 256.

57. EH to Sarah Herold and Betsy, Susan, Karl, and Duffy Heimke, 26 Apr. 1954, 2.

58. Herold, "Memory Quiz," 625.

59. Ibid., 624; EH to Betsy Heimke, 23 Feb. 1957, 2; EH to Betsy Heimke, 23 Mar. 1957; EH to Bill Herold, 4 June 1957, 2.

60. "The Philippines: Assaulting the Eagle," *Time,* 2 Feb. 1959, available online at http://www.time.com/time/printout/0,8816, 894094,00.html.

61. EH to Children Eleven, 4 Feb. 1959, 1; EH to [no salutation], 16 Feb. 1959; "A Letter from the Publisher," *Time,* 16 Feb. 1959, available online at http://www.time.com/time/printout/0,8816,894156,00.html.

62. Godfrey Hodgson, *The World Turned Right Side Up: A History of the Conservative Ascendancy in America* (New York: Houghton Mifflin Company, 1996), 69–70.

63. EH to Betsy Heimke, 24 Oct. 1957, 1.

64. EH to Betsy Heimke, 22–26 Mar. 1958, 2; EH to Children Eleven, 13 Oct. 1958, 2.

65. Dawley, *Changing the World,* 7. See also Flanagan, *America Reformed,* 212–17. On the growing importance of human rights, see Elizabeth Borgwardt, *A New Deal for the World: America's Vision for Human Rights* (Cambridge, MA: Belnap Press of Harvard Univ. Press, 2005).

66. EH to Children Eleven, 8 Sept. 1958 (p. 2), 29 Sept. 1958 (p. 1).

67. "Baguio Press Club Awardees," *Baguio Midland Courier,* 22 Feb. 1959; EH to Children Eleven, 26 Feb. 1959, 1.

68. Herold, "Memory Quiz," 677; EH to Children Eleven, 9 Apr. 1959, 1.

69. EH to Children Eleven, 1 July 1959, 1.

6. The Return of the Expatriate

1. EH to Children All, 2 Oct. 1959, 1; Herold, "Memory Quiz," 631, 633.

2. EH to Kids All, 4 May 1960, 1; Herold, "Memory Quiz," 632; Houde, *Reaching Out,* 310–11.

3. Brennan, *Wives, Mothers, and the Red Menace,* 38–39.

4. Houde, *Reaching Out,* 274–75, 278–79, 306, 313.

5. EH to Betsy Heimke, 17 May 1960, 1.

6. EH to Children Twelve, 2 June 1963, 1–2; Houde, *Reaching Out,* 323; EH to Children Twelve, 16 June 1963, 1–2; *Milwaukee Journal,* 12 June 1963.

7. William F. Thompson, *The History of Wisconsin,* vol. 6, *Continuity and Change, 1940–1965* (Madison: State Historical Society of Wisconsin, 1988), 604, 658, 673.

8. Laura Jane Gifford, *The Center Cannot Hold: The 1960 Presidential Election and the Rise of Modern Conservatism* (DeKalb: Northern Illinois Univ. Press, 2009), 53; McGirr, *Suburban Warriors,* 6, 8, 12; Phillips-Fein, *Invisible Hands,* xii; Hodgson, *World Turned Right Side Up,* 93. See also John Andrew, "The Struggle for the Republican Party," *The Historian* 59, no. 3 (Spring 1997): 613–31.

9. EH to Children, 3 Apr. 1960, 2; EH to Dear Kids, 27 Apr. 1960, 1; Thompson, *History of Wisconsin,* 682.

10. EH to Betsy Heimke, 25 Sept. 1960, 3.

11. EH to Kids, 29 July 1960; EH to Betsy Heimke, 8 Oct. 1960, 4.

12. Hodgson, *World Turned Right Side Up,* 133.

13. Reinhard, *Republican Right,* 158–63. On Goldwater's beliefs, see his book *The Conscience of a Conservative* (Shephardsville, KY: Victor Publishing Co., 1960).

14. Thompson, *History of Wisconsin,* 696; EH to Children Twelve, 14 Apr. 1961, 1.

15. Mary C. Brennan, *Turning Right in the Sixties: The Conservative Capture of the GOP* (Chapel Hill: Univ. of North Carolina Press, 1995), 4; EH to Betsy Heimke, 20 May, 1961 (p. 2), 20 Sept. 1961 (p. 3); EH to Kids, 16 Feb. 1961, 4; Gifford, *The Center Cannot Hold,* 197.

16. EH to Bill Herold, Betsy Heimke, and Sarah Herold, 12 May 1960, 2; EH to Betsy Heimke, 18 Apr. 1981, 1; EH to Children Twelve, 3 May 1961, 11 May 1961 (p. 1).

17. McGirr, *Suburban Warriors,* 172; EH to Sarah Herold and Betsy, Susan, Karl, and Duffy Heimke, 26 Apr. 1954, 2.

18. EH to Children Twelve, 14 Apr. 1961, 1.

19. "Filipino Eden No Paradise," Chicago *Daily News,* 22 Aug. 1961, 2.

20. EH to The Editor, *Chicago Daily News,* 26 Aug. 1961, 1-2; EH to Children All, 6 Sept. 1961, 1.

21. Klein, *Cold War Orientalism,* 77, 79, 85-86.

22. EH to The Editor, *Chicago Daily News,* 26 Aug. 1961, 1-2.

23. EH to Children Twelve, 21 July 1963, 1; EH to Children Twelve, 6 Oct. 1963, 2.

24. Herold, "Memory Quiz," 641.

25. EH to Children Twelve, 8 Nov. 1963 (p. 6), 16 Nov. 1963 (p. 3).

26. Herold, "Memory Quiz," 666.

27. EH to Gwendolyn and Anita Schaefer, 4 Feb. 1964, 2.

28. EH to Gwendolyn and Anita Schaefer, 4 Feb. 1964, 2; Herold, "Memory Quiz," 667-68.

29. Herold, "Memory Quiz," 667.

30. Ibid., 670.

31. Brands, *Bound to Empire,* 274-75; Karnow, *In Our Image,* 362-63.

32. Klein, 79; EH to Herolds, Heimkes, and Sarah [Herold], 27 July 1964, 2.

33. Brennan, *Wives, Mothers, and the Red Menace,* 181-82.

34. EH to Children Twelve, 4 July 1964, 2; Rymph, *Republican Women,* 174-75; Brennan, *Wives, Mothers, and the Red Menace,* 81. For a full-length consideration of Schlafly and her politics, see Donald Critchlow, *Phyllis Schlafly and Grassroots Conservatism* (Princeton, NJ: Princeton Univ. Press, 2005). For Schlafly's own views on conservatism, see her book *A Choice Not an Echo* (Alton, IL: Pere Marquette Press, 1964).

35. EH to Children Twelve, 19 July 1964, 2; Brennan, *Wives, Mothers, and the Red Menace,* 81-82.

36. EH to Children Twelve, 4 July 1964, 2-3; Gifford, *The Center Cannot Hold,* 14; McGirr, *Suburban Warriors,* 157.

37. EH to Children Twelve, 19 July 1964, 2; Rymph, *Republican Women,* 167; Reinhard, *Republican Right,* 196.

38. Rymph, *Republican Women,* 168-172; EH to Herolds, Heimkes, and Sarah, 27 July 1964, 2.

39. Editorial, "Why Lyndon Johnson Must be Elected," *Saturday Evening Post,* 19 Sept. 1964, 80.

40. Copy of letter from EH to *Saturday Evening Post,* 19 Sept. 1964; EH to Kids, 21 Oct. 1964; Phillips-Fein, *Invisible Hands,* 137; EH to Children Twelve, 18 Oct. 1964, 2. The published responses to the *Post*'s editorial can be found in the 3 Oct. and 10 Oct. 1964 issues.

41. EH to Children Twelve, 30 Sept. 1964 (p. 1), 1 Nov. 1964 (p. 1); Rymph, *Republican Women,* 171–72; Phillips-Fein, *Invisible Hands,* 143–44.

42. Phillips-Fein, *Invisible Hands,* 138–40; Brennan, *Turning Right,* 5; Thompson, *History of Wisconsin,* 729–31, 734–35.

43. EH to Children Twelve, 18 Mar. 1968 (p. 2), 9 Apr. 1968.

44. EH to Children Twelve, 7 Aug. 1968, 4 Nov. 1968.

45. Rymph, *Republican Women,* 170, 105; EH to Children Twelve, 31 May 1964 (p. 1), 4 July 1964 (p. 1). For additional information, see also Brennan, *Turning Right in the Sixties.*

46. Herold, "Memory Quiz," 632–33; EH to Children, 1 Mar. 1961; EH to [the Children?], [Mar. 1962], 3.

47. EH to Children Twelve, 23 Mar. 1967, 2; Herold, "Memory Quiz," 670; photocopy of the Lawrence Alumni Distinguished Service Award, June 11, 1967, in possession of the author.

48. Herold, "Memory Quiz," 672.

49. Ibid., 674.

50. EH to Children Eleven, 30 June 1970; "Memory Quiz," 675; EH to Children Twelve, 11 May 1971; "Memory Quiz," 682; Heimke, *Bring Cup, Plate, and Spoon,* 127.

51. Herold, "Memory Quiz," 683–84.

52. EH to Betsy Heimke, 24 Feb. 1972 (pp. 3–4), 22 July 1972 (pp. 5–6), 14 Aug. 1972 (p. 4).

53. EH to Betsy Heimke, 24 Feb. 1972 (p. 2), 16 May 1972 (p. 2), 1 Aug. 1972 (p. 6), 25 Sept. 1972 (p. 1); EH to Heimkes, Kaltenbachs, and Schaefers, 27 Jan. 1973, 1.

54. EH to Betsy Heimke, 3 May 1973, 1; EH to Billy Heimke, 25 May 1973.

55. EH to Betsy Heimke, 3 Mar. 1973, 17 Mar. 1973.

56. EH to Betsy Heimke and Bill Herold, 29 Nov. 1973 (p. 1), 14 Feb. 1974 (p. 2).

57. EH to Children All, 8 Jan. 1974, 1; EH to Betsy Heimke and Bill Herold, 14 Feb. 1974, 2; EH to Bill Herold and Betsy Heimke, 7 Oct. 1974, 4; EH to Betsy Heimke and Bill Herold, 30 Aug. 1978, 1.

58. EH to Bill Herold and Betsy Heimke, 7 Oct. 1974, 3.

59. EH to Herolds and Heimkes, 20 Nov. 1976, 2–3; EH to Kids, 26 Mar. 1980, 1; EH to Betsy Heimke, 27 May 1980, 1.

60. EH to Children Twelve, 7 Aug. 1968.

61. Herold, "Memory Quiz," 220.

62. Ibid., 220–21.

63. Ibid., 222–23.

64. Herold, "War Diary," 12.

65. EH to Florence Heald and Bill and Betsy Herold, 14 Feb. 1950, 2; EH to Bill and Betsy Herold, 15 May 1950, 1.

66. Other internee stories published in the postwar period include Alice Franklin Bryant, *The Sun was Darkened* (Boston: Chapman and Grimes, 1947), and James and Ethel Chapman, *Escape to the Hills* (Lancaster, PA: Jaques Cattell Press, 1947). None of these achieved the popularity of Agnes Keith's book.

67. EH to Sarah Herold and Bill and Betsy Herold, 30 Mar. 1950; EH to Bill Herold, 2 May 1950, 2.

68. EH to Betsy and Karl Heimke, 10 Feb. 1953.

69. Herold, "Memory Quiz," 683-84; EH to Heimkes, Kaltenbachs, and Schaefers, 27 Jan. 1973, 1; EH to Betsy Heimke and Bill Herold, 6 July 1973, 1.

70. EH to Betsy Heimke, 2 Nov. 1978, 2.

71. Crouter, *Forbidden Diary,* 20, 27.

72. EH to Betsy Heimke, 23 Mar. 1980, 1; EH to Kids, 30 Mar. 1980, 1; EH to Bill Herold and Betsy Heimke, 13 Feb. 1981; EH to Betsy Heimke, 28 Oct. 1981, 1; EH to Betsy Heimke, Nov., Day after Thanksgiving, 1981, 1. For the article that so concerned Ethel, see "Americans in Captivity: A World War II Diary Casts New Light on Tehran," *Time,* 24 Mar. 1980, 55. In an unpublished letter to *Time,* Ethel responded to the piece, claiming that Natalie Crouter had gotten only two things right in her diary: that Commandant Tomibe had been a humanitarian and that the internees had access to outside news sources.

73. Ethel Herold, "War Memories of Ethel Herold," *Bulletin of the American Historical Collection,* July-Sept. 1982 (pp. 7-25), Oct.-Dec. 1982 (pp. 44-67); EH to Karl Heimke, 1 Apr. 1977; "War Memories of Ethel Herold as told for Charles Vial and recorded by his friend Billy," [1977], copy in possession of the author.

74. EH to Betsy Heimke, 29 May 1981, 2; EH to Lewis Gleeck [spring 1981].

75. Lewis Gleeck, "Honi Soit: The Editor's Pride and Prejudices," *Bulletin of the American Historical Collection,* July-Sept. 1982, 105.

76. On women and the American Revolution, see, for instance, Linda K. Kerber, *Women of the Republic: Intellect and Ideology in Revolutionary America* (New York: W. W. Norton, 1980), and Mary Beth Norton, *Liberty's Daughters: The Revolutionary Experience of American Women, 1750-1800* (Boston: Little, Brown and Co., 1980).

77. Herold, "Memory Quiz," 678-79, 680-81.

Conclusion

1. EH to Bill Herold and Betsy Heimke, 4 Dec. 1980.

Bibliography

Ethel Thomas Herold Papers and Other Privately Held Materials

Foley, Betty Halsema. "Autobiography of Betty Halsema Foley." Unpublished manuscript.

Halsema, James J. E-mail to author, 15 February 1996.

———. Unpublished wartime memoir, 1941–1942.

Herold, Ethel Thomas. "An Autobiography," 1981 (copied August 1986 by Bill Herold).

———. Correspondence, 1947–1982.

———. *Greetings from the Monday Afternoon Club, Baguio, Philippines: Our History, July 1933–November 1954.* Privately printed pamphlet.

———. "Memory Quiz." Unpublished autobiography.

———. "War Diary, December 8, 1941–May 9, 1945."

———. "War Memories of Ethel Herold as told to Charles Vial and recorded by his friend Billy," [1977].

Herold, C. William. E-mail to author, 20 March 2001.

Resolution No. 1173, Republic of the Philippines, Mountain Province, Bontoc, Office of the Provincial Board, 19 Dec. 1958. Copy in author's possession.

Interviews

Heimke, Betsy Herold. 11 November 2000, Overland Park, KS.

Halsema, James J. 18–19 May 2001, Glenmoore, PA.

Archival Sources

Herold, Elmer, and Ethel Thomas Herold. File. The Records of the Bureau of Insular Affairs. Record Group 350, Entry 21, Box 279, National Archives and Records Administration (Archives II), College Park, MD.

Duffy, F. Ryan. Collection. State Historical Society of Wisconsin, Madison.

Lawrence College Bulletin and the *Lawrentian.* Lawrence Univ. Archives, Appleton, WI.

Marquardt, Walter W. Papers. Bentley Historical Library, Ann Arbor, MI.

Thomas, Bart. File. The Records of the Bureau of Insular Affairs. Record Group 350, Entry 21, Box 640, National Archives and Records Administration (Archives II), College Park, MD.

Wood, Leonard. Papers. Box 24–25, Library of Congress, Washington, DC.

Published Primary Sources

"Americans in Captivity: A World War II Diary Casts New Light on Tehran," *Time,* 24 March 1980, 55.

Baguio Directory and Visitors' Guide. Baguio, PI: Catholic School Press, 1937.

"Convention Between the United States of America and Other Powers, Relating to Prisoners of War; July 27, 1929." The Avalon Project at Yale Law School. Available online at http://www.yale.edu/lawweb/avalon/lawofwar/geneva02.htm.

Cornejo's Commonwealth Directory of the Philippines, 1937.

Crouter, Natalie. *Forbidden Diary: A Record of Wartime Internment, 1941–1945.* New York: Burt Franklin & Co., 1980.

Editorial, "Why Lyndon Johnson Must be Elected," *Saturday Evening Post,* 19 September 1964, 80.

Goldwater, Barry II. *The Conscience of a Conservative.* Shephardsville, KY: Victor Publishing Co., 1960.

Harding, Samuel Bannister. *The Study of the Great War: A Topical Outline, with Extensive Quotations and Reading References.* Washington, DC.: Committee on Public Information, 1918.

Heimke, Betsy Herold. *Bring Cup, Plate, and Spoon.* Laguna Vista, TX: River Road Press, 2008.

Herold, Ethel. "War Memories of Ethel Herold." *Bulletin of the American Historical Collection,* July-Sept. 1982, 7-25; Oct.-Dec, 1982, 44-67.

Keesing, Felix M., and Marie Keesing. *Taming Philippine Headhunters: A Study of Government and of Cultural Change in Northern Luzon.* Stanford, CA: Stanford Univ. Press, 1934.

Lapham, Robert, and Bernard Norling. *Lapham's Raiders: Guerrillas in the Philippines, 1942-1945.* Lexington: Univ. Press of Kentucky, 1996.

"A Letter from the Publisher," *Time,* 16 February 1959. Available online at http://www.time.com/time/printout/0,8816,894156,00.html.

MacArthur, Douglas. *Reminiscences.* New York: McGraw-Hill, 1964.

Marquardt, Frederic S. *Before Bataan and After: A Personalized History of Our Philippine Experiment.* New York: Bobbs-Merrill, 1943.

[Marquardt, W. W.] *The Philippine Islands: Information for Americans Thinking of Entering the Philippine Teaching Service.* Manila, PI: Bureau of Education, 1925.

Memoirs of Baguio. Baguio City, PI: Summer Capital Publishing House, 1960.

Miles, Fern Harrington. *Captive Community: Life in a Japanese Internment Camp, 1941-1945.* Jefferson City, TN: Mossy Creek Press, 1987.

Nellist, George F., ed. *Men of the Philippines.* Vol. I. Manila: Sugar News Company, 1931.

Onorato, Michael P., interviewer. *James J. Halsema: The Internment Camp at Baguio.* Fullerton: California State Univ., Oral History Program, 1987.
"Philippine Symphony." *Time,* 18 August 1941. Available online at http://www.time.com/time/magazine/article/0,9171,802142,00.html.
"The Philippines: Assaulting the Eagle." *Time,* 2 February 1959. Available online at http://www.time.com/time/printout/0,8816,894094,00.html.
Ream, John F. "An Interview with Lt. Col. Herbert Swick." Available online at http://www.militaryphotos.net/forums/archive/index.php.
Schlafly, Phyllis. *A Choice Not an Echo.* Alton, IL: Pere Marquette Press, 1964.
Silver, Mildred. *A View From the Ninth Decade: A Memoir.* Lawrenceville, IL: Ad Ventures, Inc., 1977.
Tomibe, Rokuro. "The Secret Story of the War's End." *Bulletin of the American Historical Collection,* Oct.-Dec. 1979, 37-45.
Volckmann, R. W. *We Remained: Three Years Behind the Enemy Lines in the Philippines.* New York: W. W. Norton, 1954.
Whitfield, Evelyn. *Three Year Picnic: An American Woman's Life Inside Japanese Prison Camps in the Philippines During WWII.* Corvallis, OR: Premiere Editions International, 1999.
Willoughby, Charles, comp. *The Guerrilla Resistance Movement in the Philippines: 1941-1945.* New York: Vantage Press, 1972.

Newspapers

Albuquerque Tribune, 1952.
Appleton (WI) Daily Post, 1913-1917.
Baguio Bulletin Supplement of the Manila Daily Bulletin, 1932-1941.
Baguio Midland Courier, 1959.
Chicago Daily News, August 1961.
Grant County (WI) Herald, 1896-1923, 1938.
Grant County (WI) News, 1918.
Kankakee (IL) Daily News, 1924.
LaCrosse (WI) Tribune, 1913.
Lancaster (WI) Weekly Teller, 1896-1923.
Manila Daily Bulletin, 1922-1927.
Milwaukee Journal, 12 June 1963.

Secondary Sources

Alvah, Donna. *Unofficial Ambassadors: American Military Families Overseas and the Cold War, 1946-1965.* New York: New York Univ. Press, 2007.
Anderson, Benedict. *Imagined Communities: Reflections on the Origin and Spread of Nationalism.* London: Verso, 1991.
Andrew, John. "The Struggle for the Republican Party." *The Historian* 59, no. 3 (Spring 1997): 613-31.
Bailey, Beth L. *From Front Porch to Back Seat: Courtship in Twentieth-Century America.* Baltimore: Johns Hopkins Univ. Press, 1988.

Barry, John M. *The Great Influenza: The Epic Story of the Deadliest Plague in History.* New York: Viking, 2004.

Bederman, Gail. *Manliness and Civilization: A Cultural History of Gender and Race in the United States, 1880–1917.* Chicago: Univ. of Chicago Press, 1995.

Bickers, Robert. *Empire Made Me: An Englishman Adrift in Shanghai.* London: Allen Lane, 2003.

Blum, Robert. "The Work of the Asia Foundation." *Pacific Affairs* 29, no. 1 (Mar. 1956): 46–56.

Bodnar, John, ed. *Bonds of Affection: Americans Define Their Patriotism.* Princeton, NJ: Princeton Univ. Press, 1996.

Borgwardt, Elizabeth. *A New Deal for the World: America's Vision for Human Rights.* Cambridge, MA: Belnap Press of Harvard Univ. Press, 2005.

Brands, H. W. *Bound to Empire: The United States and the Philippines.* New York: Oxford Univ. Press, 1992.

Brennan, Mary C. *Turning Right in the Sixties: The Conservative Capture of the GOP.* Chapel Hill: Univ. of North Carolina Press, 1995.

———. *Wives, Mothers, and the Red Menace: Conservative Women and the Crusade against Communism.* Boulder: Univ. Press of Colorado, 2008.

Brewer, Susan A. *Why America Fights: Patriotism and War Propaganda from the Philippines to Iraq.* New York: Oxford Univ. Press, 2009.

Brown, Carrie. *Rosie's Mom: Forgotten Women Workers of the First World War.* Boston: Northeastern Univ. Press, 2002.

Buenker, John D. *The History of Wisconsin.* Vol. 4, *The Progressive Era, 1893–1914.* Madison: State Historical Society of Madison, 1998.

Burrin, Philippe. *France under the Germans: Collaboration and Compromise.* New York: New Press, 1996.

Byerly, Carol R. *Fever of War: The Influenza Epidemic in the U.S. Army during World War I.* New York: New York Univ. Press, 2005.

Cabranes, Jose A. *Citizenship and the American Empire: Notes on the Legislative History of the United States Citizenship of Puerto Ricans.* New Haven, CT: Yale Univ. Press, 1979.

Callaway, Helen. *Gender, Culture, and Empire: European Women in Colonial Nigeria.* Urbana: Univ. of Illinois Press, 1987.

Capozzola, Christopher. *Uncle Sam Wants You: World War I and the Making of the Modern American Citizen.* New York: Oxford Univ. Press, 2008.

Clancy-Smith, Julia, and Frances Gouda, eds. *Domesticating the Empire: Race, Gender, and Family Life in French and Dutch Colonialism.* Charlottesville: Univ. Press of Virginia, 1998.

Coffman, Edward M. *The War to End All Wars: The American Military Experience in World War I.* Madison: Univ. of Wisconsin Press, 1986.

Cogan, Frances B. *Captured: The Japanese Internment of American Civilians in the Philippines, 1941–1945.* Athens, GA: Univ. of Georgia Press, 2000.

Colley, Linda. *The Ordeal of Elizabeth Marsh: A Woman in World History.* New York: Pantheon Books, 2007.

Conklin, Alice L. "Redefining 'Frenchness': Citizenship, Race Regeneration, and Imperial Motherhood in France and West Africa." In Clancy-Smith and Gouda, *Domesticating the Empire,* 65–83.

Connaughton, Richard. *MacArthur and Defeat in the Philippines.* New York: Overlook Press, 2001.

Corbett, P. Scott. *Quiet Passages: The Exchange of Civilians between the United States and Japan during the Second World War.* Kent, OH: Kent State Univ. Press, 1987.

Critchlow, Donald. *Phyllis Schlafly and Grassroots Conservatism.* Princeton, NJ: Princeton Univ. Press, 2005.

Crosby, Alfred W. *America's Forgotten Pandemic: The Influenza of 1918.* New York: Cambridge Univ. Press, 1989.

Crosby, Alfred W., Jr. *Epidemic and Peace, 1918.* Westport, CT: Greenwood Press, 1976.

Davies, Peter. *Dangerous Liaisons: Collaboration and World War II.* New York: Pearson Longman, 2004.

Dawley, Alan. *Changing the World: American Progressives in War and Revolution.* Princeton, NJ: Princeton Univ. Press, 2003.

Erickson, Christine Kimberly. "Conservative Women and Patriotic Maternalism: The Beginnings of a Gendered Conservative Tradition in the 1920s and 1930s." Ph.D. diss., Univ. of California, Santa Barbara, 1999.

Flanagan, Maureen A. *America Reformed: Progressives and Progressivisms, 1890s–1920s.* New York: Oxford Univ. Press, 2007.

Friend, Theodore. *Between Two Empires: The Ordeal of the Philippines, 1929–1946.* New Haven, CT: Yale Univ. Press, 1965.

Gere, Anne Ruggles. *Intimate Practices: Literacy and Cultural Work in U.S. Women's Clubs, 1880–1902.* Urbana: Univ. of Illinois Press, 1997.

Gifford, Laura Jane. *The Center Cannot Hold: The 1960 Presidential Election and the Rise of Modern Conservatism.* DeKalb: Northern Illinois Univ. Press, 2009.

Ginzberg, Lori D. "Global Goals, Local Acts: Grass-Roots Activism in Imperial Narratives." *Journal of American History* 88, no. 3 (Dec. 2001): 870–73.

Gleeck, Lewis E., Jr. *The American Governors General and High Commissioners in the Philippines: Proconsuls, Nation-Builders, and Politicians.* Quezon City, PI: New Day Publishers, 1986.

———. "Honi Soit: The Editor's Pride and Prejudices," *Bulletin of the American Historical Collection,* July–Sept. 1982, 105–6.

Glenn, Evelyn Nakano. *Unequal Freedom: How Race and Gender Shaped American Citizenship and Labor.* Cambridge, MA: Harvard Univ. Press, 2002.

Go, Julian, and Anne L. Foster, eds. *The American Colonial State in the Philippines: Global Perspectives.* Durham, NC: Duke Univ. Press, 2003.

Goldberg, Hyman. "Dr. Zipper," *Yank,* 2 November 1945. Available online at http://www.oldmagazinearticles.com/pdf/YANK%20Zipper.pdf.

Gordon, Lynn D. *Gender and Higher Education in the Progressive Era.* New Haven, CT: Yale Univ. Press, 1990.

Greenwald, Maurine Weiner. *Women, War, and Work: The Impact of World War I on Women Workers in the United States.* Westport, CT: Greenwood Press, 1980.

Gustafson, Melanie Susan. *Women and the Republican Party, 1854–1924.* Urbana: Univ. of Illinois Press, 2001.

Halsema, James J. *E. J. Halsema: Colonial Engineer.* Quezon City, PI: New Day Publishers, 1991.

Hegarty, Marilyn E. *Victory Girls, Khaki-Wackies, and Patriotutes: The Regulation of Female Sexuality during World War II.* New York: New York Univ. Press, 2008.

Heiss, Mary Ann. "The Evolution of the Imperial Idea and U.S. National Identity." *Diplomatic History* 26, no. 4 (Fall 2002): 511–40.

Higonnet, Margaret Randolph, Jane Jenson, Sonya Michel, and Margaret Collins Weitz, eds. *Behind the Lines: Gender and the Two World Wars.* New Haven, CT: Yale Univ. Press, 1987.

Hodgson, Godfrey. *The World Turned Right Side Up: A History of the Conservative Ascendancy in America.* New York: Houghton Mifflin Company, 1996.

Hoganson, Kristin L. "'As Badly Off as the Filipinos': U.S. Women's Suffragists and the Imperial Issue at the Turn of the Twentieth Century." *Journal of Women's History* 13, no. 2 (Summer 2001): 9–33.

———. *Consumers' Imperium: The Global Production of American Domesticity, 1865–1920.* Chapel Hill: Univ. of North Carolina Press, 2007.

———. *Fighting for American Manhood: How Gender Politics Provoked the Spanish-American and Philippine-American Wars.* New Haven, CT: Yale Univ. Press, 1998.

Houde, Mary Jean. *Reaching Out: A Story of the General Federation of Women's Clubs.* Chicago: Mobium Press, 1989.

Jensen, Kimberly. *Mobilizing Minerva: American Women in the First World War.* Urbana: Univ. of Illinois Press, 2008.

Kaminski, Theresa. *Prisoners in Paradise: American Women in the Wartime South Pacific.* Lawrence: Univ. Press of Kansas, 2000.

Karnow, Stanley. *In Our Image: America's Empire in the Philippines.* New York: Random House, 1989.

Keene, Jennifer D. *Doughboys, the Great War, and the Remaking of America.* Baltimore: Johns Hopkins Univ. Press, 2001.

Keesing, Felix M. *The Ethnohistory of Northern Luzon.* Stanford, CA: Stanford Univ. Press, 1962.

Kennedy, David M. *Over Here: The First World War and American Society.* New York: Oxford Univ. Press, 1980.

Kennedy, Kathleen. *Disloyal Mothers and Scurrilous Citizens: Women and Subversion during World War I.* Bloomington: Indiana Univ. Press, 1999.

Kerber, Linda K. *No Constitutional Right to be Ladies: Women and the Obligations of Citizenship.* New York: Hill and Wang, 1998.

———. "The Meanings of Citizenship." *Journal of American History* 84, no. 3 (Dec. 1997): 833–54.

Kessler-Harris, Alice. *Out to Work: A History of Wage-Earning Women in the United States.* New York: Oxford Univ. Press, 1982.

Klein, Christina. *Cold War Orientalism: Asia in the Middlebrow Imagination, 1945–1961.* Berkeley: Univ. of California Press, 2003.

Kozol, Wendy. "'Good Americans': Nationalism and Domesticity in *Life* Magazine, 1945-1960." In Bodnar, *Bonds of Affection,* 231–50.

Lane, Jack C. *Armed Progressive: General Leonard Wood.* San Rafael, CA: Presidio Press, 1978.

Laville, Helen. *Cold War Women: The International Activities of American Women's Organisations.* Manchester, U.K.: Manchester Univ. Press, 2002.

Lee, Josephine, Imogene L. Lim, and Yuko Matsukawa, eds. *Re/collecting Early Asian America.* Philadelphia: Temple Univ. Press, 2002.

Locher-Scholten, Elsbeth. "So Close and Yet So Far: The Ambivalence of Dutch Colonial Rhetoric on Javanese Servants in Indonesia, 1900–1942." In Clancy-Smith and Gouda, *Domesticating the Empire,* 131–53.

Maga, Tim. *Judgment at Tokyo: The Japanese War Crimes Trials.* Lexington: Univ. Press of Kentucky, 2001.

Maniago, Jo Anne Barker. "The First Peace Corps: The Work of the American Teachers in the Philippines, 1900–1910." Ph.D. diss., Boston Univ., 1971.

McBride, Genevieve G. *On Wisconsin Women: Working for Their Rights from Settlement to Suffrage.* Madison: Univ. of Wisconsin Press, 1993.

McConnell, Stuart. "Reading the Flag: A Reconsideration of the Patriotic Cults of the 1890s." In Bodnar, *Bonds of Affection,* 102–19.

McFerson, Hazel M., ed. *Mixed Blessing: The Impact of the American Colonial Experience on Politics and Society in the Philippines.* Westport, CT: Greenwood Press, 2002.

McGirr, Lisa. *Suburban Warriors: The Origins of the New American Right.* Princeton, NJ: Princeton Univ. Press, 2001.

Morgan, Francesca. *Women and Patriotism in Jim Crow America.* Chapel Hill: Univ. of North Carolina Press, 2005.

Newman, Louise Michelle. *White Women's Rights: The Racial Origins of Feminism in the United States.* New York: Oxford Univ. Press, 1999.

Norling, Bernard. *The Intrepid Guerrillas of Northern Luzon.* Lexington: Univ. Press of Kentucky, 1999.

O'Leary, Cecelia Elizabeth. *To Die For: The Paradox of American Patriotism.* Princeton, NJ: Princeton Univ. Press, 1999.

Perez, Louis A., Jr. *The War of 1898: The United States and Cuba in History and Historiography.* Chapel Hill: Univ. of North Carolina Press, 1998.

Petillo, Carol Morris. *Douglas MacArthur: The Philippine Years.* Bloomington: Indiana Univ. Press, 1981.

Phillips-Fein, Kim. *Invisible Hands: The Making of the Conservative Movement from the New Deal to Reagan.* New York: W. W. Norton, 2009.

Piccigallo, Philip R. *The Japanese on Trial: Allied War Crimes Operations in the East, 1945–1951.* Austin: Univ. of Texas Press, 1979.

Pixley, R. B. *Wisconsin in the World War.* Milwaukee: Wisconsin War History Co., 1919.

Purvis, June. *Emmeline Pankhurst: A Biography.* New York: Routledge, 2002.

Raftery, Judith. "Textbook Wars: Governor-General James Francis Smith and the Protestant-Catholic Conflict in Public Education in the Philippines, 1904–1907." *History of Education Quarterly* 38, no. 2 (Summer 1998): 146–48.

Rafael, Vicente L. "Colonial Domesticity: White Women and United States Rule in the Philippines." *American Literature* 67 (Dec. 1995): 639–66.

Reed, Robert. *City of Pines: The Origins of Baguio as a Colonial Hill Station and Regional Capital.* Baguio City, PI: A-Seven Publishing, 1999.

Reinhard, David W. *The Republican Right since 1945.* Lexington: Univ. Press of Kentucky, 1983.

Roces, Mina C. "Women in Philippine Politics and Society." In McFerson, *Mixed Blessing,* 159–90.

Rothman, Ellen K. *Hands and Hearts: A History of Courtship in America.* Cambridge, MA: Harvard Univ. Press, 1987.

Rury, John L. *Education and Women's Work: Female Schooling and the Division of Labor in Urban America, 1870–1930.* Albany: State Univ. of New York Press, 1991.

Rymph, Catherine. *Republican Women: Feminism and Conservatism from Suffrage through the Rise of the New Right.* Chapel Hill: Univ. of North Carolina Press, 2006.

Sato, Ryuzo. *The Chrysanthemum and the Eagle: The Future of U.S.-Japan Relations.* New York: New York Univ. Press, 1994.

Schirmer, Daniel B. *Republic or Empire: American Resistance to the Philippine War.* Cambridge, MA: Schenkman Publishing Co., 1972.

Schmidt, Jean Miller. *Grace Sufficient: A History of Women in American Methodism, 1760–1939.* Nashville, TN: Abingdon Press, 1999.

Scott, Anne Firor. *Natural Allies: Women's Associations in American History.* Urbana: Univ. of Illinois Press, 1991.

Smith, Rogers M. *Civic Ideals: Conflicting Visions of Citizenship in U.S. History.* New Haven, CT: Yale Univ. Press, 1997.

Sneider, Allison L. *Suffragists in an Imperial Age: U.S. Expansion and the Woman Question, 1870–1929.* New York: Oxford Univ. Press, 2008.

Solomon, Barbara Miller. *In the Company of Educated Women: A History of Women and Higher Education in America.* New Haven, CT: Yale Univ. Press, 1985.

Spector, Ronald H. *Eagle against the Sun: The American War With Japan.* New York: Free Press, 1985.

———. *In the Ruins of Empire: The Japanese Surrender and the Battle for Postwar Asia.* New York: Random House, 2007.

Steinberg, David Joel. *Philippine Collaboration in World War II.* Ann Arbor: Univ. of Michigan Press, 1967.

Steinson, Barbara. *American Women's Activism in World War I.* New York: Garland Publishing, 1982.

Stoler, Ann Laura. "Tense and Tender Ties: The Politics of Comparison in North American History and (Post) Colonial Studies." *Journal of American History* 88, no. 3: 1–33. Available online at http://www.historycooperative.org/journals/jah/88:3/stoler.html.

Stoler, Ann Laura, and Karen Strassler. "Castings for the Colonial: Memory Work in 'New-Order' Java." *Comparative Studies in Society and History* 42 (Jan. 2000): 4–48.

Syjuco, Felisa A. *The Kempei Tai in the Philippines: 1941–1945.* Quezon City, PI: New Day Publishers, 1988.

Thelen, David. "The Nation and Beyond: Transnational Perspectives on United States History." *Journal of American History* 86, no. 3 (Dec. 1999): 965–75.

Thompson, William F. *The History of Wisconsin.* Vol. 6, *Continuity and Change, 1940–1965.* Madison: State Historical Society of Wisconsin, 1988.

Todd, Lewis Paul. *Wartime Relations of the Federal Government and the Public Schools, 1917-1918.* New York: Arno Press and The New York Times, 1971.

Waterford, Van [Willem F. Wanrooy]. *Prisoners of the Japanese in World War II: Statistical History, Personal Narratives and Memorials Concerning POWs in Camps and on Hellships, Civilian Internees, Asian Slave Laborers and Others Captured in the Pacific Theater.* Jefferson, NC: McFarland and Co., 1994.

Watts, Margit Misangyi. *High Tea at Halekulani: Feminist Theory and American Clubwomen.* Brooklyn, NY: Carlson Publishing Inc., 1993.

Westbrook, Robert B. *Why We Fought: Forging American Obligations in World War II.* Washington, DC: Smithsonian Books, 2004.

Wilson, Dale E. *Treat 'Em Rough! The Birth of American Armor, 1917–20.* Novato, CA: Presidio Press, 1989.

Wisconsin Cartographer's Guild. *Wisconsin's Past and Present: A Historical Atlas.* Madison: Univ. of Wisconsin Press, 1998.

Wright, Patrick. *Tank: The Progress of a Monstrous War Machine.* New York: Viking, 2002.

Yoshihara, Mari. *Embracing the East: White Women and American Orientalism.* New York: Oxford Univ. Press, 2003.

Zeiger, Susan. "The Schoolhouse vs. the Armory: U.S. Teachers and the Campaign against Militarism in the Schools, 1914-1918." *Journal of Women's History* 15, no. 2 (2003): 150–79.

Zieger, Robert H. *America's Great War: World War I and the American Experience.* New York: Rowman & Littlefield, 2000.

Zimmerman, Jonathan. *Innocents Abroad: American Teachers in the American Century.* Cambridge, MA: Harvard Univ. Press, 2006.

Index

Page numbers in **boldface** refer to illustrations.